Women and Media

Women and Media

International Perspectives

Edited by KAREN ROSS
and CAROLYN M. BYERLY

350 Main Street, Malden, MA 02148-5020, USA
108 Cowley Road, Oxford OX4 1JF, UK
550 Swanston Street, Carlton, Victoria 3053, Australia

First published 2004 by Blackwell Publishing Ltd

Library of Congress Cataloging-in-Publication Data

Women and media : international perspectives / edited by Karen Ross and Carolyn M. Byerly.
p. cm.
Includes bibliographical references and index.
ISBN 1-4051-1608-0 (alk. paper) — ISBN 1-4051-1609-9 (pbk. : alk. paper)
1. Mass media and women. I. Ross, Karen, 1957– II. Byerly, Carolyn M.

P94.5.W65W656 2004
302.23′082—dc22
2003025566

A catalogue record for this title is available from the British Library.

Set in 10.5/13pt Minion
by Graphicraft Limited, Hong Kong
Printed and bound in the United Kingdom
by MPG Books Ltd, Bodmin, Cornwall

For further information on
Blackwell Publishing, visit our website:
http://www.blackwellpublishing.com

Contents

Notes on Contributors

Carolyn M. Byerly studies the relationship between social movements and communication, including the media. Her articles have appeared in journals such as *Critical Studies in Mass Communication*, *Journalism and Mass Communication Educator*, and *Journal of Mass Media Ethics*, and in several edited volumes, among them: M. de Bruin and K. Ross (eds), *Identities at Work* (2003); E. R. Meehan and E. Riordan (eds), *Sex and Money: Intersections of Feminism and Political Economy of Media* (2002); E. K. Thomas and B. H. Carpenter (eds), *Mass Media in 2025* (2001); M. Meyers (ed.), *Mediated Women* (1999); and A. N. Valdivia (ed.), *Feminism, Multiculturalism and the Media* (1995). She teaches in the Department of Communication, University of Maryland.

Ammu Joseph is a journalist and media-watcher now based in Bangalore. Among her publications are: *Whose News? The Media and Women's Issues* (co-authored/edited with Kalpana Sharma, 1994); *Women in Journalism: Making News* (2000); and *Terror, Counter-Terror: Women Speak Out* (co-edited with Kalpana Sharma, 2003). She is also co-author/editor of *Speaking in Tongues: Gender, Censorship and Voice in India* (2002). She is on the visiting faculty of the Asian College of Journalism, Chennai/Madras, and is a founder-member of the Network of Women in Media, India.

Jenny Kitzinger is professor of media studies at the School of Journalism, Media and Cultural Studies, Cardiff University. Her research spans audience reception processes, textual analysis, and journalistic production practices. Her substantive research has focused on the media and health, science and "risk," and the media and sexual violence, especially sexual violence against children. She is co-editor of *Developing Focus Group Research: Politics, Theory and Practice* (1999) and co-author of *The Mass Media and Power in Modern Britain* (1997) and *The Circuit of Mass Communication in the AIDS Crisis* (1998). Her book on the media coverage of child sexual abuse, *Framing Abuse*, is currently in press. Her work also appears in journals such as *Feminism and Psychology*, *Women's Studies International Forum*, *Feminist Review*, *Feminist Media Studies*, *Media, Culture and Society*, *European Journal of Communication*, and *Sociology of Health and Illness.*

Dafna Lemish is chair of the Department of Communication, Tel Aviv University. Her research and teaching interests include gender-related issues of media representations and consumption as well as children, media, and leisure. Her publications include: "Gender at the forefront: feminist perspectives on action theoretical approaches in communication research," *Communications: The European Journal of Communication Research* (2002) 27(1); "Gendered media: meaning and use," in S. Livingstone and M. Bovill (eds), *Children and their Changing Media Environment* (with T. Liebes and V. Seidmann, 2001); and "'Four Mothers': the womb in the public sphere", *European Journal of Communication* (2000) 15(2) (with I. Barzel).

Caroline Mitchell is principal lecturer in radio at the School of Arts, Design, Media and Culture, University of Sunderland. She has been active in community radio for the past 20 years and in 1992 co-founded Fem FM, the first women's station in the UK. She has worked in women's radio development and training in Europe, in particular with the AMARC (World Association of Community Radios) women's network. Her research is in the area of innovatory, participatory, and community radio, with a particular interest in women's and feminist radio. Her current research is about the use of radio by refugees and asylum seekers. She is a founding member of the UK Radio Studies Network and editor of *Women and Radio: Airing Differences* (2000).

Ellen Riordan is a visiting assistant professor at Gustavus Adolphus College, Minnesota. She is the co-editor of *Sex and Money: Feminism and Political Economy in the Media* (2002). Her research focuses on feminist theory, political economy, and popular culture.

Notes on Contributors

Karen Ross is reader in mass communication and director of the Centre for Communication, Culture and Media Studies at Coventry University. Her principal research interests relate to the general and media-specific aspects of (in)equalities. Her recent books include: *Mapping the Margins: Identity Politics and Media* (co-edited with Deniz Derman, 2003); *Women, Politics, Media* (2002); *Women, Politics and Change* (ed., 2002); *Black Marks: Minority Ethnic Audiences and Media* (ed., 2001); *Managing Equal Opportunities in Higher Education* (with Diana Woodward, 2000); and *Black and White Media* (1996).

Gillian Youngs is senior lecturer at the Centre for Mass Communication Research, University of Leicester. Her interests and work cover theory, practice, and policy. She has made expert contributions on information and communication technologies and women to UNESCO and the Society for International Development and has presented her research at major conferences in Europe, the United States, and China. Her publications include: *Political Economy, Power and the Body: Global Perspectives* (ed., 2000); *International Relations in a Global Age* (1999); and *Globalization: Theory and Practice* (co-ed., 1996; second edition forthcoming). She is co-editor of *International Feminist Journal of Politics* and associate editor of *Development*, and serves on the editorial board of *Political Geography*.

Acknowledgments

Our task of pulling together a collection of essays that take stock of women and media issues was made easy by a high-profile group of contributors who were enthusiastic about the project and who always met deadlines and other requests we made of them. Thus, a heartfelt thanks to Ammu Joseph, Jenny Kitzinger, Dafna Lemish, Caroline Mitchell, Ellen Riordan, and Gillian Youngs, without whose scholarship and writing there would be no book. Neither would the book exist without our wonderful editor at Blackwell, Jayne Fargnoli. From the start, she gave us her full support, guiding the project wisely and trustingly through its steps. We have enjoyed and benefited from our working relationship with her. We are also grateful to several decades of feminist scholars who laid the theoretical and empirical groundwork on women's relationship to mass media and enabled our own project to find its place and direction. Far from silent or anonymous, they make their appearance in the citations and notes that pepper (and season) this text. Last, we feel an immeasurable gratitude for electronic communication, which has made our collaborative venture across continents and oceans both possible and pleasurable over the last 18 months.

Karen Ross and Carolyn M. Byerly

1
Introduction

Carolyn M. Byerly and Karen Ross

> There is a lot of hype about the wonders of ICTs[1] in transforming the world and in the leveling of all sorts of disparities, including gender. However, we need to remember that in the final analysis, they are just tools and, just like in any technological transformation, the decisive factors regarding their impact include who has access and control of the technology, the way it is being introduced and the institutional or organisational conditions under which it is being used and organised. In other words, gender and socio-economic equality have to be ensured before women (and the poor) can be empowered to use ICTs effectively for their own advancement. (Cecilia Ng and Veena N)[2]

We live in a mediated world. Even remote geographic areas are infiltrated by advertising, newspapers, magazines, radio, television, music, films, and other print and broadcast media. The computerization of most of the world since the early 1990s further guarantees that mediated images and messages will continue to construct the very fabric of our daily lives, knowledge, and frameworks of reality, and that individuals will be linked across language and cultural borders. Less obvious to most of us are the gendered structures and relationships between human beings on the inside of media industries who control the resources and determine the images, words, and sounds that we consume. Equally obscure perhaps are the ways that media technology, messages, and the varied individuals involved in production, distribution, and consumption influence each other and, in turn, the world around them. Exposing these issues is the work of scholars.

The broader academic study of media has burgeoned over the last century but especially so in the last few years, when media research finally took its own roomy place in the newly recognized discipline of communication.[3] This dynamic discipline has evolved quickly and voluminously, particularly with regard to research on the ways in which gender, race, ethnicity, and sexual and national identity enter into the construction and consumption of media messages. Also in question are the implications that such messages hold for the political realities of those they represent. These aspects of media research emerged by way of feminist, gay and lesbian, racial justice, and postcolonial social movements in the 1970s in Europe, the United States, South Asia, Africa, Latin America, and other parts of the world. Concerned about the dual ability of the media to reinforce unequal status quo relationships, as well as to circulate new ideas and help to set political agendas leading to change, liberation movements have given significant attention to the role of the media in social processes.

The 1960s, 1970s, and 1980s were noisy years, especially in the academy, as feminist and other activist scholars from diverse class, ethnic, and national backgrounds challenged dominant intellectual paradigms, bringing into being critical, cultural, and postcolonial studies. These approaches more easily accommodated radical inquiries into gender (and other) relations of power in society, including the role of media in establishing (or changing) social hierarchies. Karl Marx's concepts and theories, for all of their shortcomings – and as ample numbers of writers have shown, there are many – offered a basic framework of analysis and social action useful to the development of new radical theories, particularly those today associated with the family of *critical theories*. Feminists following this thinking adopted Marx's conceptualization of *consciousness* about one's own predicament as arising from the context of one's life determined by the social relations one is subjected to. *Social relations* in this instance came to mean *gender* relations, referring to the underlying causes of unequal status that men and women hold in society. Critical feminists understood that women would have to move from a place of *unconsciousness* (what Marx called "false consciousness") to one of *consciousness* about their circumstances. Thus, feminist grassroots organizing has typically involved methods of *consciousness-raising*, whereby women learn to critique their own experience within the *patriarchal* (male-dominated) society. This process motivated women toward political activism, which Marx called *praxis* and feminists would later call *feminist praxis*. The outcome of praxis is *feminist struggle*, an intentional challenge to the status quo power structure of male dominance. Such struggle would take the form of a *dialectical process* that evolves over time and produces multiple (not always foreseeable) outcomes, but presumably ones that advance women's power. These basic tenets of Marx's work provided many feminists with a language, a model for organizing, and a vision for social change. However, it was most specifically Marx's *critique of capitalism* that resonated with groups of feminists who wanted to locate women's oppression in the larger structures of ownership of industries (and control of wealth), production, and consumption in society. Feminist media theorists today who follow this intellectual lineage use a feminist political economy analytical framework to examine male-owned media industries' exploitation of women's bodies and talents to increase their own profits and the social power flowing from them.

Critical and cultural feminist scholars alike adapted Antonio Gramsci's concept of *hegemony* to help explain the ways in which media and other cultural products aid in securing men's dominance in society. Hegemony describes a process by which the dominant group (in this case powerful men) maintains its power over social institutions and those in them (in this case women) by actively seeking the consent of those in society who wish to fit the established norms and practices. The appeal of the hegemony concept to feminists has been that it offers an analysis of how both men and women come to participate in a social system that is inherently unequal, and therefore undemocratic. For example, feminist media scholars have been able to consider ways that women are engaged at both the *structural level* (for example, in media professions and other aspects of the industries) and the *meaning levels* (for example, the making and consumption of media images and messages that affirm men's superiority over women) in giving their consent to men's dominant place in society. Feminist scholars who interrogate cultural issues also consider the ways in which aspects of culture, such as national or regional history, ethnic identity, religious affiliation, and sexual identity, enter into the making and consumption of media messages and social relations associated with this process.

Postcolonial feminist theorists emerged by way of national liberation movements beginning in the 1960s. This diverse group of scholars, coming from India and other regions of Asia, Africa, Latin America, and the Pacific, assumes a complex task of identifying and examining multiple ways that both they, as citizens, and their nations were affected by years of domination by foreign governments. The particular work of feminist postcolonial scholars has been to locate women in the historical colonial and liberation processes, considering the specific role of media and other cultural products.

They point out that colonial domination, far from being over, continues in today's era of globalization, which brings a proliferation of magazines, television, films, advertising, fashion, and other media and cultural forms from the powerful European and North American nations into the rest of the world.

The present volume inhabits the analytical terrain carved out by these complex, energetic new intellectual developments of the last decades – decades in which women have been major forces and players. Far from being finished, these developments continue to evolve in response to a rapidly changing world. As editors, we wanted this book to convey the dynamism of what is taking place in the realm of women-and-media today, in relation both to media enterprises and to the world to which they are integral. We recognized from the outset that limitations of space would require that the book be indicative rather than comprehensive in its contents. In addition, we wanted to ensure that it contained both the big picture, in terms of research and theoretical developments, as well as discrete local examples, geographically, in relation to women's media activism. Underlying the work of assembling this collection of authors and chapters was an abiding understanding on our parts that women's efforts to better understand and to discipline the media have always been wrapped up with women's right to self-determination, one aspect of that being women's right to communicate. Our work therefore is intellectual and political, but also deeply personal.

In this book, eight scholars representing four regions of the world take up some of these issues in relation to women's experience, both in their own nations and internationally. The recognition that runs through their writings – and serves to unify these otherwise diverse chapters – is that media have the potential not only to reinforce the status quo in power arrangements in society but also to contribute to new, more egalitarian ones. In tracking progress, all the authors acknowledge that media enterprises are not in the same place they were back in the 1970s, when women first charged the media with ignoring or stereotyping them, and with blocking their access to media message-making in various ways. On the other hand, the authors do not believe that mass media, including new media, presently serve women's interests as they might – and should. Using a range of feminist theories and methodologies, the contributors demonstrate the ways in which an understanding of gender issues in the media necessarily intersects with identity and status concerns related to social class, race, ethnicity, sexuality, religion, and nationality. In addition, the contributors report on the multiple ways that women have struggled to gain greater control over media in order to communicate and thereby participate in the public sphere. "Struggle" here is understood to be a long, continuous, dialectical process involving many and with various outcomes, some of which are in women's favor, others not. In recognizing the uneven and sometimes unpredictable nature of such historical processes, they identify the work still to be done in bringing commercial and alternative media alike more fully into the service of women.

In part I, "Representing and Consuming Women," four chapters look at the ways in which mainstream media continue to commodify and sexualize women in their routine reporting and representation strategies. Jenny Kitzinger's chapter uses complex methodology in examining the coverage of sexual violence, including child abuse, in Britain and the United States. Looking first at the evolution of such news, she then compares news accounts with the testimonies of women and children who have lived through such abuse, pointing out the discrepancies between the media's reporting of sex crimes and the lived reality. Dafna Lemish and Karen Ross both critique women and news, with Lemish looking at the way in which the Israeli media continue to exclude women from serious debates in the public spheres of Israeli society on matters such as religion and war, and instead construct the female subject as principally Madonna or whore, living almost exclusively in the private sphere. Ross interrogates the news media of Britain, Australia, and Ireland in their construction of women politicians, who, despite being elected leaders operating fully within the public sphere, are nonetheless reduced to little more than their body parts in stories by male journalists. Ellen Riordan's chapter provides a feminist political economic analysis of the international film industry's construction of what she calls "girl power feminism," arguing that this so-called feisty feminism is merely another way for large movie corporations to make money.

In part II, "Women's Agency in Media Production," the emphasis is on the ways that women have gained at least some control of news messages and images, provoking a shift in both content and context. Carolyn M. Byerly uses an historical approach to understand the contemporary situation, arguing that changes in US news are the result of both internal newsroom campaigns by women journalists and external campaigns waged by community-based women's groups making specific demands for change. In addition, she explores the tactics that women in other nations have approached in reforming the media. Ammu Joseph's chapter considers the case of India and the ways in which women in newsrooms there have had a positive impact on media culture. She suggests a number of strategies that could be employed to speed up progress. The last two chapters look at media that are specifically gendered. Caroline Mitchell traces the historical development of women's radio practice around the world, using a series of case studies to elaborate the unique characteristics of "women's radio." Gillian Youngs discusses the internet as an empowering space for women's voices, arguing that, like other media, it can provide substantial benefits to women in terms of reach and information, but that access and safety continue to be real concerns.

We believe that there is considerable wisdom in this collection of writings about where women are today in their relationship with both traditional and new media. The authors present an honest, sometimes stark look at the ambiguities, problems, frustrations, and even failures that women have encountered in their efforts to speak more publicly through the media. The contributors also inspire confidence with the many examples of women's success in accessing the mainstream media in different nations, in developing women-controlled media, and in making extensive use of new computer technologies. Grasping a working knowledge of these events, and the theoretical frameworks within which they are analyzed, is important in order to gain a full appreciation of women's self-determination in communicating within and across nations. We live in a mediated world, but scrutinized through a gendered lens, the picture is perhaps a little clearer and perhaps a little more hopeful.

Notes

1 ICTs are information communication technologies, a term mostly used in relation to new media such as cable, satellite, and digital technologies, as well as electronic media such as email and the internet.
2 Contribution to a forum discussion published in the journal *Gender and Media Monitor* (2002) August, 4–9.
3 Until recently, the study of various forms of communication, including mediated communication, was conducted by scholars in sociology, political science, psychology, rhetoric, journalism, and other social science and humanities fields. By the early 1990s, there had emerged a recognizable body of communication research, theories, and theorists focused specifically on communications phenomena. From this time, scholars began to refer to such

scholarship as the *discipline of communication* (or sometimes in the plural, *communications*). True to its roots, communication scholarship remains eclectic and highly interdisciplinary. For a more complete discussion of the field's development, and feminist theory's place within it, see Katherine Miller's *Communication Theories* (2002).

Reference

Miller, K. (2002) *Communication Theories: Perspectives, Processes and Contexts.* McGraw-Hill, New York.

PART I

Representing and Consuming Women

Researching the ways in which women have been routinely portrayed by mainstream media has been a continuing preoccupation for many media scholars over the past decades. Sadly, most contemporary studies suggest that despite the incursions which women have made into the media industry and the success of the women's movement in challenging some of the wider gender inequalities in society, the media seem stuck in a very traditional and stereotypical groove. As we will see from the chapters in the second part of this book, women *have* made and *continue* to make a difference to what we see, read, and hear in the media, but there still remain too many examples of sexist reporting in news media, and of stereotypical and sexualized characterizations in entertainment media, for the claim that we are "post-equality" to be seen as anything other than decidedly hollow.

Jenny Kitzinger, in chapter 2, charts the debate about the role of the media in representing sexual violence, a key political issue for feminist theory and intervention. She begins by presenting a broad overview of critiques of media coverage of sexual violence, in the context of feminist activism to transform such representation and incorporating critiques about definition and frameworks. The chapter goes on to present findings from an empirical study of how one form of sexual violence – child sexual abuse – came to be "discovered" by the media and how this intersected with women's experiences and social actions. This leads into a theoretical discussion about the interaction between proliferating media discourses and women's personal abuse narratives, which are themselves now subject to feminist critique.

Chapters 3 and 4 both look at news media. Dafna Lemish casts her critical eye over the way in which women in Israeli media are routinely portrayed. As Lemish points out, there are several very complicated characteristics of Israeli society, such as being deeply divided and dominated by issues of nationalism and military conflicts, which mean that the context in which the media function is quite volatile. Using a case-study approach, Lemish's chapter illuminates the complicated relationships that exist between representations of women in the media and their diverse lived realities, as well as analyzing the impact of more women in the media industry, the so-called "feminization" of the newsroom. Through her discursive and semiotic analyses, she argues that women are portrayed in a familiar range of stereotypes, mostly confined to traditional roles in the private sphere or in volunteering, education, health, welfare, and the like in their public sphere outings. Women are also seen as absolutely, and naturally, different to men, being less logical, ambitious, active, independent, heroic, and dominant and most commonly depicted either as "Madonna" or as "whore." As Madonna, "woman" is the "mother" who gives birth, nurtures, sacrifices herself, and mourns her dead son. As whore, she is sex personified, whose fate it is to be punished as a victim of violence and exploitation.

The complicated relationships between women, politics, and media are the focus of chapter 4. Karen Ross argues that it is only in recent decades that these relationships have begun to figure as a research focus, since it was only in the 1990s that women began to be elected to parliaments in sufficient numbers to make it possible to explore their representation in their regional and national media. Ross considers the ways in which women politicians are routinely portrayed in mass media, principally newspapers, as well as exploring the strategies which women themselves have developed to try and maximize their publicity – the oxygen of any politician – whilst at the same time minimizing intrusions into their personal and family lives. Drawing on content analysis as well as interview data collected from women politicians in the UK (Westminster), Northern Ireland, Australia, and South Africa, she suggests that the normative patriarchal structures that exist in the wider society masquerade in the newsroom as neutral journalist "practice" in ways that undermine not only our elected women members but also the wider democratic project.

The last chapter in this part moves away from news and provides the logical bridge between "fact" and fiction in the commodification of women's bodies and experiences. If news media rarely position women outside the narrow frame of victim, mother, partner, or second-class professional, then entertainment media have been equally assiduous in creating women-as-hero roles. The problem, though, as Ellen Riordan makes clear, is that too many of these so-called "positive" roles, such as the main characters in *Xena: Warrior Princess* or *Buffy the Vampire-Slayer*, reveal themselves to be little more than a marketing grab, with leading women wearing skin-tight leather and T-shirts as they brandish a variety of lethal weapons. Riordan examines how media organizations produce, construct, and commodify feminism, focusing specifically on the cultural construction of "girl power" by media corporations. Throughout the 1990s and early 2000s, women and girls have been portrayed in strong roles in popular shows, but these powerful female characters have sparked considerable debate: is ass-kicking Lara Croft a role model for twenty-first-century women or simply a male-ordered fantasy of the dominatrix who really wants to be daddy's girl? Riordan uses Ang Lee's film *Crouching Tiger, Hidden Dragon* as a specific case study in which to interrogate the contradictions and complexities that surround "girl-power feminism," where women can be not just strong and forceful but also beautiful and sexy. But Riordan questions whether this "new" form really represents progress for women or is simply a new way of making money by creating dedicated female consumers, while simultaneously promoting a hegemonic ideology that sustains both capitalism and patriarchy.

2
Media Coverage of Sexual Violence Against Women and Children

Jenny Kitzinger

"Read all about it!" Sexual violence as media fodder: a brief historical introduction

The sexual exploitation of women and children has played a key role in the history of the media. In 1885 scandal shook London when William Stead, editor of the *Pall Mall Gazette*, undertook a unique piece of investigative journalism. In the context of widespread debate about child prostitution and with the initial prompting of women's right campaigners, he bought a 13-year-old local girl for "immoral purposes." He had the girl, Eliza Armstrong, medically examined to confirm that she was a virgin and then packed her off to Paris. Stead wrote up descriptions of his adventure in a series of articles with headings such as "Delivered for seduction," "The violation of virgins," "Strapping girls down," and "The forcing of unwilling maidens." The newspaper was banned by major newsagents but sold out on the streets. The *Gazette* reports attracted national notoriety, provoked massive public demonstrations, and are credited with helping to raise the age of consent for girls from 12 to 16 (Pearsall 1969; Barry 1979). Just three years later, sexual violence was again the focus of intense media interest with the tale of "Jack the Ripper." A serial sex-killer loose in London was perfect fodder for the 13 national dailies in hot competition at this time. Gory details, descriptions of "fallen women," and reports of foreign-looking suspects or that the victims were ritually murdered by orthodox Jews ensured good circulation figures for the burgeoning newspaper industry. Such was the success of this story that one suggestion was that the Ripper was an enterprising newspaper man who killed in order to create "good copy" for his newspaper (Curtis 2001).

Over a hundred years later sexual violence still makes "good copy." Instead of virginal Eliza Armstrong or the specter of "Jack the Ripper" we now have, in the UK, sex murderers such as Ian Brady and Myra Hindley, who abducted and murdered children in the 1960s; the "Yorkshire Ripper" (modeled on his nineteenth-century counterpart), who raped and murdered at least 13 women before he was caught in 1980; and Fred and Rosemary West, who assaulted an unknown number of women and children over decades and were finally arrested in 1994. High-profile events in the USA include the 1984 "Big Dan" trial (involving the gang rape of a woman in a tavern, which inspired the film *The Accused*) and the 1989 brutal assault on a jogger in Central Park. There were also televised celebrity trials during the 1990s, such as those of Mike Tyson, the boxer, and William Kennedy-Smith, a member of the prominent Kennedy family, who both faced accusations of rape. However, the issues raised by articles about Eliza Armstrong or Jack the Ripper over a hundred years ago still capture many of the tensions in more recent media representations of sexual violence. Media exposure is important to inform and provoke public awareness, debate, and policy responses. Journalists, though, are highly selective in what they report and can be guilty of voyeurism and sensationalism. Coverage can decontextualize abuse, encourage racism, promote stereotypes of women (as virgins or whores), blame victims, and excuse assailants.

This chapter reviews research into how sexual abuse against women and children has been represented in the media in the UK and the US from the 1970s to the present day.[1] I outline feminist challenges to traditional understandings of sexual violence and the ways in which these have helped to transform discourse and representation, language and identity. I then review the ongoing problems with media reporting and track controversial developments such as the emergence of new discourses of disbelief.

The (re)discovery of sexual violence: the rise in media attention during the 1970s and 1980s

It is a truism to declare that sexual violence makes "good copy." However, precisely which forms of sexual violence attract the media and *how* it is defined vary across time and across cultures. In the 1940s, 1950s, and 1960s, for example, violence against women was a hidden crime, but attention to all forms of violence against women and children increased exponentially during the 1970s and 1980s:

- "*Wife beating*": The media paid little attention to domestic violence until the mid-1970s: indeed, before then the American media used the phrase "domestic violence" to mean riots and terrorism within the borders of the US rather than anything to do with violence in the home. A study of the *New York Times* shows that just seven articles explicitly discussed such violence between 1970 and 1976. However, in 1977 there were 44 articles about "wife beating" and, by the following year, "battered wives" began appearing as a separate topic in the New York Time's index: evidence that this had now been identified as a serious social issue (Tierney 1982: 213).
- *Rape*: Prior to developments in the 1970s, the mainstream media paid very little attention to rape: journalists even avoided the word, preferring phrases such as "carnal knowledge." In 1971, for example, there were just 31 reports of rape cases in the British newspapers the *Sun*, the *Daily Mirror*, and *The Times*. However, coverage more than doubled in 1978 and had almost doubled again by 1985 (Soothill and Walby 1991: 18). A similar increase in attention to sexual assault is evident in the American press, with a 250 per cent increase in coverage of this issue in the *New York Times* between 1972 and 1974 (Byerly 1999).
- *Child sexual abuse*: Child sexual abuse was not a major subject for public discussion until the mid-1980s (lagging behind the discovery of sexual violence against adult women). Analysis of *The Times* and the *Sunday Times* reveals only five articles about this topic in 1980. However, just three years later there were 66 articles about this issue, a figure which increased to 100 in 1985 and to 250 in 1986. The coverage peaked in 1987, with 413 items in *The Times* and *the Sunday Times* in this year alone (Kitzinger 1996).

In addition to this sudden expansion in news reporting about sexual violence against women, and later children, the issue also gained prominence in documentaries, talk shows, drama, and soap opera. For example, in the UK, child sexual abuse suddenly started to be discussed in documentary series such as *Brass Tacks* (7 July 1987), *Everyman* (8 May 1988),

Antenna (10 May 1989), and *Horizon* (19 June 1989). By the early 1990s, it even began to appear as a story line in police, hospital, and legal drama as well as in soap operas. The most extensive treatment was the "Beth Jordache" story on the soap *Brookside* starting in 1993, portraying a man who beat his wife and also sexually assaulted his two daughters. The story line peaked when the man's wife and elder daughter killed him and buried him under the patio (see Henderson 1996).

The Women's Liberation Movement and the feminist analysis of sexual violence

In the early 1970s, women began to organize to campaign for the equal treatment of women. This movement is often called "second wave" feminism, the first wave having peaked with the Suffragette movement and feminist campaigns at the end of the nineteenth and in the early twentieth centuries. Second wave feminism identified violence against women as a top priority, along with issues such as equal pay, access to childcare, abortion rights, and sexual self-determination. The seventh demand of the Women's liberation Movement (WLM) is reproduced in box 2.1.

Feminists exchanged experiences in consciousness-raising groups and documented and exposed sexual violence through research, fiction, and autobiography (for instance, Angelou 1969; Armstrong 1978). Activists established crisis lines and opened refuges so that women and girls who were being abused at home could escape their assailants. They also fought to put these issues on the public agenda and to transform the way sexual violence was represented in the media and understood by the public (see

Box 2.1 The seventh demand of the Women's Liberation Movement

Freedom from intimidation by threat or use of violence or sexual coercion, regardless of marital status. An end to the laws, assumptions and institutions that perpetuate male dominance and men's aggression toward women.

Smart and Smart 1978; Donat and D'emilio 1992). Alongside this, feminists worked to reform practice and legislation. Campaigns included challenging the unsympathetic way in which police treated rape complainants, the routine use of women's previous sexual history to discredit them in court, and the fact that a man could not be charged with raping his wife.

Feminist analysis re-envisaged rape and sexual abuse as a symptom of a culture of violence against and disrespect for women, which should be viewed as a form of sexist hate crime (rather than an impulsive act of sexual need).[2] Solutions had to include radical social change. Refuing to accept that such violence should be taken for granted, feminists criticized strategies which put the onus purely on women to be "sensible" (such as avoiding public parks or going out after dark, locking car doors, crossing the street to avoid groups of men, or carrying rape alarms). The tongue-in-cheek advice about "how to avoid rape" reproduced in box 2.2 sums up some of the feminist arguments at this time. The parody highlights the unrealistic nature of most advice. It also challenges the ways in which

Box 2.2 How to avoid rape

Don't go out without clothes – that encourages some men.
Don't go out with clothes – any clothes encourage some men.
Don't go out alone at night – that encourages men.
Don't go out with a female friend – some men are encouraged by numbers.
Don't go out with a male friend – some male friends are capable of rape.
Don't stay at home – intruders and relatives can both rape.
Avoid childhood – some men are "turned on" by little girls.
Avoid old age – some rapists "prefer" aged women.
Don't have a father, grandfather, uncle or brother – these are the relatives who most often rape young women.
Don't marry – rape is legal within marriage.
To be quite sure – don't exist.
(War on Rape Collective 1977, cited in London Rape Crisis Center 1984: 2–3)

women were expected to behave, such as being careful not to dress "provocatively" and obeying an unofficial curfew.

Producing cultural change: the media and feminist transformations

The WLM was very successful in achieving some reforms, even if its seventh demand is far from realized even in these so-called postfeminist days. Rape in marriage has been made a crime, a change achieved in some American states in the late 1970s and early 1980s but not realized in England and Wales until 1991. There is now a strong (if still underfunded and under-threat) network of help-lines and refuges, as well as some feminist-inspired initiatives (both local and central government) to challenge abuse (Kitzinger 1994). More and more women now talk openly about sexual assault, and the number prepared to try to seek justice has increased – although most rapes still go unreported and most brought to trial still fail to secure a conviction.

The WLM also had a profound impact on media representations. Most journalists now recognize sexual violence as a serious social issue. It is less likely to be simply treated as a titillating, salacious, and bizarre story to be juxtaposed with pictures of half-naked women, and there has been a decrease in sensationalism and overt sexism (Soothill and Walby 1991). Certain myths, such as that women "enjoy" rape, that used to be routinely invoked have all but disappeared (Los and Chamard 1997: 315), and feminist ideas and the experiences of raped women are increasingly articulated (Cuklanz 1996: 116). Many researchers also point to some excellent coverage of sexual violence issues, especially by women reporters (Soothill and Walby 1991; Mills 1997).

In fact, the media not only responded to feminist critiques, but were sometimes an ally in achieving feminist goals. Specific media events were vital to some campaigns for reform. In 1982, for example, a savvy female reporter from a major Seattle television station included footage of a veteran senator standing on the Senate floor asking: "Well, if you can't rape your wife, who can you rape?" This caused a public outcry and helped to finally remove the marital exclusion from the Washington state rape law, an exclusion now lifted in nearly all US states (Byerly 1994: 60). It was similarly a televisual event which helped to prompt outrage the same year in the UK. Police handling of rape complaints was revealed in a fly-on-the-wall documentary on Thames Television. Millions of viewers saw the vicious and bullying interrogation of a woman who had gone to the police saying she was raped. The program provoked widespread protest and helped to fuel demands for improvements in the treatment of rape complainants (Soothill and Walby 1991: 9).

In addition to the importance of such events, the impact of media recognition in itself should not be underestimated. The rapid expansion in media attention to sexual violence both reflected, and had a dramatic impact upon, changing understandings of everyday life. My own interviews and focus group discussions conducted from the early 1980s through to the mid-1990s highlight the crucial interplay between media attention, public awareness, and survivors' abilities to identify their experiences, discuss them with other people, and protest against such abuse (see Kitzinger 2001). The 11-year time span of this research highlights the media's special role, quite distinct (but not independent) from other cultural resources, in helping to confront and name sexual abuse.

Before the mid-1980s, the notion that you could be sexually abused as a child by friends and relatives was literally "incredible." The lack of cultural tools to understand what was going on and the inability to "call it something" was highlighted by mothers of abused children. One interviewee, whom I shall call Kathy, described how ill equipped she felt to confront the possibility of sexual abuse until she actually walked in on her husband with her daughter:

> [I felt] totally as though I was just in a nightmare and when daylight came I would wake up and it hadn't happened. And daylight came, and it didn't go away . . . [Finding my husband in there] confirmed what I knew, although I didn't know I knew it. (Kathy, in Kitzinger 2001: 95)

Throughout her account Kathy stressed the absence of cultural reference points and having to respond by "instinct," "like an animal," without any guidance:

> It felt just as though it were a primitive kind of instinct. I had to protect her. It was just like an animal, you know, the young have been threatened and you just have to close round them and just protect them. And that is what I did, in any way I knew how. But I had absolutely no model whatever, *that was the horrible part of it* . . . I just didn't know anything about sexual abuse. I remember thinking: "if only I had read something about it." But I had

> never read anything about it . . . only awful stories in the paper [about abduction], but no useful articles in women's magazines that said "I did so and so." These things just weren't around then. (Kathy, my emphasis, in Kitzinger 2001: 95)

More fundamentally, children and adult survivors lacked the conceptual tools to make sense of their experiences in the first place. The crime was not only unspeakable, it was literally "inconceivable." A woman who had been abused by her stepfather explained that the abuse did not feel "real" because she did not know what to call it. This sense of unreality permeated many of my interviewees' accounts of incestuous assault: "The hardest thing is trying to keep belief in it all – trying to grab hold of it. It just disappears through your fingers as you try to grasp it." One 16-year-old, Samantha, explained that she could not define what her father and other men had done to her since childhood as rape. This was because she felt that she displayed insufficient resistance: "I let them do it." In any case, she saw rape as an encounter in a dark alley-way with "a man with a knife." Samantha argued that, in fact, she could *never* be raped by anyone because "I would just lie down and take it, to get it over with" (Kitzinger 2001: 95).

The feminist exposé of sexual violence and promotion of more sophisticated ideas about power, consent, choice, and exploitation made a different version of reality available. The WLM reached some people directly; however, many more were reached via the mass media. Survivors who had grown up without their experiences being recognized by the dominant culture began to find words and images for what had happened. Prompted by mass media coverage, many began literally to "re-collect" and "re-member" abusive childhoods. Some of my interviewees described how, during the 1980s, they had begun to reassess what had been done to them – finally realizing that it was wrong or "not normal" or that they did not deserve it. Others found that media coverage forced them to confront memories that they had been trying to ignore. As Joanne commented:

> It started being talked about a bit more in the media and then I heard a radio program, that made me start thinking about it . . . Whenever he abused me he never said a word. I always found this silence around it a very loud thing. It's all been so silent. (Kitzinger 2001: 97)

Cultural recognition had an important role in legitimating experience, as Joanne went on to explain:

> [What ever it is] it legitimizes your experiences, it is saying "yes, it does happen" and you know that other people are reading it and are accepting it. Whether it's fact or fiction, whether it is research or autobiography or whatever, it's adding to this. I know when I read Sarah Nelson [a journalist who also published a book on sexual abuse in 1982] it was wonderful seeing all the basic feelings that I had there . . . [And] it moves people forward all the time, and it isn't just odd people saying things . . . it is actually down on paper . . . it's not just me having a fantasy in my head about this, many people believe this. (Joanne) (Kitzinger 2001: 97)

By the mid-1990s, fiction too had become an important source of information and could actively facilitate communication with family and friends. One girl, for example, told me how a TV film, *Liar, Liar*, had improved relations with her mother:

> My mum watched it with me. In the film the mother doesn't believe – my ma watched it and saw what pressure the girl went through and it made her see how I could feel. (Young incest survivors discussion group, group no. 48, f2)

Many incest survivors particularly valued the in-depth portrayal of incest survivor Beth Jordache in the soap opera *Brookside.* As one 15-year-old explained, she and other members of her young abuse survivors' support group would often discuss the program:

> You can watch it and say – I had those feelings like Beth, that happened to me . . . We've got some kind of communication with the telly and can talk to each other about the way Beth is. (Young incest survivors discussion group, group no. 48, f3, in Kitzinger 2001: 98)

Beth Jordache also offered an important positive image of survival – she was strong, sassy, articulate, and confident:[3]

> Victims on TV, they're like a big shadow, all blacked out. That makes me feel terrible, they're hiding away . . . I thought: "I'm going to grow up and I'm going to be scared of everything." But Beth [in *Brookside*], she's so strong, she's got a grip of everything. Before that, everything I saw seemed to say that if you were abused you'd be strange, different, keep yourself in a wee corner. Watching Beth has really helped me. (Young incest survivors discussion group, group no. 48, f3, in Kitzinger 2001: 99)

Media recognition and representation became (and continue to be) a vital part of women's process of naming and making sense of their memories and communication about the experience. Media coverage made a crucial contribution to a spiral of recognition helping to fundamentally transform private and public thinking and discussion. It encouraged the formation and expression of personal identities around this very fragmented and silenced experience and helped sexual abuse, particularly incest, to enter public discourse (Kitzinger 2001).[4]

Any account of how the media represent sexual violence should remember quite how new and crucial such media attention has been. However, that does not mean that media coverage gives cause for uncritical celebration. Although there have clearly been highly significant changes in the extent of attention, and some reform in the nature of coverage, many of the criticisms feminists were making in the 1970s still applied in the 1980s and 1990s and have remained valid into the new millennium. New problems have also emerged. It is these criticisms that are the focus of the next section of this chapter.

New and ongoing criticisms of media coverage

The following section highlights six interrelated areas in which the media in general, or certain segments of the media, are open to criticism. These are:

- the "events-based" emphasis of news reporting;
- media fatigue and declining interest in routine abuse;
- the focus on contested allegations;
- reflecting court-based discourse: excusing perpetrators and perpetuating stereotypes about victims and victimization;
- the "symbolic expulsion" of sexual violence from mainstream society, through the emphasis on stranger danger,
- evasion or misrepresentation of social analysis, positioning sex attackers as "other," "othering" sexual violence by assigning it to homosexuality, positioning victims as "other," and the reification of the law-and-order agenda;
- racism, the white gaze, and selective "color blindness."

The "events-based" emphasis of news reporting

Many media critics have noted that the news as a format tends to be led by *events* rather than *issues*. This is certainly true of news reporting about sexual violence. One study, for example, found that coverage of particular cases accounted for 71 per cent of UK press reports about child sexual abuse (Kitzinger and Skidmore 1995). This leaves little space for in-depth exploration of theoretical issues or any thorough debate about the underlying causes of, or solutions to, the problem. Indeed, the above study located just four articles that focused on the causes of child sexual abuse (out of a total sample of 1,668 items). Similar observations have been made about the reporting of the rape, battering, and abuse of adult women (Cuklanz 1996: 84; Bathla 1998: 107). The news media's bias toward focusing on events rather than issues implicitly presents sexual violence as a taken-for-granted fact of life, with the emphasis placed on intervention and judgment in *particular* accusations rather than broader social solutions. The facts that sexual violence often fits within a traditional crime beat and that much reporting relies on individual court cases also prioritize the justice system as the primary avenue of intervention.

Media "fatigue" and declining interest in routine abuse

In addition to being events-based the news media also have a notoriously short attention span. Peak interest in the 1970s and 1980s soon gave way to media ennui. Journalists interviewed in the 1990s recorded their sense that their editors and their audiences had become "fatigued" with such stories (Benedict 1992: 251; Kitzinger and Skidmore 1995; Skidmore 1998). If routine abuse quickly ceased to be news, however, that does not mean that certain "angles" on the story do not gain a hearing. A new angle has often been provided by controversial allegations and the rise of a new form of skepticism.

The focus on controversial allegations

Statistics about the prevalence of sexual violence no longer make for new, exciting stories or attract sustained reporting. Controversial cases in which allegations are disputed can, however, fit very well into the m edia's news values and routine journalistic practices. Even where such cases do not conform to standard "hard" news values (for example, having clear news "events" and high-status sources), there has been a successful backlash against women's and children's testimony. This backlash has hooked into other media and cultural values, including the "human interest story" (portraying the distressed men being "victimized" by false allegations), longstanding prejudice against the veracity of women and children, and the low status of those who intervene in suspected abuse cases.

The media now often pay more attention to supposedly false allegations than they do to established facts about sexual violence. "Date rape," "false memory syndrome," and contested allegations of child sexual abuse have all fed into a new (or revitalized) discourse of skepticism. Whether or not you believe such skepticism is justified in the particular cases under scrutiny, the diversion of media attention to these cases serves to obscure the larger problem of sexual violence. (For feminist discussion of some of the complex dilemmas around how we interpret allegations, see Reavey and Warner 2003.)

In the UK, for example, sexual abuse began to be recognized as a serious social problem in 1986. However, just one year later the biggest story in the media was about contested allegations in Cleveland. Reports focused on the anguish of those whose children had been taken into care, challenged the validity of diagnostic techniques, and vilified the professionals involved. Headlines included: "Liars and cheats: MP accuses child abuse scandal social services bosses" (*Daily Mirror*, 26 June 1987), "Sack the docs!" (*Sun*, 26 June 1987), and "Accused parents' ordeal: 'They came for my kids at bedtime'" (*News on Sunday*, 26 June 1987). This image of the "Cleveland case" was established as a media template (Kitzinger 2000) and used to make sense of future scandals, such as the 1991 controversy in the Orkney islands (part of the UK) where social workers were accused of "snatching children from innocent families." Repeated linking of Orkney with Cleveland allowed journalists and their readers a short cut to "understanding" both events. Whatever the right and wrongs of each case, the net effect of the analogy was to short circuit critical reflection and to obscure the issue of sexual violence by focusing on social workers as the real villains who "abuse" and "abduct" children (Kitzinger 1996, 2000).

Such scandals were later followed by the "discovery" of false memory syndrome. Accused parents alleged that their adult children had been prompted to incorrectly recall childhood abuse by therapists or a cultural obsession with sexual violence (see box 2.3).

Box 2.3 Examples of headlines about "false memory syndrome" in the UK press

"Therapy of danger: how this sick girl came to believe that her loving parents abused her" (*Mail on Sunday*, December 5, 1995)

"'Memories' that surface to destroy us" (*Sunday Times*, May 15, 1994)

"Total recall? How false memory syndrome reveals a past that never was" (*Guardian*, January 6, 1994)

"Father's nightmare: daughter made up rape story after therapist's counselling" (*Daily Mail*, March 29, 1995)

"Did this man abuse his child? New theories suggest that some women who claim they've been sexually molested by their fathers are, in fact, making it up" (*Daily Mail*, March 3, 1993)

As with the Orkney case, journalists took up this issue of injustice with great vigor. Journalists prioritized the voices of parents protesting their innocence and invited readers to identify with them rather than with the "alleged" victims. The fathers (and some mothers) were seven times more likely to be quoted than their accusing offspring. Again, the reporting followed problematic faultlines. There was, for example, a striking asymmetry in how the credibility of each side was assessed. The emotions of accused fathers were used to assert their innocence; the "hysteria" of those making the accusations was used to undermine their credibility. The rapid rise and nature of media attention to this issue speak volumes about gendered power and media practices. Men may have greater authority and practical/cultural resources as media sources. Men also hold more positions of power within media organizations and sometimes clearly identify with the accused fathers (Kitzinger 1998). However, perhaps more significant is the way in which a "masculine" ethos permeates news-room culture. Media coverage can be informed by subtle processes such as the selective privileging of "masculine" over "feminine" discourses and "ways of knowing" (logic versus emotion, science versus intuition), asymmetrical judgments about men's and women's emotions and credibility (such as through the notion of "hysteria"), and the gendered operation of media formats and genres ("hard" versus "soft" news) (Kitzinger 1998). (For critical reflections about false memories and the construction of sexual abuse experience through a feminist lens, see Reavey and Warner 2003.)

Reflecting court-based discourse: excusing perpetrators and perpetuating stereotypes about victims and victimization

The reliance of journalists on controversial care or court proceedings for many of their stories means that the ideas about causes of sexual violence that slip into reports are often unreflective reiterations of common-sense assumptions. Alternatively they may simply echo courtroom discourse. The latter is particularly problematic because courtrooms are places where traditional patriarchal understandings of rape are reified.

Media reporting of court cases often reflects, and sometimes amplifies, this patriarchal discourse. The victim is often invisible and silent, the anonymous object of competing discourses. She "is constantly spoken of but herself remains inaudible or inexpressible; she is displayed as a spectacle but remains unrepresentable" (Moorti 2002: 110). In the courtroom and in the media, victims are often also routinely cast either as "innocent" or as "guilty" – a dichotomy that is oppressive regardless of which category particular women and children are allowed to occupy. Children, for example, may usually be cast as inherently "innocent," but this can be equally oppressive (see Kitzinger 1990). Similar criticisms apply to the framing of adult victims/survivors of sexual violence, a category usually more "up for grabs" for adult women than for children (Kitzinger 1988; Benedict 1992).

Innocence or guilt may also depend on a woman's behavior. The woman raped by the American boxer Mike Tyson was subtly smeared in the media for driving too fast, partying, and social climbing (Benedict 1992: 257). Claims of rape against William Kennedy-Smith were challenged by declarations by the defense council, reiterated in the media, that the rape charge was made "after a night of drinking in several Palm Beach bars" (Moorti 2002: 95).

While women's behavior is subject to intense scrutiny, the men charged with their assault may have their actions obscured. Journalists often use the passive tense to describe assaults in ways which remove agency from the perpetrator and fail to hold him accountable for his violence (Henley et al. 1995). Journalists may give prominence to the defendant's claims, such as that he misread the signals or that he was provoked by the woman's behavior or by uncontrollable lust (Lees 1995). Analyses of particular cases also show how reports may obscure the nature of assaults. Some newspapers used terms such as "fondling" and "having sex" to describe the gang rape of a victim bashed in the face with a rock (Benedict 1992). An NCB news report described a rape charge against William Kennedy-Smith as a "whiff of sexual misconduct" (Moorti 2002: 91).

Such reports excuse assailants and discredit individual women. More generally they reinforce ideas about how sexual violence should be considered (as not real violence) or how consent should be deduced (for example, accepting an invitation to a hotel room). The responsibility is placed on women to avoid "provocative dress," "immodest behavior," being too assertive, or not assertive enough, or simply going out for a drink with a man.[5] The 1977 parody of advice to women reproduced above (box 2.2) is, unfortunately, just as recognizable today as it was all those decades ago.

The "symbolic expulsion" of sexual violence from mainstream society

The fifth major issue I wish to highlight here is what I shall call the "symbolic expulsion" of sexual violence. I use the phrase to highlight the fact that mainstream representations of sexual violence fail to address radical strategies for expelling this from society (involving, for example, fundamental challenges to gender and sexual norms and power inequalities). Instead, these representations often market a kind of token solution to the problem. This involves very distorted reflections of the nature of sexual violence, with an emphasis on stranger-danger and a tendency to attribute sexual violence to only a certain type of "person" ("the other"). This then sets the scene for promoting a law-and-order-agenda that tackles sexual violence purely by identifying and controlling these individuals. I will illustrate each of these themes and their interrelation below.

The emphasis on stranger-danger

Although media representations of sexual violence no longer exclusively focus on attacks by pathological strangers, this form of assault still receives disproportionate attention. The media are much more drawn to spectacular and unusual cases of serial attacks than the boring routine of ordinary sexual violence endemic in everyday life. The stranger-attack fits with traditional ideas about the nature of "newsworthiness," and the search for a missing child or serial sex-attacker, for example, has its own momentum and rationale that attract intense and prolonged coverage (Soothill and Walby 1991: 145, 157; Kitzinger and Skidmore 1995; Meyers 1997: 93). The "Jack the Ripper" type of approach to telling stories about sexual violence has its own narrative power, which evades important social questions. Analyzing an episode of Fox TV's *America's Most Wanted* about the disappearances of 31 women in Vancouver, Pitman, for example, argues that the imposition of a Jack-the-Ripper "media template" had very problematic consequences. It "displaced local and highly politicized explanations related to prostitution laws, community policing practices, and dangerous urban spaces" (Pitman 2002: 167).

Evasion or misrepresentation of social analysis

At the same time as highlighting the spectacular, and evading social implications, the media also actually often trash any research that highlights the widespread nature of sexual violence – especially if the research is identified with feminism (Soothill and Walby 1991: 145). Often the authority of such points of view is undermined by their being portrayed as biased, emotional, or incoherent (Los and Chamard 1997: 132, 302, 322). Official statistics released by government or US state bodies are harder to discredit. Such figures are more likely to be reported respectfully, but are often treated as one-off or isolated items of information that have no implications for broader media reporting strategies.

Positioning sex attackers as "other"

In addition to sidelining analysis about the widespread nature of sexual violence, and locating sexual threat in "the stranger," journalists also often position abusers as outsiders via a variety of other rhetorical tricks. They may portray an abuser as a "beast," an "animal," or a distinct type of person, almost a separate species. The very fact that there is a special noun, "pedophile," to describe those who sexually abuse children implies that those who commit such acts constitute "a breed apart" (Hebenton and Thomas 1996; Kelly 1996: 45). The concept of the "pedophile" also, of course, singles out the sexual abuse of children, as if there were no connection between abuse perpetrated against boys and girls and those perpetrated against adults.

When journalists do connect sexual violence to endemic cultural attitudes about normal sex or masculinity, it is usually in considering "sub-" or "foreign" cultures rather than taking on board the feminist critique of dominant patriarchal values. News coverage of the "Big Dan" case in 1983, for example, suggested that only the Portuguese-American community held the sort of attitudes which led to rape (Moorti 2002: 82–3). Similarly, reporting about the rape of the Central Park jogger by a group of young black men in 1989 treated "inner city youth culture" as the problem (Cuklanz 1996: 83).

These types of "cultural" explanation are even more evident in reporting sexual violence from abroad, especially from the so-called underdeveloped countries. The US media reporting of the 1991 mass rape case in a Kenyan school, for example, associated the abuse of women with "tribal tradition" and collapsed all Kenyan women into the one-dimensional category of "the oppressed" (Hirsch 1994: 1043, 1045). Sometimes the media seem happier to focus on "exotic" violence against women, so that "dowry burning," "foot binding," "female genital mutilation," or the mistreatment of women under "alien" fundamentalist regimes are treated as evidence of those countries' backwardness. In the case of Afghanistan, the denial of women's rights was even used to justify invasion by the "liberating" American and British forces in 2001.

"Othering" sexual violence by assigning it to homosexuality

Where feminists highlight the links between sexual violence, masculinity, and normal heterosexuality, the mass media often take the opposite tack. The rape of women or girls is not treated as a "heterosexual" crime; however, attacks on boys are often labeled "homosexual." For example, although most cases of sexual abuse reported in the national UK press in 1991 involved allegations of men assaulting girls, there was not a single example of an assault or assailant being described as heterosexual. By contrast, there were 50 reports[6] explicitly identifying the assault or the assailants as "gay" or "homosexual."

Positioning victims as "other"

It is not only the perpetrators who are presented as "other," outside society. The *victims* of sexual exploitation and rape can also be "othered" as if the damage done to them does not really touch "society as a whole." This was exemplified most explicitly when the serial killer "the Yorkshire Ripper" was terrorizing women in northern England in the late 1970s: the media distinguished between prostitutes and "innocent" victims. The attorney general declared that "perhaps the saddest part of this case is that . . . [t]he last six attacks were on totally respectable women," and, after one of the murders, the police warned that the next victim could be "somebody's daughter," as if the murdered prostitutes were not part of anybody's family (Lopez-Jones 1999).

The reification of the law-and-order agenda

The tendencies outlined above allow a "law-and-order" solution to be proposed as the only way forward. It can be used to justify a disproportionate application of the law to certain populations (such as gay men or black inner-city youth). It can also support a refusal to consider how "policing sex" can actually make some women more at risk (for example, curb-crawling laws which make it harder to assess "punters," or the use of condom-possession as evidence against sex workers) (Lopez-Jones 1999). Radical social solutions are ignored and rape prevention initiatives are trivialized – the media seem to prefer to orchestrate outrage about sentencing rather than looking at wider causes (Soothill and Walby 1991: 145). This has been particularly evident in recent media-led campaigns about so-called "pedophiles in the community" (for discussion see Kitzinger 1999; Bell 2003). By confining their attention to a minority of convicted multiple abusers, the media were able to focus not on society but on a few dangerous individuals within it. The problem of sexual violence was represented by the "fiend" who "prowls our streets" and could be singled out, electronically tagged, exposed, and expelled. The newspapers adopting this stance thus shifted attention "away from political solutions addressing male power and the construction of masculinity toward a range of 'problem-management' solutions [such as] . . . long term incarceration (*The Mail*); risk assessment tribunals for dangerous men (*The Guardian* and *The Times*) and individual therapy (*The Guardian*)" (McCollum 1998: 37).

The final theme I wish to highlight in this review of criticisms is that of racism. This cross-cuts many of those discussed above.

Racism, the white gaze, and selective "color blindness"

Reporting about Jack the Ripper in nineteenth-century London suggested he was a "foreigner" or a Jew. Had the sex-murderer been active in America at the same time he undoubtedly would have been cast as a "Negro." The history of media coverage of sexual violence is also a history of racism. In America stories of "black beasts" attacking white women, and the lynching of the alleged perpetrators, were the main vehicle through which sexual violence was mentioned throughout the first part of the twentieth century. Such reporting served to keep both black men and white women in their place (Benedict 1992: 30). At the same time as black men were being persecuted for the alleged sexual threat they posed to white women, black women (especially under slavery) were routinely sexually victimized by white men. This sexual violence was taken for granted, legitimized, or obscured (Moorti 2002: 55). Black women's participation in the anti-rape movement thus has diverse historical roots, including involvement in the late nineteenth-/early twentieth-century anti-lynching movement as well as the investigative journalism of pioneering reporters such as Ida B. Wells (Moorti 2002: 54–7).

Although a white-dominated feminist movement has often prioritized gender as a category of analysis, critics have pointed out that the intersections of gender and race make for specific experiences that cannot be subsumed under the category of "universal woman" as if all women were the same, living under the same conditions. These critics warn against "raceless talk of gender subordination" (Crenshaw 1992) and show how sometimes the race of victims is obscured (Pitman 2002). The inadequacies of any such "color-blind" approach were evident in the 1990s controversies surrounding accusations against black men such as Mike Tyson, the boxer, or Clarence Thomas, the nominee for the supreme court (Morrison 1992).

Moorti's study of rape on television in the US between 1989 and 1993 provides a thorough and incisive study of the problems of racism and "color blindness." She highlights, for example, the racism in the reporting of the rape trial of Mike Tyson. Before the rape allegations surfaced, the boxer was, she argues, presented as an athlete who partially transcended his race. However, once the trial was underway, news workers emphasized his racial identity. "The press offered two visions of Tyson, both informed by stereotypes of African Americans. He was a crude, sex obsessed, violent savage who could barely control his animal instincts; or he was a victim of terrible social circumstances, almost saved from the streets by a kindly overseer, who finally faltered and fell to the connivance of others" (Moorti 2002: 101).

Black women are subject to a different form of racism as it intersects with sexism. The rape of black women may receive less press attention, their allegations may be given less credibility, and the fact that this may be a racist as well as a sexist crime may be ignored (Benedict 1992: 251; Meyers 1997: 66). If the media cast a black woman as a credible and worthy rape victim then this may be achieved by erasing her race. Thus, for example, Tyson's accuser, a black beauty queen, was characterized during his trial as the all-American girl, effectively positioning her as the "white," virginal woman (Moorti 2002: 104–5). This honorary whiteness is precarious, however: after the trial her privileges were withdrawn and she was recast in the mold of the "temptress Jezebel" (Moorti 2002: 104–5).

Moorti's study identifies how "gender, race and class shape who speaks about rape in the public arena and how they speak about it" (ibid.: 14). She highlights the "white gaze" assumed in news reporting and the ways in which the audience is positioned as white; for instance, by the use of the word "we" and assumptions that viewers need to be introduced to the language and culture of "them" – inner-city youth (a code for blackness). Programs "rarely show how race and gender work together to shape individual experience of sexual violence . . . [They] either address rape as it affects (white) women or as an effect of black masculinity, rarely as a site where gender and racial discourse intersect in problematic ways" (Moorti 2002: 13–14). Thus although, for example, racial difference may be used in prime-time entertainment programs to provide dramatic tension, "when the story lines focus on race, rape tends to slide out of view. Racial oppression and gender oppression are rarely shown simultaneously" (Moorti 2002: 215).

Conclusion

In sum, the media coverage of sexual violence has been transformed since the early 1970s. The degree of recognition of sexual violence and the nature of reporting have in many cases improved. The media have been a vital conduit contributing to a radical reshaping of the public profile of sexual violence. However, problems persist. Sometimes all that has happened is that the racism or sexism, for example, has become more subtle; a "white male gaze" is still dominant. In addition, while appearing to adopt feminist perspectives, the media seem to have consistently failed to take on the more radical critiques of how society supports and perpetuates sexual violence. Instead they opt for the purely "symbolic expulsion" of sexual violence from our midst. New problems have also emerged. These include the ambivalence of reporting around issues such as "date rape," which reawakens old myths about sexual assault, and the focus on disputed allegations of child sexual abuse. Analysts of recent media coverage point to a growing media ennui with the issue of routine abuse, which is now seen as old news, as well as a backlash against women's testimony and a shift of focus whereby accused men become the real victims.

It would be wrong simply to blame journalists. The media are often reflecting popular assumptions and sometimes may even be echoing problems from within parts of feminist analysis. The "color-blind" approach, which appeals to the notion of some universal women (as if all women shared a common experience), for example, is a problem in some strands of feminist analysis as well as in the media. Efforts to understand media coverage need to take into account the source organizations and events, and other production processes which feed into reporting. I have highlighted the way court discourses are reflected in the news media and the implications of an "events-based" approach. Other factors that impact on reporting include deadlines, news values, and issues such as format constraints. One clear problem is also the lack in newsrooms of sexual violence specialists who are experienced in the complexities of the issue. (For a discussion of such constraints see Benedict 1992; Kitzinger and Skidmore 1995; Meyers 1997; Skidmore 1998.)

This chapter has tried to give an overall picture of media coverage, often focusing on news reporting. However, there are limitations to generalizing about the media without attention to genre. Many theorists argue that media formats such as one-off dramas, soap opera, and talk shows open up new possibilities for addressing sexual violence in innovative ways. (For discussion see Cuklanz 1996, 2000; Moorti 2002; Henderson 1999, 2002.) Finally, a full understanding of the role of the media in representing sexual violence would also need to analyze audience reception . . . but that, of course, is another story.

Key terms

"Big Dan" case
carnal knowledge
contested allegations
date rape
discourse of skepticism
domestic violence
false memory syndrome
"Jack the Ripper"
law-and-order agenda
media fatigue (of abuse)
rape
rape in marriage
(re)discovery of sexual violence
second wave feminism
sexual violence
spiral of recognition (of sexual violence)
stranger-danger
symbolic expulsion (of sexual violence)
victims as "other"
white gaze versus colonial gaze
"Yorkshire Ripper"

Questions for discussion

1 How has media coverage of sexual violence improved over the years, according to research by Kitzinger and others? Be sure to give some specific examples.
2 How has this improvement served to "transform private and public thinking," according to Kitzinger? What examples does she give of this transformation in thinking?
3 Improvements aside, the author writes that the media coverage of these problems is still far from acceptable. What are her specific criticisms?
4 In what ways do courtrooms serve as "places where traditional patriarchal understandings of rape are reified," in the author's analysis?

5 How has Kitzinger used interviews with survivors of sexual violence as a method for assessing media coverage of sexual abuse?
6 Most of the words that describe sexual violence (that is, the terms that Kitzinger uses in this chapter) are the product of second wave feminism, when women began to name their abuse experiences. Make a list of these words and explain how a news reporter working before 1970 might have covered a police report of a woman's rape or a child's molestation without them.

Notes

1 Media coverage has played different roles in different countries, and the form of sexual violence around which women have campaigned also varies. This chapter focuses on the US and UK context. Other issues have become important in other countries; for example, although I could find no systematic studies it is clear that the media have played a crucial, and controversial, role in campaigns against military sexual slavery when Korean women, for instance, sought to sue the Japanese government (Yoon n.d.).
2 For discussion of radical feminist analysis of sexual violence during the 1970s see, for example, the classic books: *Against Our Wills* (Brownmiller 1977) and *Female Sexual Slavery* (Barry 1979).
3 She was also a lesbian, an identity welcomed by some, but viewed with rather more ambivalence by others. Interviewees who took the latter position either felt this promoted the idea that sexual violence made women into lesbians, or viewed lesbianism as, in itself, a negative identity.
4 For discussion of women's responses to TV representations of battery and rape, see Schlesinger et al. (1992).
5 In addition the very narrative structure of some reports encourages this approach. Kay Weaver examined the representation of sexual violence on reconstruction crime programs such as *Crimewatch*. She argues that they teach women "that it is their individual responsibility to restrict and censure their activities so as to avoid becoming the victim of this form of crime . . . viewers were not provided with any alternative means of imagining how violent attacks upon women could be prevented" (Weaver 1998: 262).
6 This figure underestimates the extent of the asymmetry because it does not include the more subtle coded reference to assailants who were unmarried or "effeminate" or still lived with their mothers – common ways of implying homosexuality (Kitzinger 1999).

References

Angelou, M. (1969) *I Know Why The Caged Bird Sings*. Random House, New York.

Armstrong, L. (1978) *Kiss Daddy Goodnight: A Speakout on Incest*. Pocket Books, New York.

Barry, K. (1979) *Female Sexual Slavery*. Avon, New York.

Bathla, S. (1998) *Women, Democracy and the Media*. Sage, London.

Bell, V. (2003) The vigilant(e) parent and the paedophile: the *News of the World* campaign 2000 and the contemporary governmentality of child sexual abuse. In: Reavey, P. and Warner, S. (eds), *Challenging the Tyranny of Truth: New Feminist Stories of Child Sexual Abuse*. Routledge, London, pp. 108–28.

Benedict, H. (1992) *Virgin or Vamp: How the Press Cover Sex Crimes*. Oxford University Press, Oxford and New York.

Brownmiller, S. (1977) *Against Our Wills*. Penguin, New York.

Byerly, C. (1994) An agenda for teaching news coverage of rape. *Journalism Education* Spring, 59–69.

Byerly, C. (1999) News, feminism and the dialectics of gender relations. In: Meyers, M. (ed.), *Mediated Women: Representations in Popular Culture*. Hampton Press, Cresskill, NJ, pp. 383–403.

Crenshaw, K. (1992) Whose story is it anyway? Feminists and anti-racist appropriations of Anita Hill. In: Morrison, T. (ed.), *Race-ing Justice, En-Gendering Power: Essays on Anita Hill, Clarence Thomas and the Social Construction of Reality*. Pantheon, New York, pp. 402–41.

Cuklanz, L. (1996) *Rape on Trial*. University of Pennsylvania Press, Philadelphia.

Cuklanz, L. (2000) *Rape on Prime-Time: Television, Masculinity and Sexual Violence*. University of Pennsylvania Press, Philadelphia.

Curtis, L. Perry (2001) *Jack the Ripper and the London Press*. Yale University Press, New Haven, CT.

Donat, P. and D'emilio, J. (1992) A feminist redefinition of rape and sexual assault: historical foundations and change. *Journal of Social Issues* 48(1), 9–22.

Hebenton, B. and Thomas, T. (1996) Tracking sex offenders. *Howard Journal* 35(2), 97–112.

Henderson, L. (1996) *Incest in Brookside: Audience Responses to the Jordache Story*. Channel Four, London.

Henderson, L. (1999) Producing serious soaps. In: Philo, G. (ed.), *Message Received*. Addison, Wesley, Longman, Harlow.

Henderson, L. (2002) Serious issues in soaps. Unpublished PhD, University of Glasgow.

Henley, N., Miller, M., and Beazley, J. (1995) Syntax, semantics and sexual violence: agency and the passive voice. *Journal of Language and Social Psychology* 14(1), 60–84.

Hirsch, S. (1994) Interpreting media representations of a "night of madness": law and culture in the construction of rape identities. *Law and Social Review* 19(4), 1023–56.

Kelly, L. (1996) Weasel words: paedophiles and the cycle of abuse. *Trouble and Strife* 33, 44–9.

Kitzinger, J. (1988) Defending innocence: ideologies of childhood. *Feminist Review* 28, 77–87.

Kitzinger, J. (1990) Who are you kidding? Children, power and the struggle against sexual abuse. In: James, A. and Prout, A. (eds), *Constructing and Reconstructing Childhood.* Falmer Press, London, pp. 157–83.

Kitzinger, J. (1994) Challenging sexual violence against girls: a public awareness approach to preventing sexual abuse. *Child Abuse Review* 3(4), 246–8.

Kitzinger, J. (1996) Media representations of sexual abuse risks. *Child Abuse Review* 5(5), 319–33.

Kitzinger, J. (1998) The gender-politics of news production: silenced voices and false memories. In: Carter, C., Branston, G., and Allan, S. (eds.) *News, Gender and Power*. Routledge, London, pp. 186–203.

Kitzinger, J. (1999) The ultimate neighbour from hell: stranger danger and the media representation of paedophilia. In: Franklin, B. (ed.), *Social Policy, the Media and Misrepresentation.* Routledge, London, pp. 207–1.

Kitzinger, J. (2000) Media templates: patterns of association and the (re)construction of meaning over time. *Media, Culture and Society* 22(1), 64–84.

Kitzinger, J. (2001) Transformations of public and private knowledge: audience reception, feminism and the experience of childhood sexual abuse. *Feminist Media Studies* 1(1), 91–104. Kitzinger, J. and Skidmore, P. (1995) Playing safe: media coverage of the prevention of child sexual abuse. *Child Abuse Review* 4(1), 47–56.

Lees, S. (1995) The media reporting of rape: the 1993 British "Date Rape" controversy. In: Kidd-Hewiit, D. and Osborne, R. (eds), *Crime and the Media: The Post-Modern Spectacle.* Pluto Press, London, pp. 107–30.

London Rape Crisis Center (1984) *Sexual Violence: The Reality for Women.* Women's Press, London.

Lopez-Jones, N. (ed.) (1999) *Some Mother's Daughter: The Hidden Movement of Prostitute Women Against Violence.* International Prostitutes Collective/ Crossroads Books, London.

Los, M. and Chamard, S. (1997) Selling newspapers or educating the public? Sexual violence in the media. *Canadian Journal of Criminology* 39(3), 293–328.

McCollum, H. (1998) What the papers say. *Trouble and Strife* 37, 31–7.

Meyers, M. (1994) News of battering. *Journal of Communication* 44(2), 47–63.

Meyers, M. (1997) *News Coverage of Violence Against Women: Engendering Blame.* Sage, London and Newbury Park, CA.

Mills, K. (1997) What difference do women journalists make?. In: Norris, P. (ed.), *Women, Media and Politics*. Oxford University Press, Oxford, pp. 41–56.

Moorti, S. (2002) *Color of Rape: Gender and Rape in Television's Public Spheres*. State University of New York Press, New York.

Morrison, T. (ed.) (1992) *Race-ing justice, En-Gendering Power: Essays on Anita Hill, Clarence Thomas and the Social Construction of Reality*. Pantheon, New York.

Pearsall, R. (1969) *The Worm in the Bud*. Macmillan, Ontario.

Pitman, B. (2002) Re-mediating the spaces of reality television: *America's Most Wanted* and the case of Vancouver's missing women. *Environment and Planning* 34(1), 167–84.

Reavey, P. and Warner, S. (eds) (2003) *Challenging the Tyranny of Truth: New Feminist Stories of Child Sexual Abuse*. Routledge, London.

Schlesinger, P., Dobash, R. E., Dobash, R., and Weaver, C. K. (1992) *Women Viewing Violence Against Women*. BFI, London.

Skidmore, P. (1998) Gender and the agenda: news reporting of child sexual abuse. In: Carter, C., Branston, G., and Allan, S. (eds), *News, Gender and Power*. Routledge, London, pp. 204–21.

Smart, C. and Smart, B. (1978) Accounting for rape: reality and myth in press reporting. In: Smart, C. and Smart, B. (eds), *Women, Sexuality and Social Control*. Routledge and Kegan Paul, London, pp. 89–103.

Soothill, K. and Walby, S. (1991) *Sex Crimes in the News*. Routledge, London.

Tierney, K. (1982) The battered women movement and the creation of the wife beating problem. *Social Problems* 29(3), 207–20.

War on Rape Collective (1977) *War on Rape*. Melbourne, WRC.

Weaver, K. (1998) *Crimewatch UK*: keeping women off the streets. In: Carter, C., Branston, G., and Allan, S. (eds), *News, Gender and Power*. Routledge, London, pp. 248–62.

Yoon, B. (n.d.) Military sexual slavery: political agenda for feminist scholarship and activism. http://witness.peacenet.or.kr/kindex.htm

3
Exclusion and Marginality: Portrayals of Women in Israeli Media

Dafna Lemish

Introduction

Of all the social issues splitting Israeli society in this day and age, gender inequality is noteworthy for the low level of public discourse it has generated. Moreover, the self-image of Israeli society is one of egalitarianism and liberalism. The myth of the female kibbutz pioneer, the conscription of women into the army, the election of a woman – Golda Meir – as prime minister, and the adoption of politically correct slogans regarding family violence all promulgate the illusion of equality. Gender studies programs have been established to one degree or another at all of the Israeli universities, and their popularity, particularly among female students, is growing constantly. Most of the women who are currently Members of Knesset (Parliament) openly identify themselves as feminists. Women's organizations have been leading the struggle for equality, and in recent years they have made substantial gains in advancing the status of women in Israel in such areas as legislation and the courts. In spite of all this, perhaps precisely because feminism has apparently been embraced within the social consensus, the gender gap has largely remained outside the current discourse on social inequalities. Furthermore, its absence from the listings of the main social rifts in key intellectual analyses, (such as Horowitz and Lissak 1992; Smooha 1993) encourages delegitimization of the need to recognize the mere existence of the problem, let alone the difficulties of coping with its manifest and latent dimensions.

The reality of Israeli society, however, suggests a continuing state of gender discrimination. In the workplace, for example, women are still concentrated in a limited number of fields of employment and, within them, in specific occupations (horizontal segregation). They staff the jobs of lower status, influence, and rewards (vertical segregation). Their entry into new sectors usually occurs either when men abandon those sectors and/or when, in parallel, the status, salary, and working conditions of those jobs deteriorate (for example, in the field of education, and more recently in other areas such as family medicine, law, and the media professions).

Women's income stands, on average, at 62 per cent of men's income for the same work as a whole (Central Bureau of Statistics 2002). Not only has this gap not diminished with the growing numbers of women entering the workforce, but it has grown as a result of the increase of variable components in the salary structure (such as overtime, travel and telephone expenses, and the like). In addition, women usually aggregate fewer pension rights, since they often suspend employment for the sake of starting a family and taking care of their young children, and they also are the first to suffer from spreading unemployment. Meanwhile, their life expectancy is longer than that of men. The economic status of divorced women, widows, new-immigrant women, and single mothers also contributes to the growing feminization of poverty in Israeli society.

Similarly, in the institutional political arena in Israel – such as the political parties, the Knesset (Parliament), and local authorities – the absence of women continues to be remarkable. Their representation in the Israeli Knesset has fluctuated between 6.6 per cent and 13 per cent throughout the years. The 1996 elections resulted in the entry of nine women into the Knesset (7.5 per cent), a decline from the 9.1 per cent of the previous elections in 1992 (Fogiel-Bijaoui 1997). The current (2002) Knesset has 15 women, who constitute 13 per cent of its parliamentarians and put Israel in 49th place in the world for proportion of women in Parliament (following the USA). The various explanations offered for this gloomy situation include: the absence of socialization processes preparing women for roles in the public arena; the influence of the Israeli electoral system and the channels for achieving positions of power; the fact that the political hierarchies are ruled by men (some of them with a ladder for advancement within the party and some of them with individuals "parachuted" in from previous army careers), and the like. Political life is still perceived as being governed by relationships of power, toughness, and aggression, therefore making it seem inappropriate for women, who are perceived as passive citizens engaged in their "natural" maternal and domestic roles (Fogiel-Bijaoui 1998).

Portrayals of Women in Israeli Media

The Israeli context presents unique insights into understanding the universal discrimination against women. The traditional national emphasis on family and childbearing perpetuates woman's place in the private sphere and puts her in conflict with her activities outside its realm. "The unique mission of the woman, the mission of motherhood – there is no greater mission than that in life," declared the first prime minister of Israel, David Ben Gurion, in 1949, in a debate about releasing married women from compulsory military service. A related theme is the centrality of the army in the ongoing struggle for defense and occupation, due to the ongoing Arab–Israeli conflict since before the War of Independence in 1948, as well as the conflict with the Palestinian people in the territories occupied following the Six-Day War of 1967. These issues fertilize a system of associated masculine behaviors (such as war, conquest, repression, exploitation, violence, and rape) that have grown to dominate the public sphere and have served to marginalize women (Deutsch 1994). Indeed, participation in the public discourse that gives unequivocal preference to questions of "national security" impedes women's ability to take part in the central political sphere (Mayer 1994).

The growing status of the religious political parties in Israel and the control that the religious establishment (such as the Rabbinical courts) has over individuals' lives harm, first and foremost, the status of women and their freedom of choice with regard to marriage, divorce, and rights over their own bodies. The Israeli religious establishment has consistently demonstrated opposition to the political equality of women, including their participation in obligatory army service as a means of strengthening their status in society – personally and publicly – and to their participation in organizing religious life within their communities (Swirski and Safir 1991). Despite the fact that the majority of the Jewish population is secular, and that the Declaration of Independence proclaims equality between the sexes, every effort to realize this through legislation has been blocked by one or another overriding religious principle or interest. In general, religious interests take precedence over egalitarian principles in the Israeli legislative process. Moreover, the court system has chosen, by its lack of intervention, to prefer cultivation of the Jewish nature of the state over its egalitarian nature (Raday 1991).

The purpose of this chapter is to examine the portrayals of women in the Israeli media through an integrated overview of various studies conducted by Israeli researchers, including my own accumulated work. What can we learn from an examination of the media about women's place in Israeli society in the early years of the new millennium? The analysis of women's representation in Israeli media needs to be understood in the general context of theories and empirical evidence on representation of women globally.

Media texts are perceived to be one of the prime cultural sites through which it is possible to study the position of women in society. This is an arena within which our society presents itself publicly, defines our identity for us, establishes the parameters of consensus, and relegates what is perceived as unconventional to the margins. Worldwide studies on the representation of women, based on a variety of methodologies (both content analyses and semiotics) and of media (television, cinema, magazines, newspapers, radio, advertising, computer games), suggest similar frameworks of gender discrimination. Women are mostly relegated to the private sphere and to the emotional and sexual worlds. Women and women's issues (such as concerns for equal rights, health issues, feminization of poverty, women's peace movements and military service, and the like) are compartmentalized in media texts, formats, and schedules; a restricted set of personal characteristics and professions is considered; and women are presented mostly in subordination to men (for integrated overviews and specific issues see, among others, van Zoonen 1994; Valdivia 1995; Biagi and Kern-Foxworth 1997; Brunsdon et al. 1997; Carter et al. 1998; Meyers 1999; Sreberny and van Zoonen 2000). This framing of women by the media was defined by Tuchman (1978) as "symbolic annihilation," achieved through processes of condemnation, trivialization, and the absence of women from the media.

Portraits of women in Israeli media

Content analyses of Israeli print and broadcast media have involved documenting both reality-based genres (such as newspapers, news programs, current-events programs, talk shows, and social programs) and entertainment formats (such as quiz shows, soap operas, and children's programs) and have tended to demonstrate the marginality of women in Israeli society. While men are presented as the "normal" majority of society, women are portrayed as the minority, the "other," the exception, the incomplete, the damaged, the marginal, and sometimes even the bizarre.

An examination of Israeli media reveals fundamental principles of patriarchal thinking, including relegating the feminine to the private sphere, restricting the presentation of women to the physical functions of sex and reproduction, and locating women within the world of emotions where rational thought is lacking and behavior uncultivated. Advancing the perception of the marginality of women in society finds expression in all media. To the extent that women are shown at all, they are limited primarily to traditional roles related to the private sphere, or, if they do appear in the public sphere, it is in such traditional caring roles as voluntary activities or work in education, health, welfare, and the like. Women's personality traits are depicted as being fundamentally different in nature from those of men: they are less logical, ambitious, active, independent, heroic, and dominating. By contrast, they are portrayed as being more romantic, sensitive, dependent, and vulnerable (Tidhar and Lemish 1993). The following pages examine these claims in detail on the basis of analyses of the content of the Israeli media, by quantitative as well as semiotic research methods.

Representations of the "real world"

The main body of research on women in the Israeli media has dealt with them as subjects of the news, current events, and politics, as depicted on television and in print media. Various studies conducted have dealt with complex issues such as the degree of female presence in different genres, women's placement in the framework of various programs, the way they are presented, the traits attributed to them, and the like. In the very first study in this area, an analysis of Israeli news programs broadcast in 1988, Tidhar (1988) found that men appeared six times more frequently than women, and that men aged more than 50 spoke directly to the camera four times more often than women in the same age group, while women younger than 20 appeared six times more frequently than their male counterparts.

There were also notable differences in the roles of interviewees on news programs and talk shows: women appeared in dependent roles more often than men – such as "the wife of . . . , the mother of . . ." – while men more often appeared in professional positions. Representatives of the public were exclusively men, while women represented the volunteer sector. Ariel's (1988) study on the patterns of introducing women in Israeli television, newspapers, and magazines suggested complementary findings. While men, in print and broadcast media, were introduced with their professional credentials, women were introduced in terms of their sex and family identities. Written descriptions of men presented them as independent people working outside the home, while women were presented as immature, dependent on others, unemployed outside the home, and addressed by their first names.

Israel was one of 71 countries in which the images of women and men were examined on a random day (18 January) in 1995 (Media Watch 1995). Using a uniform research tool, the content of the "hard" news pages of newspapers and the news reports on radio and television in each country was examined. The findings reinforced what was known from previous studies: most of those interviewed or mentioned in the news were men (91 per cent on television, 90 per cent on radio, and 85 per cent in newspapers of that day). In the Israeli sample, topics dealing specifically with the world of women, such as health, employment, discrimination, and the like, were all but absent from the sphere known as "news" (10 per cent on television, 8.5 per cent on radio, and 0 per cent in newspapers of that day).

Of particular importance was the finding that the most common role for women in Israeli news was as victims (of violence, crime, accidents, and disasters). Women as victims accounted for 67 per cent of all women mentioned by or seen on television, 57 per cent of those on radio, and 72 per cent of those in newspapers. The preference of the media for dealing with women as victims (overcreative or active women, for example) is a double-edged sword. On the one hand, the media create public awareness of violence against women, thus advancing social debate and remedies. On the other hand, the media's tendency to eroticize, trivialize, and sensationalize (for example, excessive detailing of the acts of sex and violence, exaggerated use of color headlines and emotional rhetoric, invasive pictures, and so on) depicts the phenomenon as the private battles of passive, unfortunate women, rather than a structural, inherent, social problem arising from power relations and inequality. The media discussion makes extensive use of the "institutional" voice in covering these subjects – the responsible policeman, the prosecuting judge – reinforcing the impression that "everything is under control," while ignoring the female voice of the victim and her environment. One way or another, the media continue to perpetuate the impression of females as weak, passive, and in need of male protection (for similar findings in the UK and USA see, for example, Benedict 1992; Carter 1998; Meyers 1997).

Another comparative study examined the image of women in the print and broadcast media in 41 countries, on 7–8 May 1995. This study also found that in Israel women comprised less than 10 per cent of the central figures in the news and that they were almost entirely absent from the public sphere with regard to domestic politics, foreign policy, defense and security, economics, commerce, and religion (First and Shaw 1998).

A study of the portrayal of female immigrants from the former Soviet Union sheds additional light on the issues. Analysis of the content of the Hebrew press between 1994 and 1997 demonstrated that these female immigrants were presented primarily in the context of the sex industry in Israel: prostitutes, call girls, and escort girls. As such, they were depicted as the "other" of Israeli society. They were to be located in the margins of Israeli society among those living in poverty and in criminal society. Their Jewishness was called into question, and they certainly did not behave as was expected of Jewish women and mothers: they were often single mothers, they had abortions, they drank alcohol, and the like. This manner of coverage demonstrates the process by which female citizens who are part of the collective "us" are portrayed as "others" who are foreign to Israeli society and undermine morals and the desired social order (Lemish 2000).

Of particular interest is an examination of the status of the wives of prime ministers in the Israeli press (Lemish and Drob 2002). Analysis of the media coverage of Leah Rabin, Sonia Peres, and Sarah Netanyahu revealed that, while each developed a different pattern of behavior vis-à-vis contact with the media, all three had placed a high value on the family as they compromised on or gave up their own careers (in the traditional female professions of nurse, teacher, and psychologist, respectively). All three had played the role of "first lady" through some form of public volunteer work, an activity generally reserved for women in possession of independent financial means. Press coverage of these women placed particular emphasis on the private sphere: their personal appearance, descriptions of their home, furnishings, the domestic atmosphere, remodeling, the dinner parties they held, and so on. Over the years, in fact, the wives of Israeli prime ministers have been portrayed as totally conforming to the traditional profile of women in Israeli society: none presented herself, through the media, as a model for the advancement of the status of women.

Coverage of women in competitive sports is another unique area that has been examined (Bernstein 1997). Since sport is an area dealing with the physical world, it offers grounds for examining how the physicality of the male body is presented as a paradigm of superiority over female physicality. For example, "sport" is an inclusive concept, though its use is reserved for reference to masculine activities. Hence, coverage of sports activities in which women engage is depicted as "other" – "women's sports." Coverage of sports activities in which Israeli women engage is negligible. For example, in one study reported by Bernstein (1997), it was found that only 5 per cent of the items in newspaper sports sections were devoted to female athletes, and even then as small news items not accompanied by photographs. Pictures of women in the sports sections usually portrayed them in dependent roles: "The wife of . . . the girlfriend of . . ." Coverage of female athletes addressed, among other details, their external appearance, thus diminishing their athletic achievements and reducing them, as with other women, to their sexual functions (for a more general perspective, see Creedon 1994).

The inequality in how women and men are portrayed by the media is so deep that it is even perpetuated in election campaigns by parties officially committed to social equality. Lemish and Tidhar (1999b) found that promotional campaign broadcasts – which are the "calling cards" of the political parties and their public image – during the 1988 and 1996 elections deviated only slightly from the familiar images. Across all parties, women appeared on the average in 13 per cent of campaign broadcasts in 1988, and 17 per cent in 1996, and they had the following characteristics: they were younger than the men; they were more likely to be presented without being identified or without definition of professional credentials; they appeared in vox pops; and they were depicted with more emotional messages than men. They received less camera exposure during their appearances and tended to be shown in mixed groups with men. A qualitative analysis of these images highlighted how, during the 1988 campaign, pretty young women dressed in the height of fashion opened and closed the broadcasts of the large parties, providing continuity between segments, and "assisting" the public to reach the "right" conclusions. In this role, they did not express any personal political opinions, but rather narrated the party line. Most of the parties did not permit women to present the parties' position on such central issues as peace, security, and the economy. The little exposure given to female politicians focused on familiar women's areas – education, health, and welfare. Relatively anonymous women were chosen to speak about the Israeli–Arab conflict. Each was presented in her dependency role, that is, the claims and the justifications for them derived from the women's roles as "friend of . . . mother of . . . grandmother of . . ." In these roles, the women represented the civilian home front and wondered aloud about the ramifications of the possible death (or about death which had already occurred) of the men in their lives. Thus, they were relegated to the private aspect of the public sphere.

During the 1996 campaign, the "motherhood" strategy was particularly evident. Women-as-mothers was the dominant message of most of the parties. Mothers appeared with babies on their laps and children at their sides. As mothers, they spoke of their children, while the camera continually panned to the children. In this role, they spoke of peace, the future, education, equality, personal security, poverty, religion, retirement, minorities, and army service. Bereaved mothers spoke in the names of their children. Even such a senior female politician as Limor Livnat (who later became the only female minister in the Netanyahu government, and is now the minister of education in Sharon's government), in her personal appeal to the electorate, drafted in her children, Shir and Yair, who apparently feared going on their annual school trips because of the absence of peace and security. It seemed that only women's roles as mothers could legitimize their appearance on the screen and the message they were conveying.

Analysis of deviations from these expected norms is particularly interesting. In 1988, of all the campaign broadcasts, there was only one that presented a woman who was not a politician, not in a dependent position, not reading a prepared script but expressing her personal opinions on general political topics. This exceptional woman was a high-school student from a northern development town. It is interesting to note that this "extraordinary" appearance engendered extensive public reaction in the mass media and became one of the "trademarks" of that year's campaign. Using the political opinions expressed by a teenage girl of Jewish-Middle-Eastern origin – moreover, one from a peripheral town (four deviations from the "norm" of male, adult, middle-class, of Jewish-European origin) – was, it would seem, still an exceptional strategy in the Israeli media.

It is interesting to note that the trend toward change was found among small, marginal political parties with records of interest and action in the fields of human rights and women's rights. In this case, the media, as in many other instances in the history of social-political transitions (as, for example, in the case of the movement for withdrawal from Lebanon in 1982, or indeed in the American anti-war movement during the Vietnam war in the early 1960s in the USA), echoed the early signs of possible change in the existing social reality, rather than leading this new trend themselves. It seems that the media tend to break the "spiral of silence" (the process by which certain issues or perspectives are excluded from the media, reinforcing a false sense of their absence in real life) and to give a voice to alternative perspectives when they sense that the public is ripe to break through consensual views.

In her study of women in local politics in Israel, Herzog (1998) demonstrated the different ways through which the media fixated on these women's roles in the private sphere rather than on their public agendas, portraying them as interlopers trying to achieve the impossible. These themes where highlighted through the relegation of the discussion of women in politics to women's magazines and the women's sections in the national and local newspapers (instead of political-news sections); excessive emphasis on the fact that the candidate was "first of all – a woman"; depiction of the involvement in politics as threatening femininity and as being in conflict with self-fulfillment in the home and family frameworks; and emphasis on extraordinary women as being the exception to the rule.

Unique conflict situations, such as the uprising in the occupied Palestinian territories (Intifada) from the late 1980s, sharpen the problematics of the images of women in television news (Tidhar and Lemish 1993). When society is drawn into the whirlpool of a major social political conflict, people's lives naturally tend to become more politically oriented. Such situations have particular effects on women. On the one hand, as members of society they must reorganize their lives in the face of threats to social, political, economic, and/or physical existence. On the other hand, under such circumstances, women tend to become more active in the public sphere, traditionally occupied by men. However, in an analysis of the content of news over the course of several years, it was found that the Intifada was framed as a male issue on all levels: only 5 per cent of the figures that appeared on screen were women, and 18 per cent of the figures appeared in mixed groups. The decisive majority of those interviewed were men, while the minority of women interviewed appeared in dependent positions more than in any professional capacity. Only women who expressed extreme political views were identified by name and role. Further, substantial differences surfaced between the images of Jewish and Palestinian women: while Jewish women were presented stereotypically, in a manner familiar with other studies of the news, Palestinian women were presented as being more active, side by side with the men, without a clear gender distinction. This supports Ridd's (1986) argument that despite the fact that war and conflict are male territory, women are capable of actively penetrating it when the situation is perceived as an extreme and temporary crisis, such as the Palestinian struggle for independence. This accounts for the power of the image of Palestinian women with firearms, or leading violent or mournful demonstrations.

It should be emphasized that the unique contribution of both Jewish and Palestinian women – each group independently on its respective side, as well as through joint actions – has not attracted media coverage. Editors of television news, as revealed by research about the Intifada, chose to ignore women's political movements that deviated from the national consensus or sought to offer alternative ways to resolve political crisis. For example, there was a startling absence of coverage of the Women in Black, a protest movement against the ongoing occupation, who challenged the Israeli social and gendered order, raised questions about it, and proposed alternative action (Hellman and Rapaport 1997). In contrast, another political protest movement that objected to the presence of the Israeli army in Lebanon – Four Mothers – emphasized the fears of mothers for the fate of their children and openly spoke with the "force of the womb." This movement has enjoyed relatively broad media coverage, and its success in changing the national agenda can be attributed to the positive role accorded to motherhood by Israeli society. Perceived as the ultimate female sacrifice for the national collective, this role accords legitimacy to the female voice in the public sphere, whereas expression of women's political opinion as equal members of society does not earn comparable recognition (Lemish and Barzel 2000).

The aggregate picture requires our asking about "intention." Is there a media policy that intentionally prevents the voice of women from being heard? We were able to confront this question with the outbreak of the Gulf War in 1991, when women disappeared from the Israeli airwaves. In-depth interviews conducted with senior (male) personnel in broadcast organizations revealed that this disappearance was more the result of outright subconscious discrimination than of a conscious policy (Lemish and Tidhar 1999a). For these men, women in general were perceived as being less professional and as unreliable during a period of distress because of the conflict with their role as mothers and their emotionality. Similarly, policy-makers also relied on an assumption (which has never been proven empirically) that the public, comprised of both men and women, prefers the "authoritative" voice of a man (naturalized and cultivated preference). Here, too, there was one woman who was an exception that proved the rule: Orly Yaniv, who anchored a news program throughout the period of the war. As an attractive female figure, non-argumentative and non-threatening, she fulfilled her role as a supportive, non-aggressive interviewer, and represented herself as the "person in the street," rather than the "expert" professional. A clear example of the discrimination against female broadcasters during the Gulf War was illustrated by the following quotation from a senior radio editor:

> I made the manpower decisions, so I say it with full responsibility: The decision who will broadcast what was not made according to the broadcaster's sex. It was *my* decision [about] who can stand a difficult and stressful situation? I made my decisions accordingly. I think the considerations were purely professional. We purposefully chose a small group of men, only four, so that the population would identify with them and get used to them . . . The female broadcasters are mothers, they have children. There were women who stayed home or went away. There was a feeling that 6 million people were listening, and the smallest mistake could have cost many dangerous self-injections of antropin shots [the antidote for biological- and chemical-warfare materials]. There was the fear that the broadcaster will lose control during the broadcast. Imagine he hears that a Scud missile just hit the street where he lives. He is the source of authority at that moment. You can't replace him if his voice is shaky and he sounds panicked. My decision was practical. Who could we trust under such conditions. There was no discrimination. (cited in Lemish and Tidhar 1999a: 29)

Evidently, only women were perceived in terms of being the parents of children (private sphere); it was only they who might panic (emotionality); it was only they who could not be relied upon (childishness, lack of professionalism). All of this is anchored in the eyes of the above speaker as a pure, rational, and professional perception.

Advertising

Advertising is of primary interest in the discussion of gender representations because it is an essential mechanism for advancing capitalism and western patriarchal interests and therefore serves as a mobilizing force for inhibiting the possibility of change. Chief among the criticisms leveled by feminists against advertising in Israel is that it frequently and blatantly depicts women as sex objects. Semiotic analysis has identified the ways in which exposed parts of the female anatomy are displayed, in provocative body movements, enticing facial expressions, tantalizing glances, finger movements, self-caressing, emphasis on the lips, as well as extensive use of lingual and para-lingual movements. In all of these ways advertising frequently reduces women to their simple sexual functions (Lemish 1997).

In spite of the many ways in which advertising in Israel was transformed with the introduction of commercial television in the early 1990s, only a few changes have taken place in the portrayal of women in advertising over the last 20 years. Research findings comparing advertisements that appeared in Israeli newspapers and magazines in 1979 and 1994 showed that women continue to be depicted as sex objects, in provocative states, and of inferior status to men, through the use of body parts to reinforce the headings and to draw attention (First 1998). Women in advertisements frequently continue to be shown touching themselves and the product in a provocative manner, are degraded in relation to men, and exhibit less control over themselves.

Female sexuality is often woven into advertising through the use of devices hinting at violence. Thus, for example, the following motifs also associated with pornography were found in Israeli advertising: fragmentation of the female body (presenting parts of the body disconnected from the whole); bondage (portraying women in restraints or with some form of physical limitation on their freedom of movement); forced physical contact (advertisements depicting men using physical force on women); symbolic violence (advertisements portraying women in association with violence, even if expression is not actually given to the violence); and potential violence (advertisements which present women in situations known to the viewer as being potentially violent). In most of these advertisements, the woman appeared to be ignoring the violence, indifferent to it, or even enjoying it. What is more, women were even depicted as encouraging sexual violence, such as being dressed and posed provocatively and undressed or exposing parts of their bodies in manners intended to be provocative to the viewer. They exuded a willingness to initiate sexual relations under any circumstance and at any price (Lemish 1997). The objectification of women in advertisements is also expressed in how extensively they are used as objects rather than as subjects having their own existence: as fruits, colorful, juicy, and tempting to eat; as packages, such as perfume bottles; as animals, identified with the untamed, the natural, the impulsive, the uncivilized.

A quantitative study that examined commercials on Channel 2 (the commercial channel) during the years 1993–6 (Weimann 2000) revealed consistency in the discriminatory characterizations of women. They, more than men, were identified with lower-value and lower-status consumer products, particularly those associated with housekeeping, or those for improving one's external appearance. Those products are a priori identified with female stereotypes, as has been discussed above, and therefore serve to reproduce the boundaries of female representation. Such commercials project a differentiated status of men and women: men in commercials were depicted, more often, in the world of work, while women in Israel were still presented in the domestic domain, or without context. The rewards promised by advertisements centered on external appearance for women, while those for men dealt with practical benefits. Commercials directed at men or featuring men most often portrayed them as a "professional" source of information guided by rational thought, while those directed at or featuring women usually presented them on the "personal" level, characterized by emotional considerations. Most women in commercials were significantly younger than male counterparts (75 per cent were younger than 30, while 52 per cent of the men were above 40), reinforcing the value placed on women's appearance and adherence to the "beauty myth" (Wolf 1991).

With regard to the image of sexuality, significant differences were also found between men and women. Many more women than men were presented partially dressed or nude (31.5 per cent in comparison with 14.7 per cent); and employment of voyeuristic camera work was seven times more frequent for women than for men. The use of women's body parts only was almost double that of men. Three times as many commercials using women were based on sexiness as those in which men appeared. This finding also included advertisements in which girls were the lead characters.

Madonna or whore

The Israeli media, so it seems, reflect the global discourse of disrespect toward women documented in the literature worldwide. At the same time, however, the unique characteristics of the Israeli reality highlight several of the themes in their extremity. More specifically, the Israeli media often perpetuate both sides of the dichotomy reserved in patriarchal culture for women: the "Madonna" on one side and the "whore" on the other. As "Madonna," the Israeli woman is cast in the role of the mother – the one who gives birth, nurtures, raises, sacrifices herself, and, finally, the one who mourns her dead son. As "whore," she is pressed into the mold of the sexual object, the essence of whose existence is tantalizing and threatening to the male, and whose ultimate fate is to be punished as a victim of violence and exploitation. Here, media content legitimizes the dehumanization of women and regards them as objects lacking a consciousness or an individuality.

Clear examples of the social perceptions of women's role in Israeli society can be found in a number of visual projects related to the commemoration of the country's 50th anniversary of independence, celebrated in 1998. Examination of women's images presented in albums celebrating Israel's jubilee clearly reveals their place in Israeli society. Overall, the attention devoted to women is negligible, but when included, it is their social function that is portrayed, in terms of the sacrificing mother or wife. Similar evidence can be found in the highly praised television series *Tekumah* ("Revival," referring to the revival of a Jewish state). This production used leading mainstream historians and television professionals in an effort to present as multi-faceted a picture of the country's history as possible. Yet, for the most part, it ignored women. Various segments of the series were devoted to all of the possible societal divisions – "Ashkenazi" and "Mizrachi" (Jews originating from European countries versus those from North Africa and Middle Eastern countries), secular and Orthodox, veterans and new immigrants, settlers in the occupied Palestinian territories and members of the Peace Now movement, Jews and Arabs. But half of the country's populace – the women – hardly appeared on the television screen at all. Ignoring – perhaps refusing to include – documentation about the role of women in the establishment and development of the state, as foundations of the collective memory and national self-identity, is greater testament than anything else presented to date of the symbolic annihilation of women. "If you're not there, you don't exist," says a popular commercial. Simply put, the women are not "there" in the mediated world.

Extraction from invisibility?

Yet, as in other developed countries, studies are finding evidence of "creeping" change in the images of women in Israel. Lately, more than ever, women have been appearing more as professionals, in addition to being the keepers of the private sphere. This gradual transition to a more liberal model of society can be attributed to real changes in society and to the cumulative influence of the feminist revolution. Simultaneously, however, it can be further understood from at least two complementary directions. First, a major portion of the changes involves showing women more in the manner perceived as male (independent and powerful, for example, as typified by a number of female politicians and female journalists holding senior positions) or presenting men in ways that are usually perceived as feminine (as sex objects in advertisements, for example). Neither of these strategies allows for expression of the unique female experience, female worldview and values, female ways of thinking and politics. This is most evident in the discourse surrounding the Israeli–Palestinian conflict, the most central of all burning issues in Israeli society for several decades. Women's protest and peace movements analyze the continued conflict being embedded in a masculine confrontational approach to life in the Middle East and seek to demilitarize Israeli society on all levels. Their struggle incorporates a fundamentally different value system, prioritizing the sanctity of human life and civil rights over loyalty to land, nation, and heritage. In their struggle, they refuse to uphold the "motherhood" destination or become living memorials to sons and husbands lost in battle. Theirs is a perspective that undermines the very center of existence of current Israeli society.

Second, if we address the contents of media, such as advertisements, not as an unequivocal reflection of reality but as expressions of a consumer society, the image of the "new" woman can be interpreted as utilizing the feminist discourse for the sake of advancing consumerism. Recognizing and mobilizing the growing economic power of women in western society, according to some theorists, brought about a backlash in the form of a new enslavement: to an unattainable ideal of beauty, to exalting the preservation of eternal youth, and to nurturing an inferior self-image which is constantly in need of improvement (Wolf 1991). As a society so heavily influenced by the American capitalist value system, Israel is joining the rest of the Americanized world in reinforcing and naturalizing this worldview.

The claim that the growing feminization of the media industry in Israel will bring about significant change in the hegemonic worldview presented in media texts is a hotly debated proposition in Israel, as it is elsewhere (Limor and Caspi 1994; Carter et al. 1998). To what extent will the increased presence of women in this field affect or shape professional norms, blur the boundaries of the dual perceptions of reality, shift public interest to areas which are less exposed, change the accepted distinction between information and commentary? Moreover, what are the values attributed to these possibilities? For example, evidence coming from the advertising world is not encouraging. The significant growth in the number of women employed in advertising has not been accompanied by concomitant changes in the symbolic representations of women in advertisements. It seems these female advertisers internalize the value system that perpetuates the low status of women, and accept these standards, in their struggle for professional survival and success.

Within this tension between the domination by conservative images and trends toward change, a number of women stand out in expressing woman's voice in the media. Each has been perceived more than once, however, to have paid a price for daring to do so; for example, in giving up having children or by adopting a "masculine" professional character. Recently, a number of other women have begun to assume prominent roles as anchorwomen as well as field reporters and press commentators in what are normally perceived as male areas, including politics, crime, defense, sports, and economics. A weekly feminist TV program on the commercial channel has achieved a respectable audience share and seeks to contribute to the cultivation of a new definition of "women's issues" in the public mind.

In spite of these hints of possible change within Israeli media, a realistic assessment of the picture of the world presented by the media still leaves women at the margins of the social, economic, cultural, and political processes, as has been documented in many other studies worldwide. Attempts by feminist grassroots organizations engaged in media-watching and social change (in areas such as the portrayal of women in advertising) to voice criticism have been met with strong opposition by men and women (Lemish 2002). Here, we might say that Israeli women find themselves torn between their multiple identities and loyalties. As a result, they have difficulty elevating the feminist struggle to the top of the national agenda as well as their own priorities. "This isn't the appropriate time to bother society with banal questions about images in the media or the feminization of poverty," the national conscience seems to argue, "when we still have to fight a battle for existence against our external enemies." Opposing the national consensus threatens women because it shakes the foundations of their sense of belonging to the collective and the fundamental assumptions on which they were educated and about which they are expected to educate the younger generation (Deutsch 1994). Thus, accepting the underlying hegemonic militarist perception of patriotism as defining Israeli society and remaining silent is an additional price that women pay for the continuing state of political conflict.

The exclusion of women from the public sphere, including the forums of political, cultural, and economic power, is achieved through processes of negation of self-identity, abrogation of rights, and repression. This further contributes to the invisibility of women as a group within both societal and individual consciousness. The media did not invent women's inequality and victimization, and they cannot be held solely responsible for the existence of discrimination. Yet the images they present can reinforce and legitimize a patriarchal worldview by glorifying the situation, and by presenting it as the "normal" or expected state of affairs. Exposing the ideological ties between social-economic-political reality and media images representing it is but one step toward cracking the walls of hegemony.

Key terms

Four Mothers
fragmentation of the female body
Intifada
Israeli Knesset
Israeli religious establishment
Jewishness
masculine values
"motherhood strategy"
principles of patriarchal thinking
private spheres
public spheres
"spiral of silence"
symbolic violence
Women in Black

Questions for discussion

1 In what ways, according to Lemish, is the long-lasting, violent political conflict in which Israeli society has been involved since the establishment of the state reflected in the portrayals of women in the media?
2 The author observes that the Israeli news media mainly portray men in the public sphere and women in the private sphere. Explain what she means and give several examples.
3 Why does the author believe the Israeli news media portray women as victims more often than as leaders or in other contexts?
4 For what reasons does the author single out the Hebrew press for calling the Jewishness of certain women into question? What examples does she use to support her critique?
5 If Israeli news media were to cover women's leadership and other participation in the public spheres, what might they include?
6 Are there any signs of progress in the Israeli news media's treatment of women, according to Lemish's analysis?

References

Ariel, M. (1988) Female and male stereotypes in Israeli literature and media: evidence from introductory patterns. *Language and Communication* 8(1), 43–68.

Benedict, H. (1992) *Virgin or Vamp: How the Press Covers Sex Crimes*. Oxford University Press, Oxford and New York.

Bernstein, A. (1997) British and Israeli coverage of the 1992 Barcelona Olympics: a comparative analysis. Unpublished PhD thesis, Center for Mass Communication Research, University of Leicester.

Biagi, S. and Kern-Foxworth, M. (eds) (1997) *Facing Difference: Race, Gender, and Mass Media*. Pine Forge Press, Thousand Oaks, CA.

Brunsdon, C., D'Acci, J., and Spigel, L. (eds) (1997) *Feminist Television Criticism: A Reader*. Clarendon Press, Oxford.

Carter, C. (1998) When the "extraordinary" becomes "ordinary": everyday news of sexual violence. In: Carter, C., Branston, G., and Allan, S. (eds), *News, Gender and Power*. Routledge, London, pp. 219–32.

Carter, C., Branston, G., and Allan, S. (eds) (1998) *News, Gender and Power*. Routledge, London.

Central Bureau of Statistics (2002) *Women and Men. Statistical* February, 23. Israeli Government, Jerusalem. (Hebrew).

Creedon, P. J. (ed.) (1994) *Women, Media and Sport: Challenging Gender Values.* Sage, Thousand Oaks, CA.

Deutsch, Y. (1994) Israeli women against the occupation: political growth and the persistence of ideology. In: Mayer, T. (ed.), *Women and the Israeli Occupation: The Politics of Change.* Routledge, London, pp. 88–105.

First, A. (1998) Nothing new under the sun? A comparison of images of women in Israeli advertisements in 1979 and 1994. *Sex Roles* 38, 1065–77.

First, A. and Shaw, D. L. (1998) Where have all the women gone? The presentation of women in foreign news: a 1995 multi-national study. Paper presented to the annual conference of the International Communication Association, Jerusalem.

Fogiel-Bijaoui, S. (1997) Women in Israel: the social construction of citizenship as a non-issue. *Israel Society Science Research* 12(1), 1–30.

Fogiel-Bijaoui, S. (1998) Women and citizenship in Israel: analysis of silencing. *Politka* 1, 47–71. (Hebrew).

Hellman, S. and Rapaport, T. (1997) "They are Ashkenazi women, alone, whores of Arabs, don't believe in God, and don't love the land of Israel": Women in Black and the challenge to the social order. *Theory and Criticism: An Israeli Forum* 10, 175–92. (Hebrew).

Herzog, H. (1998) *Gendering Politics: Women in Israel.* Michigan Press, Chicago.

Horowitz, D. and Lissak, M. (1992) *Trouble in Utopia: Israel, an Over-burdened Polity.* Am Oved, Tel Aviv. (Hebrew).

Lemish, D. (1997) The ripple effect: pornographic images of women in Israeli advertising. In: French, S. G. (ed.), *Interpersonal Violence, Health and Gender Politics.* McGraw-Hill Ryerson, New York, pp. 285–95.

Lemish, D. (2000) The whore and the "other": Israeli images of female immigrants from the former USSR. *Gender and Society* 14(2), 339–49.

Lemish, D. (2002) Gender at the forefront: feminist perspectives on action theoretical approaches in communication research. *Communications: The European Journal of Communication Research* 27(1), 63–78.

Lemish, D. and Barzel, I. (2000) "Four Mothers:" the womb in the public sphere. *European Journal of Communication* 15(2), 147–69.

Lemish, D. and Drob, G. (2002) "All the time his wife": portrayals of first ladies in the Israeli press. *Parliamentary Affairs* 55(1), 129–42.

Lemish, D. and Tidhar, C. E. (1999a) Where have all the young girls gone? The disappearance of Israeli women-broadcasters during the Gulf War. *Women and Language* XXII(2), 27–32.

Lemish, D. and Tidhar, C. E. (1999b) Still marginal: women in Israel's 1996 television election campaign. *Sex Roles* 41, 389–412.

Limor, Y. and Caspi, D. (1994) Feminization in the Israeli press. *Kesher* 15, 37–45. (Hebrew).

Mayer, T. (ed.) (1994) *Women and the Israeli Occupation: The Politics of Change.* Routledge, London.

Media Watch (1995) *Global Media Monitoring Project: Women's Participation in the News.* National Watch on Images of Women in the Media, Toronto.

Meyers, M. (1997) *News Coverage of Violence against Women: Engendering Blame.* Sage, London and Newbury Park, CA.

Meyers, M. (1999) *Mediated Women: Representations in Popular Culture.* Hampton Press, Cresskill, NJ.

Raday, F. (1991) The concept of gender equality in a Jewish state. In: Swirski, B. and Safir, M. P. (eds), *Calling the Equality Bluff: Women in Israel.* Pergamon Press, New York, pp. 18–28.

Ridd, R. (1986) Powers of the powerless. In: Ridd, R. and Callaway, H. (eds), *Caught Up in Conflict: Women's Responses to Political Strife.* Macmillan Education, Houndsmill and Basingstoke, pp. 1–24.

Smooha, S. (1993) Divisions in status, ethnicity, and nationality, and democracy in Israel. In: Ram, U. (ed.), *Israeli Society: Critical Perspectives.* Brerot, Tel Aviv, pp. 172–202. (Hebrew).

Sreberny, A. and van Zoonen, L. (eds) (2000) *Gender, Politics and Communication.* Hampton Press, Cresskill, NJ.

Swirski, B. and Safir, M. P. (eds) (1991) *Calling the Equality Bluff: Women in Israel.* Pergamon Press, New York.

Tidhar, C. E. (1988) Women in Israel's broadcasting media and on Israeli television. In: Kawakami, Y. (ed.), *Women and Communication in an Age of Science and Technology.* Atom Press, Tokyo, pp. 112–28.

Tidhar, C. E. and Lemish, D. (1993) Women in the Intifada: a television news perspective. In: Cohen, A. A. and Wolfsfeld, G. (eds), *Framing the Intifada: People and Media.* Ablex, Norwood, NJ, pp. 142–59.

Tuchman, G. (ed.) (1978) *Hearth and Home: Images of Women and the Media.* Oxford University Press, Oxford and New York.

Valdivia, A. N. (ed.) (1995) *Feminism, Multiculturalism, and the Media: Global Diversities.* Sage, Thousand Oaks, CA.

van Zoonen, L. (1994) *Feminist Media Studies.* Sage, London.

Weimann, G. (2000) Women and men in television advertisements in Israel. *Megamot* 40(3), 466–85. (Hebrew).

Wolf, N. (1991) *The Beauty Myth: How Images of Beauty are Used Against Women.* Doubleday, New York.

4
Women Framed: The Gendered Turn in Mediated Politics

Karen Ross

Introduction

This chapter is concerned with exploring the relationship between women, politics, and the media, both focusing on the ways in which news media cover stories about women politicians and rehearsing the views of women themselves. It begins by discussing the strategies which news media use when reporting on the political process, moving to a consideration of the frames journalists use in their stories. The broad discussion of the literature is layered with and informed by the personal testimonies of women parliamentarians, gathered during an extended research study that included first-hand interviews with women from the Westminster (1995 and 2000), Canberra (1998), and Cape Town (1999) Parliaments and the Northern Ireland Assembly (2002). I aim to explore the dissonances between the rhetoric of news media, which purport to be impartially objective when reporting politics, and the experiences of women parliamentarians themselves in their dealings with and experiences of news workers.[1]

The corps of journalists are often found describing themselves as the "fourth estate" in a mature democracy, fearlessly exposing public and political wrong-doing and holding governments to account in a robust and impartial manner. Obviously, in order to ensure such high-minded independence, the news media must remain at arm's length from politics, but increasingly, their rhetoric has a hollow ring (Tunstall 1977; Baistow 1985; Jones 1995; Franklin 1997). In fact, it is more the case that the relationship between politics and the media is a necessarily inter- than in-dependent one, as each relies on the other for its survival: news media need stories and politicians need publicity. "Sources, particularly those in government, are the lifeblood of news" (Perloff 1998: 223). The media, and television in particular, ventilate the realpolitik, with presidents and prime ministers announcing important policy decisions not in Senate or the Commons but in the TV studio, live to camera (Wheeler 1997; Negrine 1998) and directly to us in our homes, a faux intimacy addressed to the masses.

Part of the rationale for that particular political strategy is a growing disquiet, on the part of the politicians, that their autonomy and ability to get their views across are too often a casualty of the political pundit or commentator who is more interested in providing her or his own interpretive inflection of the speech than in delivering the reportage straight (Steele and Barnhurst 1996; Bird 1998). Politicians are well aware, though, of the news media's need to make news exciting, as the Labor politician, Jenny Macklin, makes clear:

> The problem with the electronic media is, you know, it's only 10 seconds which is of course going to come out of Question Time, because it's the only color and movement of the day. The rest is the "normal" process of making laws, committees and there are a lot of positive things that go on but you wouldn't put it on the telly at night because it's as boring as anything. (Jenny Macklin, Labor, Australia)[2]

In addition, the savage satire which characterizes the best political comedy propels its own measure of irreverence into the public domain, further eroding the deference that politicians were once accorded (Watts 1997). The televising of politics has also brought about a shift in public perceptions of politics, making manifest not just the gladiatorial and distastefully combative stance of formal politics but the lack of an embodied physical presence amongst our elected members in what is said to be the seat of democracy.

But do we believe everything that the media tells us about the political process? Do the media really have the kind of influence they claim? The ways in which we now understand media power have undergone significant shifts in conceptualization over the 70 or so years in which we have had a mass media to analyze and observe. Early theories (for example, Lasswell 1927; Merton 1946) posited a pervasive, propagandist, and sinister role for media in the public consciousness – the "hypodermic needle" thesis – while some years later, commentators were saying the very opposite, namely that media had no or negligible effects (see Katz and Lazarsfeld 1955; Klapper 1960). More contemporary theories, though, identify highly complex sets of relations between different media and different consumers (see Shaw and Martin 1992), in which audiences attribute different levels of credibility to different media outlets. Bartels and Wilson (1996), for example, argue that an elite newspaper such as the *New York Times* shows much stronger agenda-setting proclivities than TV shows like *ABC News*. However, it is important to be cautious about claims for media influence, since so many factors are implicated when trying to disentangle what has the greater impact on whom.

Gender/agenda

However, irrespective of personal preferences as to the extent to which the media can and cannot influence public opinion, what is less controversial is to argue that the media are primarily in business to make money, not to function as a public service, although news workers might believe they do this latter as well. Accepting the primacy of the dollar, then, I further suggest that the capitalist order is also gendered, as patriarchy is promoted via the news media's circulation of a highly gendered, male-ordered paradigm of social and economic control. If it has become merely a commonplace to argue that broadcast media (especially, but other media too) regularly and routinely perform an important affirmative function in reinforcing dominant norms and values to "the public" and confirming the cherished and comfortable beliefs of most of their consumers, it still bears repeating.

The perpetuation of a hegemonic worldview of male dominance is regularly rehearsed in both fictional and factual programming strands, and the ways in which women (particularly, but also other disadvantaged groups) are represented on and in broadcast media send important messages to the public about women's place, women's role, and women's lives. The sadness and frustration are that after more than 20 years of documenting the media's representation of women (see, for example, Tuchman et al. 1978; Root, 1986; Soothill and Walby 1991; Creedon 1993; Ross 1995a, 1995b; Ross and Sreberny-Mohammadi 1997; Carter 1998; Wykes 1998), so little has changed. Importantly, part of the endurance of gender stereotypes in news discourse can be related directly to the culture of newsrooms themselves, microcosmic environments that constitute sites of considerable contestation about gender and power (Gallagher 2001; Ross 2001). While women have penetrated media organizations to a significant degree since the early 1970s or 1980s, they still find it difficult to achieve decision-making positions, even assuming that they would want to effect change when they got there, which in itself is a moot point.

Women politicians themselves are clear that there is a specifically gendered news discourse that comes into play when journalists report on activities and events involving them and their women colleagues, not just in campaign terms but more generally, as everyday occurrence (Ross 2002). Crucially, aspects of their sex are routinely incorporated into what should be "ordinary" stories of politics: they are mundanely framed as women first and then, maybe, as politicians. When 101 Labour women were elected to the British Parliament in 1997, the front-page headlines figured them as "Blair's Babes," with a photo-montage of all the new women massed outside the House of Parliament, and Tony Blair beaming in the front row. Although some of those women have argued in retrospect that doing the "Blair picture" was perhaps unwise, they were unprepared for the media response: their considerable victory was trivialized instantly not just by that possessive apostrophe, but through their sexualized figuring as "babes."

Framing serious women politicians in this way might be seen as merely irreverent or even playful, but it signals a dangerous tendency to denigrate and neutralize the potency of women to be actors and leaders on the political stage. Whilst some women take a generous view of the media's interest in them as "novelties," others see an altogether more insidious side to the media's propensity for treating them differently to their male colleagues. To be sure, women in significant numbers in any legislature (other than in the progressive Scandinavian countries) are still a rarity, but that is surely no reason to treat them in ways which are qualitatively (negatively) different to men. Women parliamentarians themselves argue that the media often appear to be operating double standards when considering women politicians, almost as if they expect "better" standards of behavior, higher moral values, more honesty, integrity, and loyalty. What seems to happen is that women are often set up as paragons and are then "unmasked," almost as quickly, as having feet of clay: the point is that they never said they were perfect in the first place, so they have undergone a doubly unfair trial by media.

Ironically, although the media make it difficult for backbench politicians to access media opportunities to address the public, the very novelty of women parliamentarians provides a reason to include them, even if the coverage is woman as commodified object rather than politician – in the end, any publicity is better than no publicity for a politician. And when women achieve senior parliamentary positions, in Senate or Cabinet or in opposition, they are even more scrutinized and their standards of behavior as well as their policy statements are all vulnerable to the investigative notebooks of journalists:

> Women politicians, particularly at Cabinet level, tend to be knocked, judged, assessed, by a criteria that is incredibly harsh, relative to their male counterparts . . . it's not that the media wouldn't want to focus on men when mistakes are made but it is more relentless and with women, it's personalized in a way that it isn't with men. (Janet Love, ANC, South Africa)

It is almost as if stepping outside the norms of "appropriate" female behavior by becoming parliamentarians at all is just about bearable, but taking up positions of authority makes women open to a highly critical form of scrutiny which is entirely gender-specific. When Carmen Lawrence (Labor) became Australia's first state premier (of Western Australia), she experienced what she describes as the "sore-thumb" phenomenon: "I just stuck out and so your actions, for good or ill, are often exaggerated and they are seen as more significant than they really are, which means that you can fly higher but you can also fall lower."

Big bottoms and Bridget Jones

As a matter of routine, news stories about powerful women are just as likely to frame the subjects of their coverage in gendered terms as to report the news item "straight." In my previous work with women politicians (see Ross and Sreberny-Mohammadi 1997; Ross 2002), I found most of them believe both that their outward *appearance* is the focus of more column inches and airtime than anything they might *say*, and that such a focus is much more likely to apply to women than to their male colleagues. Women mentioned repeatedly the way in which the media always include the age of women politicians, what they look like, their domestic and family circumstances, their fashion sense, and so on. Fiona Mactaggart believes that the media's fascination with sartorial style is partly because there is a view that the way women dress is a much more important indicator of who they are and what they stand for than is the case for men. The emphasis on style is made to undermine women; it is *not* an *un*conscious process:

> A lot of men in this place have never sent their suit to the cleaners and nobody ever says, "have you noticed the smell?," which is a perfectly reasonable question to ask. And it's done [focusing on women's externalities] to make women feel vulnerable, that's the purpose . . . I'm afraid, I don't think they are completely naïve. (Fiona Mactaggart, Labour, UK)

> I feel that the media would say things about a woman politician, even when we're out electioneering, and they'd remark on what your appearance was like and whether you were wearing something bright or dull or whatever it was. As against asking you about what you were actually fighting for, what your policies were. (Joan Carson, Ulster Unionist Party, Northern Ireland)

Women parliamentarians are very conscious that they are always on display, they are always a potential target for the media's scrutiny, even in their leisure time. This degree of hyper-surveillance makes it difficult to lead a "normal" life. Jeannie Ferris (Liberal, Australia) takes a pride in looking good, both for herself and as a pre-emptive strike against any unscrupulous journalist who might catch her wearing a tracksuit to the supermarket: "I am very conscious that wherever I am, people will know me, I feel that I have to maintain a certain standard in the way I dress, even in my leisure time, I don't think a female politicians is ever off duty." Work on newspaper photographs recently undertaken by the Women in Journalism group[3] suggested that, although it was clear that men outnumber women in public life, the way newspapers use images of women is at best old-fashioned and at worst complacent.

Of course, women choose to dress in stylish and/or provocative ways because they can and because it is a way of achieving a media presence quickly. This strategy is useful for women in opposition and especially for women in minority parties who would otherwise find it hard to get coverage. Often women will do or wear or say something unexpected in the hope that they might be able to slide in a policy statement along with the expected quote and picture. But there is also a political point in expanding the scope of our perceptions of who politicians are and what they look like, although this is always a precarious strategy, because it is surprisingly difficult to "get it right" in the eyes of the media:

> Women are never the right age. We're too young, we're too old. We're too thin, we're too fat. We wear too much make-up, we don't wear enough. We're too flashy in our dress, we don't take enough care. There isn't a thing we can do that's right. (Dawn Primarolo, Labour, UK)

The media will often undermine the credibility of women as serious political actors by framing them in sexual situations with male colleagues, a strategy that has a particular potency when used in cartoon form. Many women in interviews talked about being pictured in this way, especially when they were suddenly taken up as a news item because of a particular prominence. For example, when Cheryl Kernot crossed the floor of the Australian Parliament in 1997, giving up her leadership of the Australian Democrats to become a Labor candidate, the media responded, in picture form, with cartoons of her in bed with Kim Beasley (the then Labor Party leader). Similarly, when the Australian Pauline Hanson was dominating public discourse in early 1998 because of her spectacular success in the Queensland state elections, she was immortalized in cartoons showing her in bed with a variety of political colleagues but also as a puppet, with men pulling the strings. Journalists characterized her as a "not very bright woman who's being manipulated and is too dumb to even know that she's being manipulated" (Sue West, Labor, Australia). Such presentations convey several negative and sometimes even contradictory messages simultaneously: that women are being "used" by men; that they are in thrall to and carrying out the orders of men; or that they use their sex to advance their political careers. "It's almost as if you can't think of a woman without thinking of her sexuality simultaneously." (Carmen Lawrence, Labor, Australia). A woman politician is always described as a *woman* politician in the media, her sex is always on display, always the primary descriptor. She is defined by what she is *not*, that is, she is not a "typical" politician who, in principle, bears no gendered descriptor but who is clearly marked as male (Ross and Sreberny 2000).

If elections are won or lost in the public gaze of the media, as the media themselves have often claimed, then it is easy to argue that the privileging of form over function, presentation over policy, means that *all* politicians are subject to the tyranny of needing to be telegenic and *all* must surrender to inappropriate sartorial scrutiny, not just the women. While this is, in principle, true, the objectification of male politicians is noticeable because of its infrequency. With women politicians, on the other hand, it is almost the rule. Even women in positions of considerable power, such as previous prime ministers Golda Meir, Indira Gandhi, or Margaret Thatcher, nonetheless received broadly similar media coverage, suggesting that although there was very little that was traditionally "feminine" about these women and nothing very similar about them apart from their shared gender, the "woman politician" frame was used as a handy catch-all, regardless of their differences: "If women leaders are described in a common way in the news, despite these differences, this suggests the media are viewing women through a sex stereotyped lens (Norris 1997: 155).

What also emerged from Norris's study, though, was the identification of a number of thematic frames which positioned emergent women leaders as breaking the mold, as outsiders winning against the odds, and as agents of change. These are all very "positive" frames at a superficial level but the first two at least are unsustainable over the lifetime of a woman leader's career, once she is an established rather than a "new" leader. The third frame is equally problematic since it could, by its emphasis on change (challenging the barren desert of "politics as usual"), set women up to fail as they prove unable to achieve the unrealistically high expectations. Beyond the media obsession with the physicality of women politicians, the gendered assumptions about politicians are manifest in the discourses used. The differential use of language signals the media's opprobrium against women who transgress the orthodox boundaries of what "real" women are and what "real" women do. What they don't do, apparently, is become politicians:

> If a woman goes out at 6 o'clock in the morning to clean offices to keep her family together, to raise her children, she will be presented as a heroine. If she wants to run that office she will be presented as an unnatural woman and even worse, as an unnatural mother. (Glenda Jackson, Labour, UK)

Women, politics, media: a problem for democracy

Despite the complacent cry of the media that they provide merely a looking-glass service to the public, mirroring back to us what we ourselves create and believe, such crass disingenuousness is less and less tenable in a media environment in which the sector actually relies on the public's knowledge of media manipulation, journalistic opportunism, and general mendacity for its success. One example is *Spin City*. This show and others like it make clear the ways in which media industries are economical with the truth in order to sell a good story. While the public do not necessarily believe all they read or hear, they nonetheless continue to consume news products in a mostly uncritical way. The point is that the mass media do much more than the selfless act of reflection that they claim; they do more than hold up a mirror and give our diverse and disparate selves and circumstances, our various hues and tones and varieties, back to ourselves. Rather, they function simultaneously as both modern agenda-setters (Entman 1989; Ansolabehere et al. 1991) and orthodox gatekeepers of traditional social mores and values. Unfortunately, the end result of both impulses is the presentation of a world dominated by men and male concerns, where women's voices and women's perspectives are marginal and peripheral to the main event: *his*tory is made every day, *her*story struggles to reach the back page. The media's largely stereotypical portrayal of the relationship between women and politics is symptomatic of this wider news perspective, which rarely strays outside the conventional frame of male–political–public and female–personal–private. Notwithstanding the generalized tendency of the news media to use their own interpretative lens though which to analyze politicians *per se*, male (rational) politicians receive coverage on what they say and what they believe while women (emotional) politicians receive coverage on what they wear and what they feel, in the gender-dependent articulation of style vs. substance politics (Whittaker 1999).

Part of the answer to the question "why is it a problem for democracy?" is that many women (and men) who could make an important contribution to the democratic project are put off pursuing a career in politics because of the way they think the political process works, and this perception is largely grounded in the media's coverage of politics and politicians. Women parliamentarians are particularly poorly treated by the news media and this harms democracy itself. Jeannie Ferris (Liberal, Australia) worked as a journalist for many years before entering politics, and she laments the direction which reporting has taken with regard to women:

> If you look at what has happened to some of the high-profile women in the last five years, the media has been very very tough on them. I think that many professional women who see that think, "why should our families have to endure that scrutiny?" I don't find it hard to believe that women are reluctant to come forward for that reason. It must be difficult for younger women with children in primary or high school where they are vulnerable to peer contact.

The kinds of stories, perspectives, and interests we see and read in the media are inextricably bound up with the socio-economic relations that exist in news organizations themselves, as sites of news production. The political economy of the newsroom provides a strongly gendered context in which the traditional power-plays of patriarchal relations – men on top and women underneath – are played out in abidingly conventional, for which read "sex-stereotyped," ways (van Zoonen 1998; Riordan 2002). Women in this study recognized that most media professionals and certainly all the owners and controllers of media institutions are men and that the way in which politics is reported is determined, to a large extent, by a male-oriented agenda that privileges the practice of politics as an essential male pursuit. The journalist Joanna Coles suggests that the atmosphere at a typical political press conference resembles that of a boys' public school, where a few clever girls have been allowed into the sixth form (Coles 1997). The men on the platform address the journalists in their midst by their first names; the few women in the press corps are not similarly addressed, still less invited to put their question. This is not to say that more women in the news would necessarily change news output, but rather to argue that different (gender) perspectives would produce different "takes" on news stories and events. In other words, whilst the subject matter might remain constant, the orientation of the story, the actors invited to speak, and the underlying point of view presented could all be different in the hands of women as opposed to men reporters.

It seems clear that the ways in which women are represented in the media are inextricably linked with who produces those media outputs, which in turn is linked with who owns those means of production. As Carter et al. (1998: 3) point out, "feminist and gender-sensitive studies of journalism are becoming increasingly concerned with the changing patterns of news media ownership [especially] within local, national and global contexts." Although space does not permit a fuller discussion of the implications of the increasing convergence and concentration of myriad small media organizations in the hands of a few "big" players, the one big global problem of conglomeration (see, for example, International Institute of Communications 1996) provides part of the environmental back-cloth to the discussion on gender, space, place, and portrayal that I have sketched out here. Sex, politics, and money have always enjoyed intimate relations and the media's involvement in that triumvirate merely adds another player to the field.

The light in the tunnel

If lobby and other political journalists persistently fail to report those issues with which women politicians are specifically involved and on which they have campaigned vigorously, then perhaps it is not so surprising that the electorate at large believes that our women politicians are no different from their male colleagues, that is, they are held to do very little to earn their salary. However, there is some positive evidence to suggest that the media are not always and everywhere hostile to women politicians and that some journalists, women and men, are attempting to shift the agenda through their own reporting of a different range of stories. Braden (1996: 131) argues that greater numbers of women in Congress after the 1992 elections has not only meant a shift in the policy agenda but also encouraged the media to cover those changes, and she argues that the ways in which the media chronicled stories about women's first few months in office were far more persuasive than the hype that surrounded the Year of the Woman, when "stories were frequently patterned on the traditional formula of David vs. Goliath or the new kid on the block taking on the bully."

Roberts (1994) cites a particularly poignant example that perfectly captures the patronizing tone in which women politicians have become used to being addressed by male colleagues, and the way in which women are challenging the status quo. The assured response of the politician in question quickly dispatches the casual put-down, but the anecdote also reveals an unease with the competence of women politicians. In an exchange on firearms control, Senator Dianne Feinstein was accused by a male Republican Senator of being a "gentle lady" who needed to do her homework on the power of guns. Feinstein's response was personal and deadly:

> I became mayor as a product of assassination . . . I proposed gun control legislation in San Francisco. I went through a recall on the basis of it. I was trained in the shooting of a firearm when I had terrorist attacks, with a bomb at my house, when my husband was dying, when I had windows shot out. Senator, I know something about what firearms can do. (Feinstein cited in Roberts 1994: 4)

Press reporting of such exchanges has encouraged a better understanding of the kinds of experiences which women politicians in male-dominated legislatures must endure and the robustness of their responses when their credibility is challenged. In a *Washington Post* article, the African-American journalist Kevin Merida quoted the feelings of intimidation reported by a white, middle-aged Republican representative (Henry J. Hyde), on being verbally "attacked" by a group of African-American women representatives, because of his use of racially offensive and paternalistic language in a debate over funding abortions for working-class women. Merida gave the last word to the women protagonists: "We're shaking up the place . . . If one of the godfathers says you can't do this, my next question is, why not? And who are you to say we can't?"

The commitment, by some sections of the media, to cover stories involving women politicians which show them as capable, competent, and professional goes some way to providing a corrective to the more routine, sensational, and trivializing proclivities which push so many journalists to portray women politicians negatively. And if backbenchers – and most women politicians are in this category – find it hard to achieve prominence in the national media because of news-room pressures to deliver to increasingly tight deadlines, which mean less time to obtain quotes from other than the usual suspects, then local media offer far more opportunities for publicity and self-promotion. As the British MP Tony Wright argues, "when backbench politicians perform in Parliament, their real eye is frequently on their local media" (Wright 1998: 21). An intervention from the floor, be it a prepared speech, the introduction of an amendment or a new policy intention, or an impromptu point, can all be quickly (re)packaged and delivered to a news-hungry local news desk as a press release: "local MP challenges . . ." and so on. Ensuring at least a local profile is crucial for parliamentarians who rely on their local constituents to get out and vote for them next time round. As Jane Morrice (Northern Ireland Women's Coalition) points out, perhaps cynically, local people are always pleased to see their elected representative in the media, especially on TV, as if this exposure is evidence of their working for the constituency, regardless of what they are actually doing or saying:

> I'm also Deputy Speaker, so any time that the Assembly is shown, I'm often seen in the Chair, in the background. And people say they saw you on TV, and you weren't necessarily doing anything but you were there! My Deputy Speaking role has helped us [the Coalition] a lot. For example, there was a big controversy last week about consulting gay and lesbian groups and I was in the Chair at the time. In all the clips of the exchanges between [. . .] and

> the others, I was having to keep control, so my voice and me saying, order, order, was there in all the clips. It's about having a presence. (Jane Morrice, NIWC, Northern Ireland)

What's the big deal? Gender, media, and affect

The agenda-setting power of the mass media has been well documented over the past few decades (Iyengar 1987; Entman 1989; Ansolabehere et al. 1991), to a point where it is now recognized that the media's impact is less about actively changing values and beliefs than about determining what issues are important, and the extent to which media scholars attribute power to media organizations has also shifted considerably. If the public is to be able to discriminate between different candidates and their policies and thus make an informed choice about who they want to lead and govern them, then they must "acquire sufficient information about matters under public discussion to avoid being easily duped about the facts by self-interested candidate misinformation or distortion" (Buchanan 1991: 22). What Buchanan is implying here, although not quite saying, is that the political "default" position (that is, that they're all pretty much the same) is one that assumes the category "politician" is more rather than less likely to manipulate the voter/public, so the latter needs to be awake to evidence of willful intent to deceive.

That agenda-setting push is important to understand in general terms, but the everyday power-play which is a routine part of the politico-media dance is thrown into even sharper relief when the stakes are raised as they are in dynamic situations such as elections. Recent research studies exploring more precisely the contours of that relation and the media's potential and actual role in influencing voting behavior have identified a complex set of effects with several variables, such as gender, party, education, and ethnicity, all playing a part (LeDuc 1990; Kahn and Goldenberg 1991; West 1991). What is a little less clear cut, though, is the specific identification of cause-and-effect relations between exposure to political campaigning and actual voting decision, although most studies suggest that the media are more likely to reinforce existing attitudes than change them, and therefore have a negligible real effect on influencing final outcomes.

The ways in which women candidates and parliamentarians are covered by news media find obvious parallels with the way in which women and women's issues more generally are marginalized as legitimate topics of media discourse: whilst a particularly "gendered" item might make the women's page in daily newspapers, it will rarely feature as a news item in the mainstream sections (Kahn and Goldenberg 1997). Successive studies of the media's portrayal of women politicians and political candidates are unequivocal in their findings that women and men politicians receive differential coverage at the hands of the media, and that this differentiated coverage may have important effects on the way candidates are evaluated by the electorate. Caroline Flint, one of the so-called "Blair's Babes," who was elected along with 100 other Labour women MPs in the 1997 British elections, is exasperated with a media discourse that is only interested in her views on facilities in the House of Commons:

> [I am] ready to throttle the next journalist who asks me about toilets and crèches in the House of Commons . . . there are enough toilets for women MPs . . . and as for the crèche – there are very few women with children under five. They [the media] should focus on the diversity of women in Parliament. We are a mixed bunch and hopefully in many different ways represent the variety of women in Britain. (Flint cited in McDougall 1998: 79)

The media's persistent domestication of women parliamentarians in this way, and the power of media workers to frame their female subjects as constantly in thrall to their bodily functions, send out clear messages to the public that this is indeed what preoccupies our women politicians. Is it any wonder, then, that stereotypes of the "weaker" sex continue to hold sway in the collective public consciousness? If that's the discourse, then that's the story. In Kahn's (1994) comparative study of American Senate candidates during the 1982 and 1986 elections, she found that women generally received less media attention than men and that this could adversely affect their chances, because less information about candidates could mean that intending voters had little to inform them about the specific policy positions of women candidates, and therefore voter recognition of women candidates is weak. Kahn also found that the substance of media coverage was qualitatively different; for example, more time was devoted to the "horse race" – that is, who was ahead of whom – when reporting on women candidates than to considering their policy positions, and more time was spent discussing negative "horse-race" elements than was the case with male candidates.

This focus on competitive advantage (and especially *dis*advantage) can harm women's chances, since it could suggest, in the minds of voters at least, that winning is itself an issue for women candidates outside of whether or not they promote a politics to which voters subscribe. In an interesting study comparing media coverage of candidates from Northern Ireland standing for the 1997 British general election and the local elections in Northern Ireland (which were held simultaneously), Whittaker (1999) suggests that women candidates for both elections were significantly and consistently underreported across the 22 newspapers which were monitored for her study, that women were virtually absent from leader comments, and that women candidates themselves were overwhelmingly dissatisfied with their treatment by the media.

The image and language of mediated politics support the status quo (male as norm) and regard women politicians as novelties, viewing with considerable hostility strategies that encourage even more of them into elected office; for example, through mechanisms such as all-women shortlists. I would suggest that male paranoia and fear lie at the root of much women-bashing copy, where such displays conceal an orthodox male chauvinism dressed in the cynical garb of a faux appeal to equality: positive action is inherently unfair. As all the old certainties about women's roles and men's roles are increasingly brought into question, the privileged position of white, middle-class men is being challenged. But strangely, there appears to be a marked antipathy amongst many women parliamentarians to the implied suggestion that their sex might yet cause their political undoing, even as women accept that the media *do* operate a gendered reporting practice which *can* undermine their credibility as serious politicians. In other words, no publicity is bad publicity, although some of the more astute politicians can easily see the dangers in adverse publicity, particularly that which undermines the authority of women's political voice.

A case in point is the departure of the highly successful Cabinet minister Mo Mowlam from politics in 2001, after which she claimed that a vicious whispering campaign, begun by her own colleagues and slyly articulated by eager media, had made it impossible for her to continue to do her job effectively, hence her decision to leave politics. In January 2000, for example, an article appeared in the British *Independent on Sunday* newspaper stating that senior government sources thought Mowlam did not have the "intellectual rigour" to do her job.[4]

Conclusion

Ironically, the current chilly climate for politicians generally may well encourage an upturn in the fortunes of women politicians, as the media's continuing fascination with sex and scandal routinely fixes a male subject in their lens, enabling women to claim the moral high ground, often by default in the eyes of the voters if not by virtue of their own moralizing rhetoric. But women need to make much more concerted efforts to get themselves and their messages into the public domain, and using the media for such profiling activities would seem to be a fairly crucial part of any strategy to win votes, especially when conservatism amongst voters means that the "best" politicians are those who are male and middle-aged.

Even taking the most generous view of the media's role in the articulation of a normative social world order that privileges men and male concerns over those of women – that is, taking the media as unwitting agents of control – it is nonetheless irresistible to contend that there must be *some* element of complicity, some sense of collusion with the circulation of words and pictures that routinize what it is to be female and male in contemporary society. And it is precisely the "packaging" of politics and, in this current context, the "packaging" of women politicians that we need to read more carefully. If news is a commodity and we are all consumers, then how women politicians are "sold" to us in qualitative terms is as important as how often they appear in the news: volume matters but context matters more. Commenting on the way in which women Members of the Scottish Parliament (MSPs) had quickly begun to influence the political agenda after their election in May 1999, the Fawcett Society (1999: 24) argued that the media had nevertheless ignored their impact:

> The lobby correspondents are predominantly men who have developed a particular style of reporting . . . sections of the media simply ignore certain stories. For example, in a debate on domestic violence – an issue which affects one in five women in their lifetimes and as many as 100,000 children in Scotland alone – the press gallery was virtually empty.

Women in politics, as in many other competitive, male-dominated professions, tend to work longer hours (on average, 10 hours more per week) and spend more time on the less "glamorous" side of politics, that is, on constituency work, than do their male colleagues (Norris 1996: 101). With a greater critical mass of women in many Western parliaments as we move through the early years of the new millennium, perhaps the best sign of success for women politicians will be when the media criticize them for their politics rather than their personalities. Some women *are* making a difference but the media seem uninterested in reporting their achievements. In Britain, the successes of women parliamentarians documented in Fiona Mactaggart's (2000) report on the first 1,000 days of the Blair administration are little understood by the woman (or man) in the street, because the media are rarely interested in good news, especially, it seems, about women.

The ways in which the news media regularly cover stories about political women damage not only these women, but also us as citizens and democracy more generally. This is not to argue that women parliamentarians deserve special or different treatment at the hands of the media – quite the contrary, in fact, as I want to see women and men treated as politicians first and foremost. Whilst gender attributes may well be important to mention if the policy under discussion is specifically gendered (for example, breast cancer or paternity pay), is the public interest really served by our knowing about this politician's domestic circumstances or where that Senator went on vacation? If the personal is political, is the political also the personal? With a few exceptions, I just don't think so, and the sooner the news corps get to grips with that reality, the more seriously we might begin to take their claim to be our fourth estate.

Key terms

agenda-setting
"Blair's Babes"
collective public consciousness
gatekeeper
gendered news discourse
hegemonic worldview of male dominance
*his*tory vs. *her*story
news framing
"packaging" of politics
political economy of the newsroom
politico-media dance
primacy of the dollar

Questions for discussion

1. How does Ross apply the public–private dichotomy in analyzing media coverage of women politicians?
2. In what ways are both journalists and politicians mutually involved in setting the policy agenda, in Ross's assessment? What examples from research does she use to support this conclusion?
3. Explain the various ways that gender frames news stories about political issues and politicians, according to the author, and give several examples of when this has occurred.
4. In what ways do media ownership and news-room hierarchies contribute to unfavorable news about female politicians, according to Ross?
5. In explaining what is misrepresented and left out of the news about women politicians, the author also implies how such coverage might be improved. What would be included in this improved coverage?
6. Ross understands that the news reflects larger structural problems in gender relations. How are these structural problems defined?

Notes

1. Parts of this chapter are derived from my previously published book, *Women, Politics, Media* (2002), and I would like to thank Hampton Press for their permission in allowing me to draw from that source.
2. From here on, all the quotations from women parliamentarians are taken from the four sets of interviews I undertook with women in the Westminster (UK), Cape Town (South Africa), and Canberra (Australia) Parliaments and the Northern Ireland Assembly during the years 1995–2002. After each parliamentarian's name, I include her party affiliation and the national parliament or assembly in which she sits or, in the case of some women, where she sat before resigning or being defeated in an election subsequent to being interviewed.
3. Women in Journalism is a British network group comprising women journalists from all UK media, which provides support for members and undertakes research on their own profession's practice, particularly focusing on issues of gender.
4. Mo Mowlam in *Mo Mowlam: Inside New Labour* (dir: Nick Kurwin, Channel 4 Television, 6 May 2002).

References

Ansolabehere, S., Behr, R., and Iyengar, S. (1991) Mass media and elections: an overview. *American Politics Quarterly* 19, 109–39.

Baistow, T. (1985) *Fourth-Rate Estate: An Anatomy of Fleet Street.* Comedia, London.

Bartels, L. and Wilson, W. (1996) Politicians and the press: who leads, who follows? Paper presented at the annual conference of the American Political Science Association, San Francisco, August.

Bird, S. E. (1998) News we can use: an audience perspective on the tabloidisation of news in the United States. *Javnost/The Public* 5, 33–49.

Braden, M. (1996) *Women Politicians and the Media.* University of Kentucky Press, Lexington, KY.

Buchanan, B. (1991) *Electing a President: The Markle Commission's Report on Campaign '88.* University of Texas Press, Austin, TX.

Carter, C. (1998) When the "extraordinary" becomes "ordinary": everyday news of sexual violence. In: Carter, C., Branston, G., and Allan, S. (eds), *News, Gender and Power.* Routledge, London, pp. 219–32.

Carter, C., Branston, G., and Allan, S. (eds) (1998) *News, Gender and Power.* Routledge, London.

Coles, J. (1997) Boy Zone story. *Guardian* April 28.

Creedon, P. (ed.) (1993) *Women in Mass Communication* (2nd edn). Sage, Newbury Park, CA, London, and New Delhi.

Entman, R. M. (1989) How the media affect what people think: an information processing approach. *Journal of Politics* 51, 347–70.

Fawcett Society (1999) *Winning Women: Lessons from Scotland and Wales.* Fawcett Society, London.

Franklin, B. (1997) *Newszak and News Media.* Arnold, London.

Gallagher, M. (2001) *Gender Setting: New Agendas for Media Monitoring and Advocacy.* Zed Books and WACC, London and New York.

International Institute of Communications (1996) *Media Ownership and Control in the Age of Convergence.* University of Luton Press, Luton.

Iyengar, S. (1987) Television news and citizens: explanations of national affairs. *American Political Science Review* 81, 815–31.

Jones, N. (1995) *Soundbites and Spin Doctors: How Politicians Manipulate the Media – and Vice Versa.* Indigo, London.

Kahn, K. F. (1994) The distorted mirror: press coverage of women candidates for statewide office. *Journal of Politics* 56(1), 154–74.

Kahn, K. F. and Goldenberg, E. N. (1991) Women candidates in the news: an examination of gender differences in US senate campaign coverage. *Public Opinion Quarterly* 55, 180–99.

Kahn, K. F. and Goldenberg, E. N. (1997) The media: obstacle or ally of feminists? In: Iyengar, S. and Reeves, E. (eds), *Do the Media Govern? Politicians, Voters and Reporters in America.* Sage, Thousand Oaks, CA, London, and New Delhi, pp. 156–64.

Katz, E. and Lazarsfeld, P. F. (1955) *Personal Influence: The Part Played by People in the Flow of Mass Communications.* Free Press, New York.

Klapper, J. T. (1960) *The Effects of Mass Communication.* Free Press, New York.

Lasswell, H. (1927) *Propaganda Technique in the World War.* Knopf, New York.

LeDuc, L. (1990) Party strategies and the use of televised campaign debates. *European Journal of Political Research* 18, 121–41.

Mactaggart, F. (2000) *Women in Parliament: Their Contribution to Labour's First 1000 Days.* Fabian Society, London.

McDougall, L. (1998) *Westminster Women.* Vintage, London.

Merton, R. K. (1946) *Mass Persuasion: The Social Psychology of a War Bond Drive.* Harper, New York.

Negrine, R. (1998) *Parliament and the Media: A Study of Britain, Germany and France.* Royal Institute of International Affairs and Cassell, London.

Norris, P. (1996) Women politicians: transforming Westminster? In: Lovenduski, J. and Norris, P. (eds), *Women in Politics.* Oxford University Press, Oxford, pp. 91–104.

Norris, P. (1997) Women leaders worldwide: a splash of color in the photo op. In: Norris, P. (ed.), *Women, Media and Politics.* Oxford University Press, Oxford, pp. 149–65.

Perloff, R. M. (1998) *Political Communication: Politics, Press and Public in America.* Lawrence Erlbaum, Mahwah, NJ.

Riordan, E. (2002) Intersections and new directions: on feminism and political economy. In Meehan, E. R. and Riordan, E. (eds), *Sex and Money: Feminism and Political Economy in the Media.* University of Minnesota Press, Minneapolis, pp. 3–15.

Roberts, J. (1994) *Dianne Feinstein: Never Let Them See You Cry.* HarperCollins, New York.

Root, J. (1986) *Open the Box: About Television.* Comedia series no. 34. Channel 4 and Comedia series no. 34, London.

Ross, K. (1995a) Gender and party politics: how the press reported the Labour leadership campaign, 1994. *Media, Culture and Society* 17(3), 499–509.

Ross, K. (1995b) Skirting the issue: political women and the media. *Everywoman* 199: 16–17.

Ross, K. (2001) Women at work: journalism as en-gendered practice. *Journalism Studies* 2(4), 531–44.

Ross, K. (2002) *Women, Politics, Media: Uneasy Relations in Comparative Perspective.* Hampton Press, Cresskill, NJ.

Ross, K. and Sreberny, A. (2000) Women in the house: media representations of British politicians. In: Sreberny, A. and van Zoonen, L. (eds), *Gender, Politics and Communication*. Hampton Press, Cresskill, NJ, pp. 79–100.

Ross, K. and Sreberny-Mohammadi, A. (1997) Playing house: gender, politics and the news media in Britain. *Media, Culture and Society*, 19(1), 101–9.

Shaw, D. L. and Martin, S. E. (1992) The function of mass media agenda setting. *Journalism Quarterly* 69(4), 902–20.

Soothill, K. and Walby, S. (1991) *Sex Crime in the News*. Routledge, London.

Steele, C. A. and Barnhurst, K. G. (1996) The journalism of opinion: network news coverage of US presidential campaigns 1968–1988. *Critical Studies in Mass Communication* 13(2), 187–209.

Tuchman, G., Daniels, A. K., and Benet, J. (eds) (1978) *Hearth and Home: Images of Women in Mass Media*. Oxford University Press, Oxford and New York.

Tunstall, J. (1977) *The Media are American*. Constable, London.

van Zoonen, L. (2002) One of the girls: the changing nature of journalism. In: Carter, C., Branston, G., and Allan, S. (eds), *News, Gender and Power*. Routledge, London, pp. 33–46.

Watts, D. (1997) *Political Communication Today*. Manchester University Press, Manchester and New York.

West, D. M. (1991) Television and presidential popularity in America. *British Journal of Political Science* 21, 199–214.

Wheeler, M. (1997) *Politics and the Mass Media*. Blackwell, Oxford.

Whittaker, R. (1999) *Reading Between the Lines*. Northern Ireland Women's European Platform, Belfast.

Wright, T. (1998) Inside the whale: the media from parliament. In: Seaton, J. (ed.), *Politics and the Media*. Blackwell and Political Quarterly, Oxford, pp. 19–27.

Wykes, M. (1998) A family affair: the British press, sex and the Wests. In: Carter, C., Branston, G. and Allan, S. (eds) *News, Gender and Power*. Routledge, London, pp. 233–47.

5

The Woman Warrior: A Feminist Political Economic Analysis of Crouching Tiger, Hidden Dragon

Ellen Riordan

How long will audiences – especially with increasing access to the tools and technologies of culture – continue to play the role of consumers of cultural values and products not of their own making?

(Wasko 1995: 254)

Introduction

I begin my chapter with this quote by a political economist because although it makes no explicit reference to women or gender, it invokes a very real concern for many feminist media scholars. With the onslaught of home computers, digital cameras, and editing systems touted as revolutionary by media corporations, one would think that images of women should be undergoing some change, particularly if increased numbers of women – or better yet feminists – have access to them. As this chapter points out, certain images of women have remained the same even while undergoing changes to fit the times.

Ideological messages in media occur at the textual, structural, and political economic levels, and it is necessary and of importance to examine them. With the advent of new technologies allowing for wider and faster distribution of information in globalized markets, examining commodity culture is crucial. This is especially so since cultural commodities are developed with profit in mind, rather than other normative values such as diversifying representations and increasing access to information, which perhaps could enrich society and bring us to a more equitable or at least socially just place.

Since the late 1990s, dissatisfaction with corporate global domination has become increasingly visible. Public protests against corporate globalization and world trade have taken place in Seattle, WA, 1999, against the World Trade Organization (WTO); in Davos, Switzerland, January 2000, against the World Economic Forum; in Prague, Czechoslovakia, September 2000, against the International Monetary Fund and World Bank; and in Genoa, Italy, July 2001, against the G-8. In these various protests taking place around the world, activists have disrupted meetings being held by the world's economic elites, in order to draw attention to some of the problems of globalization, such as the profiting of corporations at the expense of fair-wage jobs for workers.

Many people have criticized the lack of fair and representative news media coverage of these events, at least in the United States. However, condemnation for global entertainment or media companies has not been a major focal point in the discussions of corporate global domination. Perhaps this is because on an economic scale of global dominance, entertainment corporations seem to have less financial power than other major corporations.[1] However, entertainment companies are not like other corporations. Because they also operate on an ideological dimension, they circulate values and beliefs, thereby making them distinct from other businesses (Meehan 1994). Even though all global corporations naturalize, or present as common sense, the ideological dimensions of capitalism, entertainment and media corporations also reproduce and re-present significant cultural values and beliefs, particularly about gender.

Because of relaxed government regulations since the 1980s, companies have merged into mega-corporations, controlling large portions of global cultural production through synergistic practices (Wasko 1995: 249). For example, when Disney merged with ABC in 1995 the corporation was able to use many of its newly acquired television networks to distribute Disney-created commodities. Synergy, in addition to allowing for one concept to be spun off into many commodities, in effect quelling the circulation and distribution of new and diverse ideas, also economically rewards the corporation for recycling already produced culture. Corporate synergistic effects on culture are the very reason why many people feel outraged about the freer trade of cultural products with the United States. Even though many people in the US view media properties such as film, books, and magazines primarily as economic entities, citizens in other nations view such material products as central to the production and reproduction of their history and culture. For this reason, many outside of the US defend their right to exclude cultural industries and products from WTO negotiations (McPhail 2002: 215), while corporate elites find little problem with their inclusion.[2]

Concern for the effect of globalization on culture dates back to discussions regarding cultural imperialism. The cultural imperialism thesis suggests that Western media products will contribute to a decline in local values and culture, while simultaneously promoting the ideas associated with capitalism. Communication scholars such as Herbert I. Schiller (1971) and Ariel Dorfman and Armand Mattelart (1975) were among the first in our field to draw attention to these issues. This early articulation of cultural imperialism has been critiqued extensively for not allowing people agency, and communication scholars today tend to conceptualize media processes as complex interactions between people and products.

Cultural studies scholars and feminists such as Barrett ([1982] 2001), Radway (1984), Modleski (1984), and Ang (1991) have made significant contributions to the literature of cultural domination, underscoring the point that audiences are not passive recipients but actively engage texts, and therefore are not simply controlled by media corporations. Nonetheless other feminist cultural scholars have noted a continuing unequal relationship between women and cultural production (Gallagher 1980; Steeves 1993), suggesting that women's influence in the realm of cultural production and the circulation of symbolic ideas is underrepresented. Despite critiques of cultural imperialism, one cannot discount the fact that a disproportionate number of cultural commodities are produced by predominantly male-controlled corporations in industrialized capitalist countries and then exported to other parts of the world. This position does not necessarily minimize the importance of the increasing number of media products coming out of smaller countries. Rather, it acknowledges the asymmetrical relationship between the relatively small number of films (and more notably television shows) imported into the US, and the significantly larger number of Hollywood exports to many other countries. As the work of feminists has suggested, the relationship between production and consumption is also skewed vis-a-vis gender.

The remainder of this chapter highlights some of the major concerns for feminist political economy of the media. Integrating feminism and political economy, the chapter examines the film *Crouching Tiger, Hidden*

Dragon and how it constructs and commodifies culture and feminism. Primarily, this chapter focuses on how the industry marketed the film and how a male gaze dominates and recuperates the potential of a feminist message. Finally, the chapter will discuss the implications of commodified culture, particularly the consequences for feminism.

I begin with a brief synopsis of the film. *Crouching Tiger* takes place in nineteenth-century China during the Qing dynasty rule. Adapted from a novel, the story revolves around a mythical sword, the Green Dynasty, and those into whose hands it passes. The warrior Li Mu Bai, vowing to put his fighting days behind him, asks Shu Lien, a long-time woman companion, to take the sword to Beijing to be retired. During this trip, Shu Lien meets an aristocratic young girl, Jen Yu, who is about to be wed in an arranged marriage. Unbeknownst to almost all, Jen is an extraordinarily gifted swordswoman. Since childhood, she has been secretly training under Jade Fox, her governess. Jade Fox, however, does not realize Jen has surpassed her in skill and mastery of the sword until Jen steals the sword and challenges the warrior Li Mu Bai. Dark Cloud, an outlaw bandit who lives in the desert, loves Jen. Yet this love is not to be realized because Jen is moving toward an arranged marriage. A tension sustained throughout the film is that Jen is jealous of Shu Lien, who possesses the freedom to be a Wudan warrior, and Shu Lien is in awe of Jen because Dark Cloud loves her, a sentiment that Li Mu Bai cannot openly express for Shu Lien.

Feminist political economy

Feminist scholarship is a heterogeneous field of inquiry, rich in diversity of theoretical approaches and methods. Most feminist work is interdisciplinary with respect to theories and methods, and underlying assumptions frequently are not fixed. While feminists may not agree upon what constitutes "woman," they repeatedly agree that the everyday moments in women's lives are valuable, important, and political. Yet the meaning ascribed to these terms is fiercely contested, meaning feminists continue to debate the philosophical significance of these ideas. Likewise, there is not one approach to political economy. Theoretical positions within the field range from classical (mostly descriptive) to critical (often more prescriptive). In addition to a continuum of theoretical approaches, political economy analyses vary in subject matter. Whether presenting an analysis of policy, regulation, corporate structure, labor, or production, political economic studies tend to examine the macro-level, rather than the individual or micro-level.

Feminist political economy integrates an examination of capitalism and patriarchy. In addition to offering a critique of macro-level social structures, feminist political economy stresses the importance of understanding issues of identity, subjectivity, pleasure, and consumption as well as visible and invisible labor in the day-to-day lives of women. Drawing from both feminist and political economic theories, it offers ways to think about how knowledge is simultaneously gendered and economic. For example, while a political economic approach to the study of corporate-controlled production may examine social relations as shaped by capitalist exploitation such as labor conditions, a feminist political economic approach would look at how capitalist exploitation is also gendered and patriarchal; for example, how women's work is often deskilled and underpaid. This is precisely what happens at an entertainment corporation like Sony, where Asian women using highly technical machinery to assemble electronic parts are often concentrated in low-wage jobs while male owners and managers are earning substantially more for decision-making. Whereas a political economic analysis might look at how the commodity audience is bought and sold, a feminist political economic analysis might look at how the process is also gendered. More specifically, a study may examine how corporations use women either as a commodity audience to sell to advertisers or as an object used to attract a demographic niche that becomes the commodity audience.

Work in feminist political economy in the field of communication varies. Some scholarship looks toward gendered and economic relations and how they affect women's work. For example, Canadian political economist Michele Martin has focused on how technologies are gendered, yet also have the potential for progressive appropriation by women (1991, 2002). Other researchers integrating feminism and political economy look not only at the cultural and legal implications of women's work, but also at representations of that work. For example, Karen Ross (2002) has examined how news establishments in the UK treat female politicians and voters, and simultaneously sexualize and underpay female journalists. Nancy Hauserman (2002) has analyzed Swedish and United States news accounts of women workers who were sexually harassed by corporate executives, and how press coverage devalued women's experiences.

Others scholars are concerned with understanding how entertainment and consumption practices can inform identity. For example, Fred Fejes (2002) has argued that gay men and lesbians are targeted by advertisers as niche markets and valued consumers, yet they are continually and systematically denied basic civil rights. Ramona Curry and Angharad Valdivia (2002) have demonstrated how work practices and assumptions about gender used by television producers in the United States limit importation or adoption of non-US programming. Still others researchers look toward policy issues and how they affect women's lives. Ellen Balka (2002) has focused on how telecommunication policies and deregulation combine to deskill and destabilize women workers in Canada. Roopali Mukherjee (2002) has used discourse analysis to examine how news reportage of public policy can be gendered and racialized. As is evident from this brief review of work, scholars working in the area of feminist political economy integrate multiple methodologies to unlock complex relationships between highly abstract concepts – patriarchy and capitalism – that have very real consequences for the lives of women and men.

This chapter starts from an assumption grounded in feminist political economy: global production of culture has both positive and negative consequences, particularly for women. Given that only a handful of industrialized nations has the ability to produce and circulate culture globally, those creating cultural commodities, and how culture shapes national identities, are important considerations. A general concern for feminists is that women, and particularly women of color, have little control of the means of production and have less access to resources than men do.

In *The Political Economy of Communication*, Vincent Mosco (1996) suggests three points of entry for political economic investigations: commodification, spatialization, and structuration. According to Mosco, commodification is predicated on the ideas, derived from Marxist theory, that a use value (the usefulness of the commodity to the consumer) is changed into an exchange value (what the commodity can command on the market). Spatialization, based on the ideas of Henri Lefebvre (1979), is concerned with issues surrounding the transformation of space and time by changes in the technology and information; and structuration, originating in the work of Anthony Giddens (1984), deals with how to think about the impact of human agency on macro-level structures.

While a discussion about the film *Crouching Tiger* could occur at any of these points, I start with the commodity itself, the film, and examine how social relations are reproduced by marketing strategies and the representation of feminism. Implicit in my discussion are issues of spatialization and structuration: spatialization because the film's potential to spread ideological messages is staggering, particularly since it was released in many countries; structuration because this chapter assumes that feminist analyses of micro-level events, such as this film, can indeed change the nature of macro-level structures, such as how the industry represents women. Conversely, this chapter expresses concern regarding the significance of mass-produced culture for micro-level politics because of its representation of feminism.

Constructing and commodifying culture

As mentioned previously, the concern about commodified culture is connected to issues raised by cultural imperialism (Dorfman and Mattelart 1975; Schiller 1971). Concerns regarding commodified culture also bring up the issue of the corporate take-over of public expression (Schiller 1989; Mosco 1999; Klein 2000). Much of the concern for the debasement of public culture links back to the work of Frankfurt School scholars Theodor Adorno and Max Horkheimer (1972). While many critique their work as pessimistic and reductionist, it nevertheless offers some insight into the problems with mass-produced culture.

Grounding their assumptions in Marxism, Frankfurt scholars made connections between the nature of monopoly capitalism and its relationship to mass-produced popular culture. Adorno and Horkheimer argue that modern capitalist societies create affluence and consumerism, while the culture industries create ideological control through mass media; thus the working class become so entrenched in the system that they see no need to revolt.

These concepts are central to understanding why one should approach the analysis of a film such as *Crouching Tiger* from a feminist political economic standpoint. While scholars mentioned above as working in the areas of cultural imperialism, commodified public expression, and the Frankfurt School do not attend to issues of gender, they nevertheless raise the concern about corporate-produced culture and the reproduction of ways of life.

Crouching Tiger offers us a way to examine how global entertainment corporations naturalize patriarchal and capitalist ideology. Because the marketing and press coverage of the film suggest it is an "independent" collaboration with "strong women" as central characters, *Crouching Tiger* puts forward the idea that it is something very different than a mainstream Hollywood motion picture. A closer look at the film, however, reveals that even though the rhetoric suggests *Crouching Tiger* is different than mainstream, corporate-financed motion pictures, it continues to work in patriarchal and gendered ways.

As Wasko has suggested, "the notion of competition in the traditional film industry is a legendary myth" (1995: 250). When looking at the financing of *Crouching Tiger*, one can see some truth in this. Although the film was touted as a collaboration amongst different groups, it becomes evident that *Crouching Tiger* is a Sony commodity, organized with maximum profit as the underlying motivation. *Crouching Tiger* was co-financed by the Hong Kong-based Columbia Pictures Film Production Asia (a subsidiary of Sony Pictures Entertainment) and distributed in North America by Sony Pictures Classics (Sony Annual Report 2001: 39). Additionally, a separate music rights deal to finance the film's soundtrack was made with Sony Classical Music (Eller 2000). After its release on DVD and VHS, *Crouching Tiger* debuted at number 1 on sales and rental charts, and was the fastest-selling DVD title ever for Columbia TriStar. According to Marshall Forster, executive vice-president for Columbia TriStar North America, the film has become "a hugely popular mainstream title crossing several genres – foreign film, martial arts/action, romantic – generat[ing] more than $200 million in global box office receipts" (as quoted in *PR Newswire*, June 15, 2001). Sony Pictures Entertainment's revenue for the fiscal year ending March 31, 2000, rose 12 per cent to $4.4 billion, much of that credited to the film (Souccar 2001: 12). In 2000, the film became the highest-grossing foreign-language film ever in North America, topping $120 million and winning four Academy Awards, including best foreign film (Sony Annual Report 2001: 39).

While the cultural imperialism thesis has been critiqued, looking at ways in which power occurs – not primarily in the form of one country over another, but in terms of how the logic of capitalism becomes a prevailing social relation – is still quite valuable. Evident in the financing of the film, the discourse surrounding *Crouching Tiger* naturalizes the function of capitalism as it suggests the film is an international collaboration, one that not only benefits major Western nations, but also benefits an Eastern nation, Japan (Sony is Japanese owned), and a developing nation, China. While this arrangement does benefit both Western and non-Western countries, it more specifically benefits economic elites in private industry and state-owned organizations. Commonly these types of arrangements often benefit the state and economic elites, but rarely do good for ordinary citizens.

Because government regulations in China require all foreign films to have a state firm involved in the film's release, the rights to release *Crouching Tiger* in China were shared by a private production firm, Asian Union Film and Entertainment. Asian Union invested 80 per cent of the $1 million cost to release the film, and China Film Co-Production Co., one of 16 state-run film companies in China, invested 20 per cent (Chu 2001). Much of the film's $15 million budget came from the advance sale of rights in Asia, North America, and Europe (Eckholm 1999). While these figures may suggest the film was an international collaboration, the success of *Crouching Tiger* continued to primarily benefit Sony.

Slightly more complex and subtle is that the rhetoric naturalizing the film as an international collaboration takes attention away from real problems involved with the global economy. For example, in a global economy the generation of capital occurs largely through the exploitation of labor by transnational corporations and the state. A consequence is that this allows for gender and racial ideologies to be played out (Moghadam 1999). More specifically, naturalizing the rhetoric of the global economy shifts our attention from the fact that those who tend to benefit from the exploitation of labor by transnational corporations and the state are predominantly men, while the exploited labor tends to come from women and people of color. So in the interest of profit-making – a perfectly legitimate assertion in the logic of capitalism – we lose sight of the *process* of profit-making and focus only on the *result*, which tends to benefit elite men.

A *Los Angeles Times* interview with James Schamus, the executive producer for the film, points to how the rhetoric about *Crouching Tiger* being a global production naturalizes the ideology of capitalism. For example, Schamus was quoted stating the following:

> I'd start the day about 6 in the morning, because I had to talk to everybody in Hong Kong and Taipei before they closed for business. When I finished those discussions, I worked with our attorneys in New York and our international sales company and start interfacing with Europe. We'd have to get all the European business done before noon. Then, we'd start talking to Columbia and our bond company in Los Angeles and their lawyers, who would be opening for business at 1 o'clock our time. We'd spend the afternoon wrangling with the Sony attorney and the bond company. And

> then, at the end of the day, I'd pick up the phone and fill in my partners in Asia, Hong Kong, Taipei and Beijing because they'd just be waking up. (quoted in Eller 2000)

Although this quote does suggest a production that involves corporate global companies, it fails to acknowledge that most of these corporations are tied to economic elites who are mostly male. So while the companies involved are not all major United States corporations, they are all motivated by the logic of capital to increase profits and market share, drawing our attention away from the day-to-day experiences of laborers, and instead focusing on abstract concepts such as the benefits of compressing time and space through technology. Additionally, many of these businesses represent transnational corporations with control residing primarily in core nations, illustrating what McPhail has suggested about the international communication industry: "These corporations are tied closely into a subtle and invisible network of Western political, ideological, and economic elites who use the communication industry to perpetuate certain 'needs,' tastes, values, and attitudes so as to increase profits" (2002: 38–9). Even though different nations are involved in the negotiations, the logic of capitalism still primarily benefits a handful of elites.

In addition to *Crouching Tiger* being represented as a global production, it is also touted as an independent production, further masking the ideology of capitalism. As mentioned above most of the financial backers for the film are connected to transnational corporations. Yet popular press articles, such as the one in the *Los Angeles Times*, refer to *Crouching Tiger* as a "must-see independent film" (Eller 2000). In the same article, executive producer James Shamus reinforces the idea of the film as independent, suggesting that it serves as "a good snapshot" of what the international independent film business looks like today. This statement does contain some truth in the sense that proportionately fewer women work in independent film production, and *Crouching Tiger* is a film written, produced, and directed by men. While it is true that it was "cheap" to produce (about $12 million) (F. Kaplan 2001), and the marketing budget was *only* $7 million – comparatively low when considering that usually in excess of $20 million is spent on mainstream Hollywood releases (Lippman 2001) – this hardly qualifies as "independent."

Although the acquisition, promotion, and distribution strategies at Sony Picture Classics are not identical to the blockbuster model, the film still relies on many conventional practices of the mainstream industry. For example, co-presidents of Sony Picture Classics Michael Barker and Thomas Bernard pride themselves on their success with *Crouching Tiger*. Rather than relying on a typical Hollywood model, which stresses one major hit to cover the losses of many releases, Barker and Bernard's strategy over the years has been to get more modest-success films rather than a few big winners. They suggest that the big-winner mentality is evident even with film companies promoting "independent" films like *Crouching Tiger*, and most companies buy 10 or 12 specialty films, relying on one hit to make up for the losses (Souccar 2001: 12). The blockbuster economic model drives film producers to look for the synergistic potential of a film, and given that primarily eight major corporations control the industry, this has consequences for the reproduction of culture. If the most desirable niche market is white males aged 18–34, a blockbuster mentality and synergistic logic have real consequences for women because the majority of reproduced culture excludes women.

Corporate synergy has also promoted a form of "cultural synergy" as cautioned against by Wasko. As she suggests, "The economic logic is compelling, as once a character or story is created and developed (and of course, owned), there are advantages in moving it into different formats" (Wasko 1995: 252). As can be seen with *Crouching Tiger*, the economic incentives prompted quite a bit of synergy and the recycling of culture. For instance, Ubi Soft Entertainment, one of the top 10 interactive entertainment publishers worldwide, acquired the license from Sony to develop and publish worldwide games based on the film, such as PlayStation 2, GameCube, Game Boy Advance and Xbox. As well as developing original properties, Ubi Soft Entertainment has also steadfastly partnered companies such as Disney, Warner Bros, and DreamWorks (*Business Wire* 2001). Additionally, Art Asylum, a New York-based company, has the license to create action figures based on the main characters of the film.[3]

Yet for all of *Crouching Tiger*'s "independence," there seems to have been a lot of tried and true film industry tactics applied to it. For example, it was directed by Ang Lee, who has a strong track record of producing successful films, such as *Sense and Sensibility*, *The Wedding Banquet*, *The Ice Storm*, and *Eat Drink Man Woman*. Using established directors with track records often excludes women from entering into the upper echelons of film production, because fewer women film directors have been able to break through the glass ceiling, so they cannot establish a solid track record.

Another convention is to use big-name actors to help promote the film. The main actors of *Crouching Tiger* are two of Asia's biggest stars, Michelle Yeoh and Chow Yun Fat, both of whom have gained some popularity in the West. The director also relied on the choreography of Yuen Wo-Ping, the Hong Kong kung fu master who worked on the Hollywood special effects blockbuster *The Matrix* (Eckholm 1999). Another practice becoming more commonplace in the production of mainstream big-budget films is the use of locations that provide favorable economic conditions (Litman 1998: 194). Countries that can supply qualified yet cheap labor entice foreign investment. On-location shooting was certainly economically beneficial for *Crouching Tiger*, which was shot over a five-month period in Beijing and in China's western provinces.

Constructing and commodifying feminism

Since the early 1990s or so "pro-girl" images have been increasing in popular culture. However, not all "pro-girl" rhetoric offers an opportunity for girls to transcend individual consumption and enact collective change in social relations. The ideas behind "pro-girl" rhetoric or "girl-power" feminism are that as a society we should value girls and traditionally girl (that is, feminine) activities more than we currently do. The logic follows that if we start to value girls more and celebrate their culture, girls in turn will feel positive about themselves and achieve higher self-esteem, allowing them agency and voice. Girl-power images have become reified in popular culture as commodities bought and sold primarily by entertainment corporations. These commodities are most evident in popular culture such as music (Britney Spears), television (*Buffy the Vampire Slayer*), and the internet (gURL sites). All of these examples point to how a use value – the idea of valuing girls – is changed into an exchange value – commodities intended to empower girls.

With this in mind, one can examine the film *Crouching Tiger*. It was presented as a "strong woman" film and marketed with the idea of "power feminism." According to Michael Barker, co-president of Sony Pictures Classics:

> [*Crouching Tiger*] is the ultimate kind of independent film that really addresses so many demographics and so many different groups. It's really the first action film of its kind that is aimed at women. Women really appreciate

> the strong characters and the romantic story. And the men and the younger crowd really appreciate the entertainment.[4]

This particular type of marketing allowed the film to command the largest possible audience – men between the ages of 18 and 34, who are the most desirable commodity audience, but also the niche market of upwardly mobile women aged 18–34. By creating a film that not only crosses genres, but also appeals to educated, upwardly mobile audiences, Sony was able to ensure a sizable profit.

Part of constructing *Crouching Tiger* as a "strong woman" film meant that the marketing of it would have to target feminists. However, it didn't target all types of feminists; it specifically targeted "power feminists." Frequently, power feminism becomes equated with "postfeminism," or the idea that women have achieved equality, so they no longer need feminism and should just get on with it. To this end, one of the marketing strategies used to promote the film included having the magazine *Sports Illustrated for Women* host a screening for 150 graduates of a women's leadership institute conducted by power feminist Naomi Wolf (Lippman 2001). This is problematic on many levels, but one issue that I will develop later on is that because *Crouching Tiger* presents a monolithic view of feminism and is hugely successful, fitting with the current trend of "girl power," it helps reify one type of feminism – power feminism – *as* feminism. And the media have been doing this for quite some time.

The selling of strong women as feminists fits with the typical mainstream studio film. Strong women sell right now and the film industry is very willing to capitalize on this trend. Regarding the current wave of strong action heroines, Paul Dergarabedian, president of Exhibit Relations (a firm that analyses box office trends), stated:

> [they are the feminine counterparts of] the Dirty Harrys of the world . . . rugged guys who everybody's rooting for to beat the heck out of the bad guys and save the day. Now you have these really powerful women who are physically adept and able to express their feelings in a way that's usually reserved for men. (quoted in Puig 2001)

Simon West, who directed Angelina Jolie in the film *Lara Croft: Tomb Raider*, confirmed this point by stating:

> I suppose on a purely mercenary level the studios may have stumbled across something: We can have the best of all worlds – exciting action and

> beautiful, sexy women to look at the same time. Why restrict yourself to big, sweaty men in that genre of film? Instead of romantic comedies for women and action for men, we can appeal to both sexes and have them queuing around the block. (quoted in Puig 2001)

As this quote suggests, the film has been crafted to command the largest possible commodity audience without threatening patriarchy.

In addition to *Crouching Tiger* being marketed as a strong woman film, and subsequently thought about as a "feminist" film, it also constructs feminism in a way that is not threatening to patriarchy. So while this may be a film where women "kick butt," its success is due to the fact that women are still "women," meaning still feminine and to be looked at. According to Ang Lee, the director, "The key to the cross-gender appeal of these mighty heroines is that they harness their strength without trading in their femininity" (quoted in Puig 2001). Retaining this "feminine" attribute is another critical factor in the success of the film. While strong women characters appeal to many women, feminine women appeal to many men without disrupting patriarchy. Since according to media analysts the "babe quotient is critical to ensuring male attendance" (Puig 2001), feminine action heroines are less menacing than butch ones. As Joanne Morreale (1998) suggests about the title character in *Xena: Warrior Princess*, her popularity as a strong woman is OK because Xena still retains enough feminine characteristics (scant, tight-fitting clothing) to make her desirable rather than threatening to men. This, however, is not the case with the film *Thelma and Louise*, which received harsh criticism because the two lead characters were not acting feminine enough.

There is little dispute that *Crouching Tiger*, along with other films and television shows featuring strong women characters, has elements that are both empowering and *dis*empowering. One the one hand, these cultural commodities inspire young women and make girls and women feel powerful; undeniably this shifts consciousness. However, the representation of strong women characters does not necessarily shift structural power relations, which are often roadblocks to prevent women achieving their fullest potential in a world that is patriarchal. One could argue, as does Susan Faludi, that "girl power" feminism is watered down because "no guy goes to sleep worrying that this little girl is going to take his job or stand up to him as an equal. [Therefore], the underlying message to women is you don't really need to question social structure, you just need to go to the gym more often" (quoted in Puig 2001).

A feminist reading of *Crouching Tiger*

While the women in *Crouching Tiger* are never called feminists, the marketing of the film and the discourse surrounding it suggest that they represent a popular form of feminism. Since the film fits in with fashionable constructions of "powerful women," it thus serves to reify a monolithic and ultra-contemporary version of feminism. Because images of physically strong women are popular in present-day television shows and films, "power feminism" becomes the accepted imagining of feminism. Rather than posing a real threat to patriarchy, the women in power feminism films attract both men and women because they simultaneously fit conventional notions of powerful and sexy. As a matter of fact, in the case of *Crouching Tiger* the two principal women characters present a type of feminism that is complicit with patriarchy, while another female character who does not comply with patriarchy is eventually killed. As discussed below, using the concept of the "male gaze" helps us understand how this film can be read as a non-feminist text.

The concept of the "male gaze" in feminist film theory originates with Laura Mulvey's (1975) classic contribution to psychoanalytic film theory. In her groundbreaking article "Visual Pleasure and Narrative Cinema," Mulvey argues that mainstream Hollywood films position women as objects of a male or dominating gaze. She argues that film texts do this in two ways: first, women become the object of the male protagonists' gaze in the film; second, women are positioned as objects by the camera, rather than actively forwarding the narrative. Thus, these two conditions allow the audience to only look at women with a controlling male gaze. Scholars have written numerous responses to and critiques of Mulvey's argument. For example, many feminist film scholars argue that Mulvey's description of the male gaze is not adequate because it does not theorize female spectatorship adequately (Doane 1990; Gaines 1990; E. Kaplan 1983). Furthering this, other feminist film scholars have worked to formulate a more complex understanding of female spectatorship (Gledhill 1999; Stacey 1994; Gamman 1989).

Two primary themes work to construct and reify feminism throughout *Crouching Tiger*: (1) women are in opposition to each other, and (2) strong women are complicit with patriarchy. The theme of women in opposition is not necessarily new in literary or media texts, and mainstream Hollywood narratives often use the strategy of rivalry and opposition (Gamman

1989). However, because *Crouching Tiger* is being represented as a "strong woman" or pro-woman film, the theme of women in opposition seems even more problematic. Throughout the film, opposition is represented between "older" and "younger" women. The rivalry between the two main women, Shu Lien (the woman warrior) and Jen (the aristocratic girl), is a main plot device throughout the narrative. Another less emphasized rivalry throughout the film is between Jen and her older governess, Jade Fox.

The opposition between Shu Lien and Jen centers on jealousy and betrayal. Jen is jealous of Shu Lien's life because the latter is free to be a warrior – exactly what Jen would like. Likewise, Shu Lien wishes her life could be more like Jen's because Dark Cloud freely and devotedly expresses his love for Jen, while Li Mu Bai cannot do the same to Shu Lien. The jealousy expressed primarily on the part of Jen creates the rivalry between the two women.

Jealousy is the undercurrent that fuels betrayal. Throughout the film, Jen acts like a spoiled and selfish child, only wanting her way. Although Shu Lien has spoken with her about the qualities of a good warrior – friendship, integrity, and trust – Jen refuses to follow these warrior codes, seeking only self-gratification. At various points throughout the film, Jen turns on Shu Lien, starting with the first betrayal when she steals the sword. The rivalry between the two escalates until they have a sword battle, prompted by the betrayal of friendship. This scene is symbolic because it stresses that the friendship between the two women is over (literally in the English subtitles, and metaphorically in the battle). Also, in the English dubbed version the dialogue stresses that they are no longer sisters, invoking the idea of second wave feminist sisterhood.

The rivalry between Jen and Jade Fox can also be read as an "old vs. young" rivalry, again centering on the idea that younger women betray older women. Jade Fox, Jen's governess, secretly raised her to be a Wudan warrior fighter. After 10 years of being cared for and instructed by Jade Fox, Jen reveals that she has been secretly studying the Wudan manual, which in turn, allows her to become a superior fighter and surpass Jade Fox.

This theme of women in opposition also can be read as second wave feminism versus third wave feminism. The character of Shu Lien represents an example of a liberal feminist position – wanting equality with men and also still very much committed to heterosexual love to complete her. Jade Fox represents an example of a radical feminist – one who would prefer a separate community for women, one with a matriarchal system of governance. Although space does not permit a fuller discussion of this, Jade Fox can also be read as lesbian throughout the film. Moreover, she is the only woman character to pose a threat to patriarchy in her rejection of it, and in the end, she is the only woman punished by death.

Both women, Shu Lien and Jade Fox, oppose Jen, whose character is most certainly coded as third wave feminist or more specifically girl-power feminist. Jen retains her femininity even though she is strong and skilled enough to fight like a male warrior. Her interactions with men throughout the film also reveal their desire for her. For example, when she interacts with men – Li Mu Bai and Dark Cloud – she is sexualized, and becomes the object of their gaze. In fight scenes with Li Mu Bai, body language conveys that he is always in control. He is poised and his movements are graceful. Conversely, Jen is overly zealous and her movements flailing. While the narrative presents us with moments where she stands up to patriarchal challenges, these are more consistent with moments of spectacle, rather than activity. For example, Jen's most active moments occur when she is fighting, yet in the two most significant fight scenes with men, the camera objectifies her, making her an object of desire. Furthermore, her active fighting scenes are often recuperated because she is portrayed as a disruptive child needing protection and guidance from Li Mu Bai.

Jen's relationship with Dark Cloud also suggests she is complicit with patriarchy. While she appears to be Dark Cloud's equal in terms of fighting ability, she is captured and "rescued" by him on two separate occasions. In keeping with stereotypical portrayals of female desire, Jen sexually longs for her captor, reminiscent of a mythical rape-fantasy. Although the two appear to have consensual sex, the plot establishes Jen's sexual desire as coming from her being overpowered. In addition, the on-screen portrayal, including costuming, body posture, and camera angles, frequently suggests that Jen is an object for the male gaze, rather than a subject. For instance, right before the two engage in a struggle that leads to sex, Dark Cloud removes a splinter from her foot, while Jen lies seductively reclined, framed by a slightly higher camera angle looking down on her, and with her shirt partially open. In another scene, somewhat uncharacteristic for the film, Jen is blatantly sexualized for the camera. She has been drugged by Jade Fox, and in a state of delirium she rips open her shirt (white, completely drenched by rain and see-through), asking if Li Mu Bai has come for her. As these examples suggest, even though Jen is a strong fighter, she is not a threat to patriarchy, and is in fact complicit with it because of her need to be desired by men.

While space does not permit an exhaustive reading of *Crouching Tiger*, the brief analysis above suggests that while having moments of pleasure for female spectators because women in the film are skilled martial artists, the film ultimately succumbs to a dominant male gaze. This reading of a conventional narrative film is not unusual. However, analyzing *Crouching Tiger* as both text and commodity points to multiple ways in which asymmetrical power relations between men and women persist.

Conclusion

This chapter uses a particular commodity (or text), *Crouching Tiger*, to illustrate how a feminist political economic approach can further our understanding of commodification. As discussed above, the discourse surrounding *Crouching Tiger* tends to naturalize the extension of capital by suggesting the film is both independent and an international collaboration between East and West, thereby enabling a set of social relations that benefit all parties involved, rather than revealing that globalization benefits some at the expense of others. The rhetoric of the film as a global production and as an independent production assuages the fact that it is financed, produced, and distributed by major media corporations that operate under the logic of capitalism and Western ideology, both patriarchal. Additionally, this chapter illustrates how the patriarchal structure of capitalism poses problems for women, girls, and feminists who have their identities co-opted, repackaged as commodities, and sold as feminism.

The corporate recycling of culture has serious consequences for women, and more specifically feminism. We are in a period in which "girl power" and images of strong women sell. As I have discussed elsewhere, the idea of girl power has become reified into tangible commodities bought and sold most notably by entertainment corporations (Riordan 2001). In the process of transformation of a use value into an exchange value, the idea of "girl power" or empowerment becomes watered down so that it means something to everyone, allowing it to be rearticulated in a number of ways and appeal to the widest audience. Part of hegemonic expansion (Mouffe 1979), by which I mean the way dominant societal ideas (often repressive) are assumed as common sense and go unchallenged, is that the ideas of marginal groups become adopted into the mainstream. In the process, radical messages are co-opted and lost, and feminism is rearticulated as part of the mainstream. *Crouching Tiger* demonstrates how the strong woman image has been subsumed in the dominant culture and in the process, has become neutralized. Dominant culture changes in so far as it takes on and rearticulates once-marginalized images, but through the adoption process, the feminist message about structural change is lost. Moreover, this adoption of once unpopular images compromises the ideas of third wave feminism. While it may feel empowering to see women in strong roles, upon closer examination it is evident that these images of women are being packaged and sold by media industries, rather than women themselves. There is nothing new about the representation of women in this film. And because images of fighting women are heralded as progressive, the message is more insidious. *Crouching Tiger* constructs women in opposition, divided by patriarchal constructions of femininity, and ultimately complicit with patriarchy. This poses very real consequences for the way feminism is articulated and understood by the public.

Feminism is not one thing, it is a contested area of activism and theory. Yet mainstream notions of feminism become popularized and recirculated by entertainment conglomerates. The power of these conglomerates is to put forth a particular worldview, intentional or not, and this particular worldview is one that minimizes the achievements of feminism, constructs women in opposition to one another rather than as supportive of each other, and creates women as desirable objects for men. A feminist political economic analysis suggests that this is problematic and should be challenged.

Key terms

commodification
commodity audience
corporate synergistic effects on culture
cultural synergy
economic elites
female spectatorship
feminist political economy of media
"girl power" feminism
global production
ideological dimensions of capitalism
independent production
macro-level social structures

male gaze
micro-level social structures
postfeminism
"pro-girl" rhetoric
spatialization
structuration
third wave feminism

Questions for discussion

1 How does Riordan define "feminist political economy of media"?
2 The author challenges marketing claims that the film *Crouching Tiger, Hidden Dragon* is an independent production. What are her arguments?
3 Why does the author believe that *Crouching Tiger* is another example of what she calls "global cultural imperialism"?
4 In what ways does *Crouching Tiger* exemplify what Riordan calls "girl-power feminism"? How might the film be different if it reflected a truer representation of feminism?
5 Why does Riordan believe that characters like Lara Croft (*Tomb Raider*) and Xena (*Xena: Warrior Princess*) are ultimately disempowering to women?
6 Where does the matter of "male gaze" fit into Riordan's analysis of *Crouching Tiger*?

Notes

1 In 1999 General Motors ranked twenty-third in the list of the top 200 economies, with sales of $176.6 billion. GM's sales were more than those of many countries, including Denmark, Norway, Venezuela, Colombia, and Ireland. See Anderson and Cavanaugh (2000). This compares to the Sony Corporation with net sales of approximately $53.8 billion in 2001.
2 During the General Agreement on Tariffs and Trade (GATT) negotiations in 1995, the French prime minister stuck firmly to his position opposing the importation of Hollywood films (Segrave 1997).
3 http://actionfigures.about.com/gi/dynamic/offsite.htm?site=http://www.artasylum.net.

4 As quoted in Valerie Morris in an interview with Michael Barker, co-president of Sony Pictures Classic, *Biz Buzz*, CNN FN Network, 18:00 ET, January 31, 2001.

References

Adorno, T. and Horkheimer, M. (1972) *The Dialectic of Enlightenment.* Herder and Herder, New York.

Anderson, S. and Cavanaugh, J. (2000) *Top 200: The Rise of Corporate Global Power.* Institute for Policy Studies, London.

Ang, I. (1991) *Desperately Seeking the Audience.* Routledge, London.

Balka, E. (2002) The invisibility of the everyday: new technology and women's work. In: Meehan, E. and Riordan, E. (eds), *Sex and Money: Feminism and Political Economy in the Media.* University of Minnesota Press, Minneapolis, pp. 60–74.

Barrett, M. ([1982] 2001) Feminism and the definition of cultural politics. In: Robinson, H. (ed.), *Feminism-Art-Theory: An Anthology, 1968–2000.* Blackwell, Oxford, pp. 308–12.

Business Wire (2001) Ubi Soft and Sony Pictures unleash the Tiger! May 18.

Chu, H. (2001) *Crouching Tiger* can't hide from bad reviews in China. *Los Angeles Times* January 29, A1.

Curry, R. and Valdivia, A. (2002) Xuxa at the borders of US TV: checked for gender, race and national identity. In: Meehan, E. and Riordan, E. (eds), *Sex and Money: Feminism and Political Economy in the Media.* University of Minnesota Press, Minneapolis, pp. 240–56.

Doane, M. A. (1990) Film and the masquerade theorizing the female spectator. In: Erens, P. (ed.), *Issues in Feminist Film Criticism.* Indiana University Press, Bloomington, pp. 41–57.

Dorfman, A. and Mattelart, A. (1975) *How to Read Donald Duck: Imperialist Ideology in the Disney Comic.* International General, New York.

Eckholm, E. (1999) A filmmaker reroutes the flow of history. *New York Times* December 16, E1.

Eller, C. (2000) Company town; the biz; funding for *Crouching Tiger* a work of art. *Los Angeles Times* December 12, C9.

Fejes, F. (2002) Advertising and the political economy of lesbian/gay identity. In: Meehan, E. and Riordan, E. (eds), *Sex and Money: Feminism and Political Economy in the Media.* University of Minnesota Press, Minneapolis, pp. 196–208.

Gaines, J. (1990) Women and representation: can we enjoy alternative pleasure? In: Erens, P. (ed.), *Issues in Feminist Film Criticism.* Indiana University Press, Bloomington, pp. 75–92.

Gallagher, M. (1980) *Unequal Opportunities: The Case of Women and the Media.* UNESCO, Paris.

Gamman, L. (1989) Watching the detectives: the enigma of the female gaze. In: Gamman, L. and Marshment, M. (eds), *The Female Gaze: Women as Viewers of Popular Culture.* Real Comet Press, Seattle, pp. 8–26.

Giddens, A. (1984) *The Constitution of Society: Outline of a Theory of Structuration.* University of California Press, Berkeley, CA.

Gledhill, C. (1999) Pleasurable negotiations. In: Thornman, S. (ed.), *Feminist Film Theory: A Reader.* New York University Press, New York, pp. 166–79.

Hauserman, N. (2002) Sexual harassment as an economic concern: Swedish and American coverage of Astra. In: Meehan, E. and Riordan, E. (eds), *Sex and Money: Feminism and Political Economy in the Media.* University of Minnesota Press, Minneapolis, pp. 88–99.

Kaplan, E. A. (1983) *Women and Film: Both Sides of the Camera.* Routledge, New York.

Kaplan, F. (2001) Producing the Tiger neglecting his dissertation, James Schamus has found unlikely success in film. *Boston Globe* March 25, N29.

Klein, N. (2000) *No Logo: Taking Aim at the Brand Bullies.* Picador, New York.

Landler, M. (2001) It's raining tigers and dragons: Asian filmmakers rush to repeat an Oscar winner's success. *New York Times* July 2, E1.

Lefebvre, H. (1979) Space: social product and use value. In: Frieberg, J. W. (ed.), *Critical Sociology: European Perspectives.* Halsted Press, Irvington, pp. 285–95.

Lippman, J. (2001) The creation of a buzz: marketing has transformed *Crouching Tiger, Hidden Dragon* from an art house obscurity to an academy award contender. *Ottawa Citizen* January 12, D3.

Litman, B. (1998) *The Motion Picture Mega-Industry.* Allyn and Bacon, Needham Heights.

Martin, M. (1991) *"Hello Central?": Gender, Technology and Culture in the Formation of the Telephone Systems.* McGill-Queen's University Press, Montreal.

Martin, M. (2002) An unsuitable technology for a woman? Communication as circulation. In: Meehan, E. and Riordan, E. (eds), *Sex and Money: Feminism and Political Economy in the Media.* University of Minnesota Press, Minneapolis, pp. 49–59.

McPhail, T. (2002) *Global Communication: Theories, Stakeholders, and Trends.* Allyn and Bacon, Boston.

Meehan, E. R. (1994) Conceptualizing culture as commodity: the problem with television. In: Newcomb, H. (ed.), *Television: The Critical View.* Oxford University Press, New York, pp. 563–72.

Modleski, T. (1984) *Loving with a Vengeance: Mass Produced Fantasies for Women.* Methuen, London.

Moghadam, V. M. (1999) Gender and the global economy. In: Ferree, M. M., Lorber, J., and Hess, B. B. (eds), *Revisioning Gender.* Sage, Thousand Oaks, CA, pp. 128–60.

Morreale, J. (1998). *Xena: Warrior Princess* as feminist camp. *Journal of Popular Culture* 32(2), 79–86.

Mosco, V. (1996) *The Political Economy of Communication.* Sage, London.

Mosco, V. (1999) Political economy, myth and place. Paper presented at the Union for Democratic Communications conference, Oregon, October.

Mouffe, C. (1979) *Gramsci and Marxist Theory.* Routledge, London.

Mukherjee, R. (2002) Single moms, quota queens, and the model majority: putting "women" to work in the California civil rights initiative. In: Meehan, E. and Riordan, E. (eds), *Sex and Money: Feminism and Political Economy in the Media.* University of Minnesota Press, Minneapolis, pp. 100–11.

Mulvey, L. (1975) Visual pleasure and narrative cinema. *Screen* 16(3), 6–18.

PR Newswire (2001) June 15.

Puig, C. (2001) Hollywood heroines get tough: films bank on strong, savvy, sexy women to score at the box office. *USA Today* January 23, 1A.

Radway, J. (1984) *Reading the Romance: Women, Patriarchy and Popular Literature.* University of North Carolina Press, Chapel Hill, NC.

Riordan, E. (2001) Commodified agents and empowered girls: consuming and producing feminism. *Journal of Communication Inquiry* 25(3), 279–97.

Ross, K. (2002) Selling women (down the river): gendered relations and the political economy of broadcast news. In: Meehan, E. and Riordan, E. (eds), *Sex and Money: Feminism and Political Economy in the Media.* University of Minnesota Press, Minneapolis, pp. 112–29.

Schiller, H. (1971) *Mass Communications and American Empire.* Beacon, Boston.

Schiller, H. (1989) *Culture Inc.* Oxford University Press, New York.

Segrave, K. (1997) *American Films Abroad: Hollywood's Domination of the World's Film Screens from the 1890s to the Present.* McFarland, London.

Sony Annual Report (2001) www.sony.co.jp/en/SonyInfo/IR/Financial/AR/2001/BR-pictures.html

Souccar, M. K. (2001) Putting on the indie hits: Sony pictures classics masters the art of finding big audiences for small films. *Crain's New York Business*, May 14, 12.

Stacey, J. (1994) *Star Gazing: Hollywood and Female Spectatorship.* Routledge, London.

Steeves, H. L. (1993) Gender and mass communication in a global context. In: Creedon, P. (ed.), *Women in Mass Communication.* Sage, Newbury Park, CA, pp. 32–60.

Wasko, J. (1995) *Hollywood in the Information Age: Behind the Silver Screen.* University of Texas Press, Austin, TX.

PART II

Women's Agency in Media Production

The chapters in this half of the book show that women's persistent efforts to take control of their own representational image, as producers, directors, journalists, and editors, have reaped significant rewards for the way in which women are portrayed in mainstream media and the range of issues which now count as news. While there is clearly a long way to go before the media reflect the multiplicity and diversity of real people's real experiences, the contribution which women media professionals have made to shifting the agenda has been substantial. The first two chapters in this part look at the ways in which women work in newsroom cultures and the strategies they use to thrive within essentially male-dominated working environments.

Chapter 6, by Carolyn M. Byerly, begins by taking an historical look at the involvement of women in newsrooms over a 30-year period from 1970 to 2000. In surveying several examples of success and failure, Byerly argues that we need to apply the concept of "change" broadly, in order to account both for events that have succeeded and for those that have been stymied. Crucially, she suggests that change in the newsroom is linked to the fluctuating success of feminist movements in influencing social institutions at any given historical point. The chapter includes a history of organized feminist pressure on news media, both on the inside of newsrooms (through women journalists organizing) and through external campaigns by feminist advocacy groups seeking specific changes. Individual groups of women journalists in various nations over the years have also been important, as has women's alternative journalism, which has developed considerably since the late 1970s, and especially during the UN Decade for Women (1975–85).

Chapter 7 focuses on the complex relationship that women have with the media in India, and in doing so provides important insights into an underresearched topic and a region which is mostly unknown to many Western media scholars. Ammu Joseph's contribution attempts to describe the complicated reality of the ways in which women are involved in and reported by the media, in order to highlight the challenges and opportunities presented by the prevailing situation. Using content analysis to look at the ways in which women journalists in both print and TV are affecting the news agenda, she discusses some of the measures and strategies currently being tried in an effort to enhance media professionals' ability to tackle gender-based disparities within the sector and in society more generally, as well as to empower women both as professionals and as citizens. Joseph argues that although there have been very positive changes that have benefited women media professionals, much remains to be done. She suggests that organizations, associations, and/or networks of women in the media should call attention to the need for change through research and documentation, dissemination of information, discussion and debate, advocacy and lobbying. They could also initiate mutually supportive strategies – such as sharing resources, training, and mentoring – to enhance women's confidence, capabilities, and potential for advancement within the media.

The second pair of chapters looks at media that are consciously gendered inasmuch as they were set up to appeal directly to women, and women are the principal media players in terms of the output delivered. In chapter 8, Caroline Mitchell explores the development of women's radio practice during the late twentieth century, briefly documenting some of the key historical moments in this emergent medium as well as using specific case studies as the route along which to examine the wider concerns and issues involved in such a targeted media practice. She also focuses on the particular structures of production, program content, style, and forms of (audience) address contained within women's radio output, in order to define the ways in which women's radio practice is actually different to mainstream processes. Because of continuing hostility amongst regulators such as the UK Radio Authority toward community radio generally, women's radio stations are precariously positioned and cannot provide a sustained service to their many listeners. This not only stifles women's voices and denies them access to their audiences (and vice versa) but puts a brake on women's talent and creativity. Nevertheless, Mitchell argues that women's radio stations have increased the diversity of voices across the airwaves as well as improving the skills of women in community radio, despite the short broadcasting life of those stations.

The final chapter looks at gender and cyberspace. Gillian Youngs considers the theoretical and practical meanings of cyberspace for feminist activism, linking ways in which women have used the internet, individually and collectively, to contemporary debates about feminist politics and identities. Drawing on the meanings associated with "frontier," the chapter considers what is "new" about virtual space for women, their lives, their practices and opportunities. It focuses, in particular, on the politics of virtual environments, including the many problems associated with safety and danger. Youngs considers the degree to which presence and access on the internet is gendered and can be politically empowering and productive as well as opening up new forms of vulnerability. The chapter draws directly on Youngs's practice-related cyberwork in international settings, and on her diverse contributions to policy debates both in the UK and in international and non-governmental organizational contexts. In that vein, the chapter discusses the importance of practice-driven thinking for new feminist theorizing on, through, and about the net.

6
Feminist Interventions in Newsrooms

Carolyn M. Byerly

> *[W]omen's selfhood, the right to her own story, depends upon her ability to act in the public domain.*
>
> *Carolyn Heilbrun, Writing a Woman's Life*

Introduction

One could read any academic study of women and news these days – including several included in this text – and come away with the sense that women must not work in the newsrooms that spew out the daily fare of stories that still focus mainly on the deeds and ideas of men. An even more cynical view might be that women *do* work there but have done little or nothing to confront the enduring sexism that characterizes both the newsroom hierarchy and its products, even after three decades of modern feminism and women's advancement in the workplace and elsewhere. Neither scenario is accurate or true, of course. The explanations surrounding women journalists' relationship to their newsrooms present a different, more complex picture than either of these scenarios suggests, and it is a picture set against a backdrop of all women's broader relationship to *all* communications media, as well as to the larger society in which they live. In this chapter, I examine the women-and-news relationship, which has evolved over time and in response to feminist activism that has specifically targeted the news media, both inside and outside of newsrooms. In the process, I explore masculine newsroom hegemony, review the feminist critique of news, summarize numerous examples of feminist[1] news interventions, and explore why these matter in relation to women's right to communicate.

The analysis draws on and extends my earlier research in this area, which includes surveys and interviews among both women and men working as journalists on major US daily newspapers and in alternative media in the US and elsewhere since the late 1980s (Byerly and Warren 1996; Byerly 1995), critiques of the political and economic structures of news organizations (Byerly 2002a, 2002b, forthcoming a), and historical analyses of feminist, gay, and lesbian media interventions (Byerly 1995, forthcoming b). My academic concern with women's (and by extension, gays', lesbians', and racial minorities') relationship to news and other media is grounded in my years as a journalist, public relations professional, and feminist activist (who inevitably ended up trying to bring reporters and movement leaders together). These multiple identities as professional, activist, and academic have taught me that women will never gain full social participation or political power until they are able to speak about women's concerns, indeed all matters of public interest, in the mainstream news of their nations. At the same time, I have come to see more clearly that the ability to have any meaningful control of those media to assure they serve women's needs and interests will not come easily. In other words, the struggle is not yet over.

Feminist media critique

Feminist criticisms of the news (and to a large extent also other mass media) can be organized under three main problems. The first focuses on women's absence in most serious news content. Such invisibility has the effect of reinforcing women's marginality through what Tuchman (1978a) called a "symbolic annihilation of women." Women as relevant, accomplished social actors remain unknown and therefore unimportant when they are not seen or heard from in routine information purveyed by news media. Agenda-setting theory (McCombs and Shaw 1972) helps us to understand the seriousness of this problem, which essentially explains why women's concerns have historically been slow to appear in public discourse created by news and public policy that flows from it. The second problem has been one of representation, or portrayal. When women are included, the news media misrepresent and distort them, for example, by focusing on their sexual attributes as women instead of their ideas, activities, and accomplishments. Charges of sex-role stereotyping also fall under this problem, that is, the portraying of women as less intelligent and less capable than men, or showing them in their traditional private sphere roles of mother, wife, sister, caretaker, or servant rather than in light of their deeds or more complex identities. The third problem is one of access to the news-making apparatus. The main concerns here have been women's employment and advancement within news (and other media) industries where news is defined, formulated, and distributed.

It is significant that feminists throughout the world have essentially agreed in this overarching media critique, as shown in research across nations and in documents in global forums like the United Nations. Such convergence in thinking has enabled strategies for change to emerge, both within and among nations, as the ensuing discussion reveals.

Theoretical terrain

The ensuing analysis is informed by current traditional research on women and news and by feminist and other critical theory. Critical theories are cross-disciplinary in nature and share a number of characteristics that include: (1) understanding the role of ideology in establishing and maintaining hierarchies and relations of power among groups in society; (2) seeking the connections among systems of oppression based on gender, social class, race, ethnicity, and sexual orientation; and (3) having the goal of using scholarship to advance consciousness and emancipation in oppressed communities (Miller 2002). I am beholden to a burgeoning literature of feminist news and media research that goes back to the early 1970s. Tuchman's (1978a, 1978b) and Gallagher's (1979, 1980, 1995) foundational and more recent theoretical and empirical work on women and media has inspired others to interrogate everything from women's structural relations to media, to representational issues, to audience research. Current work by feminist political economists like Eileen Meehan and Ellen Riordan (Meehan and Riordan 2002) contributes to the present discussion by revealing the ways that patriarchy (male domination) and capitalism are intertwined systems that perpetuate a male hegemonic system in media industries. Work by feminist scholar Bernadette Barker-Plummer (1995) and feminist journalists Anita Anand and Gouri Salvi

(1998) show how feminist media activism has helped to change the situation.

Critical race theorists Mari Matsuda and Charles Lawrence remind me that critical theory is also grounded in the social reality of the researcher's experiences, as well as "the collective historical experiences of our communities of origin" (Matsuda et al. 1993: 3). These theorists look to their own backgrounds as minorities for direction in their scholarship on communication issues, which they acknowledge is "avowedly political" (ibid.). They inspire a white academic like myself to be more aware of the ways that gender intersects with economic, racial heritage, sexual identity, nationality, and other signifiers of status.

In the present discussion, I am also pushed to return to the work of Italian Marxist Antonio Gramsci (1987), whose original explication of hegemony theory enables feminist theorists like myself to ferret out some of the specific ways that the masculine systems of power are kept in place, not so much through force or even the threat of force as through routines that serve to manufacture the consent of the oppressed through mechanisms of punishment and reward (Gramsci 1987: 12–13). This is not to minimize the real violence (or fear of such) that women experience every day in their lives through physical, sexual, and emotional assaults by men or its coercive ability to reinforce men's power over women, in both private and public spheres. Much of my own professional and political work has been a response to sexual assault, domestic violence, and war, and my scholarship and teaching have often focused on media coverage of these (Byerly 1994, 1999). However, here I want to consider the non-violent mechanisms that work more subtly alongside overt acts of coercion to manufacture the consent of both women and men in perpetuating particular masculine systems in newsrooms and, by extension, the stories those newsrooms produce.

In earlier work, I have argued that feminist media analysis should move beyond the "paradigm of the misogynist media" that has dominated feminist media research since the 1970s. Instead, I've suggested that feminist analysis might seek to reveal "how feminism, over time, has deeply embedded itself in the fabric of media messages and the industries that produce them" (Byerly 1999: 383–4). This chapter incorporates this same reasoning by focusing on feminist newsroom interventions over a thirty-year period. But it also seeks to better theorize the context of the newsroom culture in which feminists have interceded on women's behalf.

Hegemony and its discontents

Economic power in the news business proceeds from the fixed *structural relations* – in Marxist terms, the base – determined by ownership and executive control over resources, strategic plans, formulation of personnel policies, etc. by those in top echelons. In the United States (the primary focus of this chapter), news corporations are almost exclusively the domains of very wealthy white men, with only minuscule involvement by women and persons of non-European heritage above the journalistic ranks. In 2001, only 14 women could be counted among the chief executive officers or boards of directors governing the largest global media conglomerates – AOL-Time Warner, Disney, Viacom, News Corporation, Bertelsmann, and Vivendi – the first three of which are US.-based (Byerly forthcoming a). In terms of employment in the industries, women comprise just over a third of those employed in newspapers (37 per cent), but less than a fourth (22 per cent) hold supervisory positions, with only a small percentage of all women journalists being ethnic minority. Women employed in broadcast journalism fare about the same overall, as they comprise about a fourth (26 per cent) of local TV news directors, 17 per cent of local TV managers, and 13 per cent of general managers at radio stations (Annenberg Public Policy Center 2002). Available data also suggest that those who staff and control newsrooms are overwhelmingly heterosexual, with gay and lesbian journalists generally few in number but lesbians particularly invisible (Aarons and Murphy 2000).

Men, who on the whole have not exhibited the will to make women equal shareholders in either boardrooms or newsrooms, have always controlled the corporate structures in which mainstream commercial news is defined, produced, and distributed. There are some exceptions, of course. My earlier research has revealed, for instance, that many male journalists today identify with feminism and, indeed, have taken their feminist colleagues' side to protest sexist news coverage as well as to demand more egalitarian newsroom policies; similarly, not all women align themselves with feminism or its activities to advance women's status (Byerly and Warren 1996). Fortunately, gains continue incrementally as enlightened persons in policy positions within news organizations pursue progressive hiring and promotion policies or revise journalistic standards for journalism to better reflect gender-related changes in society. I will review some of these recent changes in the course of the discussion, but here it is important to observe that such enlightened gatekeepers are still insufficient in number to influence broad changes that would require a significant restructuring of organizations and practices to allow women anything close to equal control over resources or news content within news industries.

The situation is similar internationally. Bettina Peters's (2001) survey of women in journalism for the International Federation of Journalists (IFJ) – the largest journalists' association in the world – shows that the numbers of women journalists range widely, from only 6 per cent in Sri Lanka to around 50 per cent in Scandinavian nations like Finland. But the numbers are much more in agreement (and "shockingly low") regarding decision-making, where women account for only about 6 per cent of the editors, department heads, and media owners. The percentage is highest (10–20 per cent) in Cyprus, Costa Rica, Mexico, and Sweden (Peters 2001).

These data are sufficient in and of themselves to reveal the gendered, racial, and sexual nature of today's newsrooms in the United States and other nations. However, it would be neither fair nor accurate to allege that all those belonging to this dominant class think or behave the same. Gender, race, or sexual identity, either alone or together, are not the only predictors of what reporters believe or how they will behave in their professional roles with respect to women and others of less social power (Byerly 2002a; Byerly and Warren 1996). However, there is obvious value in problematizing and critiquing what is undeniably a *masculine newsroom hegemony*. Such hegemony is accomplished not through a sheer exercise of overt authoritarian control by those in charge but rather through institutionalized hiring and promotional practices that privilege white men over others, and that rely on nineteenth-century criteria to determine which events should be covered (and from what perspective), which facts and sources should be included in a story (and which not), and how headlines should be written and pages laid out (or, in broadcast industries, how stories should be sequenced and given time allotments).[2] Routines might also be said to include the customary (and expected) rules for professional interaction and self-identity that give greater authority to men and greater credence to traditional feminine and masculine gender roles for women and men. These routines play themselves out in ways that contribute to a newsroom culture that remains decidedly white, male, and heterosexual in its values and standards; these in turn define a genre of news defined by an ideology of heterosexual, white male superiority that is sometimes reinforced by hostility to feminism and its followers.

That such a newsroom culture and a corresponding news ideology exist first occurred to me during the 1960s and 1970s when I worked for a series of news and other organizations as a writer and public relations specialist. Naïve and underpaid but determined to learn the profession, I found myself first prey to the advances of male supervisors and others who seemed more amused and attracted by my physical presence than impressed with my professional assets or potential. Title VII (making workplace discrimination on the basis of race and gender illegal) was not passed until 1972, and the major lawsuits by women and racial minorities would not be filed and settled until later in the decade. The US Supreme Court did not recognize sexual harassment as a violation of Title VII until 1986. My experiences in these years thus reflected the gender inequalities of the times. Some of the more troubling of these included being backed up against a filing cabinet by one newspaper publisher trying to kiss me ("Hey, it's after 5!" he insisted), being asked by a Pulitzer-winning journalist whom I was interviewing if I would spend the night with him after the interview, and being told by a male editor to buy some new, presumably more feminine clothes for an interview he had assigned me to do with a retiring male political leader. While reporting for the English national daily in Brazil in the mid-1970s, I earned the designation of "the women's libber" after I wrote a feature about the difficulties encountered by well-educated women who left their own professional lives behind in Europe or the United States to come to Brazil with their executive husbands.

In the early 1990s, life in the newsroom of a Seattle-area daily, where I worked the night copy desk while finishing graduate school, was little improved, with all but one of the major gatekeepers male and the nightly newsroom patter full of men's commentary about sports, women, and war. The Persian Gulf war broke out during this time, and as a copy editor, I encountered not personal affronts so much as the daily dose of men's fixation on violence. The menu of wire stories was bad enough, with lengthy articles on the daily body count (that is, casualties), weaponry, and the miracles of high-tech warfare, touted as being so precise that bombs could surgically spot and destroy only the intended target – something that would turn out to be a myth. By contrast, few stories were emerging through either the wire services or our paper's own reporting on the fairly spontaneous, extensive anti-war responses erupting both locally and around the nation. Remembering how many years it had taken for the Vietnam anti-war movement to mobilize, I was struck by this phenomenon and thought it worth covering. In Seattle, the anti-war movement was a diverse collection of groups and individuals, many of them women, so such coverage would have lent itself well to bringing in divergent voices and views. But so energized by the fervor of war were our writers and editors that they barely took notice, even when thousands of students and faculty from the University of Washington stopped traffic on Interstate-5 not once but twice during the three weeks of the US offensive against Iraq.[3]

Toward the beginning of the war, the paper's graphic artists created a series of banners to "package" the daily war stories, thereby giving them more prominence than other news of the day. I first objected to this blatant promotional device, and then later stopped using it in laying out my pages (which contained the international stories), but my omissions were caught and corrected. The war also created a sudden context for my male colleagues to conjure up their own tales of war – one veteran treated us to the nightly retelling of combat in Vietnam, another to being a reporter for various military newspapers. Women in the newsroom rarely entered into these discussions – indeed, we had very little exchange with our male colleagues until President Bush called a cease-fire and things got back to "normal."

The managing editor interpreted "normal" as meaning news that didn't offend our advertisers and readers. Unfortunately, this meant the most banal mainstream agenda imaginable, one that excluded feminist perspectives in reporting. I thought I saw a ray of hope one day when I spotted a book by a feminist author on incest on one junior reporter's desk, but she quickly informed me that she got "those kind of books" all the time from publishers but never read them. "You don't?" I asked. No, she said, it might affect her point of view when she went to the next court case. This same reporter also avoided "biasing" her stories by calling staff at rape crisis centers for comment or background information on sexual assault stories, an amazing situation since the Seattle-area hospitals and women's groups had pioneered many of the advances in forensic medicine, law, and victim services for sexual abuse and domestic violence. To my knowledge, neither the editors nor this young reporter's colleagues ever suggested to her that reading more feminist books and talking to local experts might substantively improve her reporting and serve to include women's perspectives on problems that harmed women disproportionately.

Though admittedly some years ago, my experience with the male newsroom hegemony is neither outdated nor isolated. Instead, it fits into a larger context established (and therefore validated) by both empirical and anecdotal data. Reporters and editors, male and female, continue to report similar situations at all sizes of newspaper and in the newsrooms of television and radio stations.[4] Those who interrupt the norm by challenging it or suggesting alternatives risk discipline or ridicule. One *Los Angeles Times* reporter known for challenging the system with her aggressive style was given a jockstrap for a going away present by her male colleagues, with a card that read "Sniff this for luck" (Byerly and Warren 1996: 11). Gay and lesbian reporters and editors, though increasingly open about their identity, are still low-key or altogether closeted in many newsrooms and at most radio and television stations (Alwood 1996; Aarons and Murphy 2000).

As mentioned already in relation to my own experiences, the news media are consistent in their exclusion of women's perspectives on war and terrorism, something that Lemish also examines in her chapter (this volume) within the Israeli context. Particularly noticeable were the airwaves and pages of newspapers, in both the US and world media, during and following the September 11, 2001, attacks on the World Trade Center and Pentagon, which were monolithically middle-aged, white, male, and official in both news and commentary. Madeleine Bunting, a journalist for Britain's *Guardian* newspaper, analyzed five British daily newspapers and confirmed what she had perceived to be a decline in women's views about the attacks. On September 20, 2001, she wrote:

> The people handling this crisis are men. It is men who perpetrated this violence and men who organize the response. The power structure is exposed at such times, as the token women slide into the background, leaving war to men . . . Condoleeza Rice seems to be the one exception. Virtually the only female faces in the media at the moment are the victims; women are cast as passive. (Bunting 2001)

In the early days of 2003, as the US prepared for and then engaged in war against Iraq, journalism again absented women as concerned citizens, activists, participants, and commentators, even with massive protests against the war across the United States and other nations. Empirical research will eventually give us a systematic analysis of the gender dimension of reporting on the Iraq situation, which this researcher's routine daily monitoring finds to be deeply troubling. At a theoretical level, the phenomenon suggests again the presence of an ideology of male superiority in war news growing out of masculine newsroom hegemony. One might ask how such hegemony is implemented.

The masculine hegemonic newsroom culture – which Joseph also takes up in chapter 7 in this volume – enters the content of news by means of selection, framing, and sourcing, all of which extend the ideology of male superiority. As Joseph observes, mainstream news is event- rather than issue-oriented. The events selected are almost entirely those that occur in the public sphere and concern the activities of men. One logical explanation for this is that men are still the primary actors in social institutions. While this is true, the situation is a bit more complicated, as traditional news values defining who and what shall become news also enter into the process. News values, or standard criteria, emerged with the commodification of news in the late 1900s in the United States and England at a time when technology allowed newspapers to be printed in mass quantities. To facilitate a daily publication schedule and expanded format, and to ensure that papers were sold, publishers determined a set of criteria still used today (Tuchman 1978b). These standard industry criteria include a focus on timeliness, prominent people (not ordinary ones), conflict and drama over cooperation and harmony, and unusualness (or oddity). The most important events are the dramatic, conflict-oriented ones that involve traditional institutions with a location, identified leaders with status, and legitimate responsibility for deliberations and decision-making affecting the general public. News reporters particularly seek sources who are elite by virtue of "holding the reins of legitimate power" (Tuchman 1978b: 133).

All of these criteria have steered reporting in the direction of white powerful men, their activities and organizations, up to and including the present time. The lives of women and others traditionally at the social margins cannot always best be understood with this kind of reporting, and reporters are little inclined or encouraged to look to the margins for their news. In the 1960s and 1970s, feminist movement leaders and activities operated in those margins, outside of what Tuchman called the "news net," that array of established public and private institutions that reporters cover on their beats. Feminism then was happening in the margins, someplace between the private and the public spheres. Bumper stickers, tee-shirts, and lapel buttons insisted that the "personal is political," as feminists struggled to articulate their personal problems in political ways that would enable them to move from one sphere to the other. Their groups tended to be ad hoc and non-hierarchical, as they mobilized other women through a consciousness-raising processes that produced no definable news "events." Moreover, the early movement had no established offices or identified spokespeople. The coverage of feminism activities increased after it institutionalized itself, with organizational offices, leaders, and measurable feats in the form of new laws and other changes (Tuchman 1978b: 133–55).

While certainly neither monolithic nor altogether unchanging, the news coverage of women and women's perspectives has been at best an uneven, rocky road in years since. The prevailing pattern continues to be mostly one of women's absence in newspapers and broadcast news, even in times and places where women and their interests are clearly relevant. Take human rights, for example. Though the United Nations incorporated women's rights under the larger umbrella of human rights in 1993 after a worldwide feminist campaign, most news about human rights violations and gains has continued to ignore women. Systematic analysis of news surrounding the fiftieth anniversary of the Universal Declaration of Human Rights on December 10, 1998, for instance, a date and event clearly relevant to women around the world in all sorts of ways, produced only a dozen stories, in a sea of hundreds, in either English or Spanish, circulating on international wires, that included at least a paragraph about women in relation to human rights (Byerly 2002a). Ninety-six per cent of the stories in the sample of 300 selected for analysis mentioned women only in passing; for example, the day was one "to mark men's and women's human rights." The study showed that the gender of the journalist made little difference in the reporting, a finding that suggests women and men are both responsive to the ideology of male superiority that is manifested through journalistic consciousness and professional routines used in the coverage of events (ibid.).

Other international research reveals a similar tendency on the part of reporters to privilege all things male in news coverage, particularly the portrayal of women newsmakers. One recent report by the European Commission, titled *Images of Women in the Media* (1999), shows that when women step outside of their accustomed roles (presumably those in the domestic, or private, sphere), the news media respond by focusing on their feminine characteristics rather than their ideas or activities. Referring to research in Italy, the UK, Denmark, and Ireland, the EC report mirrors Ross's analysis (this volume) of news on women politicians in the UK, South Africa, and Australia, which showed that news reporters use women's femininity rather than their politics or accomplishments to frame stories.

Feminist interventions

Feminist action to change the situation has been longstanding, both in the US and around the world. Women have employed various kinds of *feminist news interventions*, which can be defined as specific strategies and programs whose goals are to interrupt sexist policies or practices in newsmaking and to replace them with policies and practices more inclusive of (and favorable to) women. It is useful to divide these interventions into categories of external and internal campaigns (Byerly forthcoming b). *External campaigns* are interventions led by independent advocacy groups that lodge particular complaints about treatment of women (or sexual minorities), or that engage in strategic activism of some kind. *Internal campaigns* are those waged within newsrooms by journalists themselves, often with support from their professional organizations and labor unions. The boundaries are not clean, however, as women (and men) journalists often hold membership in feminist groups outside their workplaces and may, additionally, be motivated to align themselves with progressive social movements like feminism through contact with leaders in their reporting (Byerly and Warren 1996).

External intervention campaigns

Bernadette Barker-Plummer's (1995) research provides a lens on some of the earliest external feminist interventions in the US. The National Organization for Women (NOW) was formed by US feminist and journalist Betty Friedan and others in 1966 to lobby for legal changes that would advance women's rights. NOW focused on mobilizing mainstream, middle-class (and, in its early stages, mostly white) women. Friedan and her colleagues realized if they were to gain broader public support for NOW's legislative agenda, leaders would need an effective news media strategy to "speak" to the public. By 1968, NOW had adopted media guidelines and press kits to help leaders in its national and local chapters put out press releases, give interviews and generally promote its activities (Barker-Plummer 1995: 312–13). Among the requirements were learning the routines of local media and the professional practices of journalists. The goal was to build a "network of women's issue reporters" to carry new messages and images of women's political lives to the citizenry

(Barker-Plummer 1995: 313). When NOW leaders became aware of how few women worked inside newsrooms, and how many of those had very little consciousness of feminism or their own relationship to it, NOW leaders first educated female reporters about women's issues, and then supported them as they struggled with their supervisors for agreement to cover women's politics. Some ended up covering events in their own time, but the process of mentoring–supporting–prodding produced the movement's first important stories in elite newspapers and some network TV news by the late 1970s (ibid.: 314).

Beasley and Gibbons (1993) observed ways that NOW also applied legal pressures on news organizations. In 1972, the group filed a petition opposing license renewal of WABC-TV in New York, charging the station with deficiencies in three areas: (1) ascertaining women's opinions on community issues; (2) news and programming on women's concerns; and (3) employment of women. The petition also criticized negative coverage of women, such as one editorial by Howard K. Smith in which the celebrated journalist said that sex discrimination was too inconsequential for federal action (Beasley and Gibbons 1993: 23–4). Word spread through the industry, and, nervous that the Federal Communications Commission (FCC) would begin to intervene in station policies all across the country, owners began to negotiate with NOW members. Other women's groups followed suit. In 1974, the Los Angeles Women's Coalition signed agreements with two network-run stations, which led to the establishment of women's advisory councils and other fair treatment mechanisms (ibid.: 24).

Founded in 1972 by the late Donna Allen, the Women's Institute for Freedom of the Press (WIFP) in Washington, DC, has played a unique role in mobilizing feminist action around media issues. Allen founded WIFP to establish a political framework for what she called "media democracy," which she believed entailed both the restructuring of mainstream industries and the expansion of women-owned media. She participated in the latter by publishing the newsletter *Media Report to Women*, beginning in 1972, and putting out a range of directories and other publications. Allen was also among the first to criticize the concentration in media ownership, which she recognized had specific implications for women and other less powerful groups (WIFP 2002).

Allen's work in feminist media interventions continues, with WIFP now under the direction of her daughter Martha Allen. In early 2002, WIFP joined NOW, a new feminist media watchdog group called Women in Media and News (WIMN), and other groups to intercede on women's behalf in federal policy on telecommunications conglomeration. Their activities marked a greatly needed feminist intervention in the media mergers and globalization that began in the 1980s and accelerated after the US Telecommunications Act of 1996 was passed. In March 2002, WIFP, NOW, WIMN, and other groups demonstrated outside the FCC offices in Washington, DC, to protest rulings a month earlier that further dismantled regulations against media mergers and acquisitions in telecommunications (Byerly 2002b). Reiterating the longstanding feminist vision of a feminist media democracy, WIMN chief organizer Jennifer Pozner said:

> [T]he implications for diverse representation, local coverage, equal access to media and independent perspectives are dire when media consolidation continues at a break-neck pace. Parodying and speaking out against the FCC's lack of concern for public interest matters, the protest aims to force the FCC to re-examine what the public wants and needs and how to create a truly democratic media system.[5]

In testimony before the FCC in June 2002, NOW political director Linda Berg emphasized the need for equal employment regulations in the broadcast industry, which she said "consistently overlook women and minorities for job opportunities" (quoted in Voices for Media Democracy 2003). At that same hearing, NOW vice-president Terry O'Neill emphasized the need for women and minorities to advance into decision-making within broadcast and telecommunication industries (ibid.). In January 2003, WIFP joined a long list of US advocacy groups in filing comments with the FCC to object to further deregulation of telecommunication industries, something they argued would further marginalize employment of women and minorities (ibid.).

These interventions have a historical, global context that underscores their significance. Media issues emerged strongly as shared cross-national concerns during the UN Decade for Women, 1975–85, reflecting the three-part critique explained earlier. The United Nations had made gender equality part of its original mission (DPI 1995), and even prior to designating a special decade for women, the agency had taken steps to advance women's well-being and status through its programs. The plan of action, adopted by delegates at the Mexico City conference in 1975 (the first of three meetings during the decade), called for sexism in media to be addressed through a range of measures, from research on media treatment of women to programs that would increase women's visibility in the media and introduce new ideas about women's social roles into the public discourse (Byerly 1995; Gallagher 1980). Regional and cross-national studies on women in media grew out of this meeting, producing the first global baseline literature on women and media.[6] One major interventionist outgrowth of the Mexico City meeting was the Women's Feature Service (WFS) Project, funded by UN agencies from 1978 until 1983. WFS programs were independent women-run news services that operated within established news agencies in Latin America, Africa, Asia, the Middle East, and the Caribbean regions. Their job was to generate news stories about women from a progressive women's perspective using the development news format, which emphasized issues over events, historical context for problems, voices and views of ordinary (non-elite) persons, and a focus on efforts to change or solve problems. Two of these agencies survive today, one in India, the other in the Philippines (Gallagher 1980; Byerly 1995). Subsequent UN Decade for Women meetings in Copenhagen (1980) and Nairobi (1985), as well as the follow-up meeting in Beijing (1995), continued to shine a light on women's marginalization by most media of the world and to advance ways of improving the media.

Around the world, women employ a range of interventions. Recently, in Jamaica, the Women Media Watch organization began "cleaning up the image of women in media" in local media. WMW members use a non-confrontational strategy, meeting with media managers and "encouraging them to look at their work from a gender perspective" (Virtue 1998: 73). In Zimbabwe, men's and women's groups work together to tackle the problem of women's media representation. These efforts include holding workshops and other meetings for male journalists (Matambanadzo 1998).

Internal intervention campaigns

Women in both broadcast and print news were affected by the emergence of feminism in the 1960s, and as they began to see its relevance for their own lives, some sought to make it part of their reporting. Marlene Sanders (Sanders and Rock 1988) recounts her own and other women's efforts in the early 1970s to persuade male producers that stories about women's issues were newsworthy. Male managers were resistant on the whole, and women journalists began to file grievances about content, believing that their mission was to serve the public interest. They also started documenting the way that management treated them as employees. They formed newsroom groups like ABC's Women's Action Committee. Discrimination suits were filed, both by individual women and by groups of women, once Title VII was passed in 1972. These were won, and thus, Sanders says, more women were hired and promoted, but discrimination persisted in the form of the "glass ceiling" (that is, barriers to promotion into higher-ranking jobs), age discrimination, poor news assignments, and lower pay than men's (Sanders and Rock 1988). Women at the *New York Times* and other major papers found their militancy through Women's Caucuses in these years, and bolstered by numbers, they, too, began to file sex discrimination suits. The *Times* settled its suit, lodged by six women, in 1974, for only $350,000, but 550 women in their employment class benefited through back pay. The *Times* also agreed to revise its personnel policies to advance women into management (Robertson 1992: 207).

Women in journalism who filed similar suits in the 1970s and 1980s nearly always won, but journalists like Sanders note that discrimination did not go away, it just became more subtle. Her insider observations are supported by survey research among journalists at major newspapers, but it's important to note that challenges to such discrimination did not go away either. Newsroom activism of varied kinds was both *continuous* (organizations already in place tended to continue, though with perhaps less steam) and *episodic* (ad hoc groups tended to form around specific grievances) during the 1980s and into the 1990s (Byerly and Warren 1996). Episodic activism was often the response to dramatic news events in which sexism or racism was a central problem. One of these occurred during the US Senate's confirmation hearings for Supreme Court nominee Clarence Thomas in 1991, when it was discovered that law professor Anita Hill had accused Thomas of sexual harassment when she worked with him years earlier.[7] Hill's disrespectful treatment by an all-male Senate judiciary committee – sensationalized and sometimes trivialized in the media for days on end – caused a resurgence of newsroom activism among journalists who believed Hill's experience should have been given more serious treatment (Byerly and Warren 1996).

Associations begun by women in US journalism represent significant newsroom interventions, both historically and presently. Elizabeth Burt (2000) takes stock of this, observing these "played an active role in the preparation, professionalization, recognition, and assimilation of women in journalism," beginning in the early 1880s (Burt 2000: xvii). These associations, active in nearly all US states, have often been closely related to feminist movements and served "to help put women's issues on the public agenda," Burt said (ibid.). Though they have not succeeded in obliterating the presence or effects of a masculine newsroom hegemony, they have been able to keep women's journalistic demands alive and to support legal suits and other specific action. For example, Linda Steiner (2000: 169) noted that by end of the 1990s, the *New York Times* Women's Caucus had succeeded in "virtually closing the salary gap between men and women." As the nation's agenda-setting newspaper, the *Times* has also adjusted its reporting on gay and lesbian experience, in response to pressure exerted by journalists belonging to the National Lesbian and Gay Journalists Association (NLGJA) and the media activist group Gay and Lesbian Alliance Against Defamation (GLAAD). In August 2002, the paper announced it would begin running same-sex commitment notices in its engagements and weddings section. GLAAD spokesperson Monica Taher said the *Times*'s policy set an immediate trend (Venema 2003). In fact, the *Times* had been slow to follow dozens of other newspapers in Alabama, California, Massachusetts, Michigan, Montana, Utah, Washington, DC, and elsewhere around the country that had quietly begun to run such notices over the preceding few years (ibid.).

Women journalists have also supported internal campaigns for women's advancement by forming external organizations like the International Women's Media Foundation (IWMF). Established in 1990 and headquartered in Washington, DC, IWMF cites its central mission as strengthening "women in the news media around the world, based on the belief that no press is truly free unless women share an equal voice" (IWMF website). The group's members span more than 100 nations, and its leadership is drawn from high-profile female veteran journalists, many of whom were among those who years earlier filed and won discrimination lawsuits against their US news organizations. IWMF conducts research, education, and other activities, but none stands out so much as its annual "Courage Awards" to women who have risked life and reputation to cover war, crime, corruption, poverty, and other dramatic events. The 1992 recipients included Anna Politkovskaya of Russia, who covers the war in Chechnya for the biweekly *Novaya Gazeta*, despite threats from the Russian military; Sandra Nyaira of Zimbabwe, the only political editor in her nation, whose investigations of former president Robert Mugabe's corruption brought daily threats; Kathy Gannon, chief of the Associated Press at the Afghanistan–Pakistan bureau, who reported on the Taliban and its aftermath in the region; and the *Washington Post*'s Mary McGrory, for two decades of commentary on political and international issues (IWMF 2002).

In considering interventions, it would be a mistake not to include the crucial work of unions composed of both men and women who have made the advancement of women in the profession a major goal. The Brussels-based IFJ is particularly active in this regard, with stated goals of raising women's wages (to the level of men's) and industry standards on women's portrayal, creating structural mechanisms (like women's committees and equality councils) in news organizations to address women's inequality (Peters 2001).

Conclusion

In assessing the range of feminist newsroom interventions, it is important to establish that we are talking about a lot of loosely connected activities that together represent a dialectical process involving many persons widely dispersed geographically, throughout both the United States (the primary focus of this chapter) and other nations. Processes occur over time; therefore, they always have a historical context formed by the events and issues of any particular moment. As with all social movements, feminist news interventions have succeeded incrementally and unevenly, making the situation one that feminist media scholar Margaret Gallagher (1995) has deemed an "unfinished story." The chapters in this volume show that feminist challenges to men's authority over message- and image-making have made measurable gains but there is still much to be done. Women's alternative media – newsletters, newspapers, news services, films, and the internet – give women maximum control over articulating their own experiences and ideas about the world. But these do not always reach the broad publics that mainstream news media do. Therefore, considering women's strategic, intentional interventions in mainstream news provides both a theoretical and a methodological framework for understanding feminist agency within male news structures whose products influence and serve to construct public opinion, public policy, citizens' understanding of society, and their daily lived experience in it. The perennial question of "What do women want?" might be adapted here to read "What do feminists want?" This chapter has sought to provide some answers to that question, as it relates to mainstream news.

Key terms

agenda-setting theory
continuous vs. episodic newsroom activism
critical race theory
critical theories
feminist critical theory
feminist media critique
feminist news interventions
hegemony theory
ideology of male supremacy
internal vs. external intervention campaigns
manufacture of consent
masculine newsroom hegemony
"news net"
paradigm of the misogynist media
patriarchy
"personal is political"
traditional news values

Questions for discussion

1 Describe the ways that Byerly applies various critical theories in her analysis of feminist news critique and interventions.
2 How does the author develop her thesis of masculine newsroom hegemony? What evidence does she bring to bear?
3 Summarize what the author calls the feminist media critique. What evidence does she give to show that this critique has been applied by feminists both in the United States and in other countries?
4 How do traditional news values contribute to an ideology of male superiority in the news, according to Byerly?
5 What kinds of newsroom interventions have feminist journalists and others used to try and bring women more fully into the news, according to the author? Your answer should include the relevance of internal and external campaigns.

6 How does Byerly apply the dichotomy of public and private spheres in her analysis of women and news?

Notes

1 "Feminist" is used in this chapter in its noun form to refer to women working for women's social advancement within women's liberation movements, and in its adjective form to refer to principles, ideas, and events associated with those movements. The author recognizes that many men also embrace a feminist identity and take part in women's advancement – I bring men's participation to light in several parts of the discussion.

2 See Tuchman (1978b) for a fuller discussion of the ways that news values and practices established in the nineteenth century still prevail today. See Byerly (1995) for a discussion of how these values have come under feminist scrutiny, as well as that of the world community during the New World Information Order debates of the 1970s and 1980s.

3 To be fair, I should say that neither did other Seattle media pay much attention to these anti-war events; and nationally, the anti-war mobilization was a non-story.

4 For a more complete set of discussions, see research on the experiences of female, minority, gay, and lesbian experiences in the newsroom environment in Aarons and Murphy (2000), Alwood (1996), Beasley and Gibbons (1993), Byerly (forthcoming b), Byerly and Warren (1996), Marlane (2000), Gross (1993), and Weaver (1997). For first person accounts, see Robertson (1992), Sanders and Rock (1988), and Mills (1988).

5 Personal email correspondence with Jennifer Pozner, 2002.

6 Among these publications are Ceulemans and Fauconnier (1979), Gallagher (1979, 1980), and Cuthbert (1981).

7 Both Thomas and Hill were African-American, and, through the course of the hearings and in reporting, race became conflated with sex.

References

Aarons, L. and Murphy, S. (2000) Lesbians and gays in the newsrooms, 10 years later (report). Annenberg School for Communication, University of Southern California, Los Angeles, CA, and National Lesbian and Gay Journalists Association, Washington, DC.

Alwood, E. (1996) *Straight News: Gays, Lesbians and the News Media*. Columbia University Press, New York.

Anand, A. and Salvi, G. (eds) (1998) *Beijing! UN Fourth World Conference on Women*. Women's Feature Service, New Delhi.

Annenburg Public Policy Center (2000) No room at the top? (study). University of Pennsylvania, Philadelphia.

Barker-Plummer, B. (1995) News as a political resource: media strategies and political identity in the US women's movement, 1966–1975. *Critical Studies in Mass Communication* 12(3), 306–24.

Beasley, M. and Gibbons, S. (1993) *Taking their Place*. American University Press, in cooperation with Women's Institute for Freedom of the Press, Washington, DC.

Bunting, M. (2001) Special report: terrorism in the US. *Guardian*, September 20, www.guardian.co.uk (last accessed January 10, 2003).

Burt, E. V. (ed.) (2000) *Women's Press Organizations, 1881–1999*. Greenwood Press, Westport, CT.

Byerly, C. (1994) An agenda for teaching news coverage of rape. *Journalism Educator* Spring, 59–69.

Byerly, C. (1995) Women, news and social participation: the contribution of Women's Feature Service to world news. In: Valdivia, A. N. (ed.), *Women, Multiculturalism and the Media: Global Diversities*. Sage, Thousand Oaks, CA, pp. 105–22.

Byerly, C. (1999) News, feminism, and the dialectics of gender relations. In: Meyer, M. (ed.), *Mediated Women: Representations in Popular Culture*. Hampton Press, Creskill, NJ.

Byerly, C. (2002a) Gender and the political economy of newsmaking: a case study of human rights coverage. In: Meehan, E. and Riordan, E. (eds), *Sex and Money: Feminism and Political Economy in the Media*. University of Minnesota Press, Minneapolis, pp. 130–44.

Byerly, C. (2002b) Facing Goliath: feminism and communication policy. *Feminist Con/text* Spring, www.icahdq.org/divisions/feminist/context/2002Spring (last accessed January 10, 2003).

Byerly, C. (forthcoming a) Women and the concentration of ownership. In: Creedon, P., Oukrup, C., and Rush, R., *The Search for Equity: Women in Journalism and Mass Communication – A 30-year Update*. Lawrence Erlbaum, Mahwah, NJ.

Byerly, C. (forthcoming b) Shifting sites: feminist, gay and lesbian news activism, in the US context. In: de Bruin, M. and Ross, K. (eds), *Identities at Work: Gender and Professionalism in Media Organizations*. Hampton Press, Cresskill, NJ.

Byerly, C. and Warren, C. (1996) At the margins of center: organized protest in the newsroom. *Critical Studies in Mass Communication* 13(1), 1–23.

Ceulemans, M. and Fauconnier, G. (1979) *Mass Media: The Image, Role and Social Conditions of Women.* United Nations Educational, Scientific and Cultural Organization, Paris.

Cuthbert, M. (1981) *Women and Media Decision-Making in the Caribbean.* United Nations Educational, Scientific and Cultural Organization, Paris.

DPI (Department of Public Information) (1995) *United Nations and the Advancement of Women 1945–1995.* Department of Public Information, United Nations, New York.

European Commission (1999) *Images of Women in the Media: Report on Existing Research in the European Union.* Employment and Social Affairs, European Commission, Luxembourg.

Gallagher, M. (1979) *The Portrayal and Participation of Women in the Media.* United Nations Educational, Scientific and Cultural Organization, Paris.

Gallagher, M. (1980) *Unequal Opportunities: The Case of Women in the Media.* United Nations Educational, Scientific and Cultural Organization, Paris.

Gallagher, M. (1995) *An Unfinished Story: Gender Patterns in Media Employment.* United Nations Educational, Scientific and Cultural Organization, Paris.

Gramsci, A. (1987) *Selections from the Prison Notebooks.* International Publishers, New York.

Gross, L. (1993) *Contested Closets.* University of Minnesota Press, Minneapolis.

IWMF (International Women's Media Foundation) (2002) Courage Award winners risk hazards in search of the truth. *IWMF Wire* (newsletter of International Women's Media Foundation) 10(1).

IWMF (International Women's Media Foundation) website: www.iwmf.org (last accessed January 5, 2003).

Marlane, J. (2000) Barriers to women in TV lowered – not dismantled. *IWMF Wire* (newsletter of International Women's Media Foundation) 10(1), 9, 11.

Matambanadzo, I. (1998) Media: men on women. In: Anand, A. and Salvi, G. (eds), *Beijing! UN Fourth World Conference on Women.* Women's Feature Service, New Delhi, pp. 71–2.

Matsuda, M, Lawrence, C. R. III, Delgado, R., and Crenshaw, K. (1993) Introduction. In: Matsuda, M, Lawrence, C. R. III, Delgado, R., and Crenshaw, K. (eds), *Words that Wound: Critical Race Theory, Assaultive Speech, and the First Amendment.* Westview Press, Boulder, CO, pp. 1–16.

McCombs, M. and Shaw, D. (1972) The agenda setting function of mass media. *Public Opinion Quarterly* 36, 176–85.

Meehan, E. and Riordan, E. (eds) (2002) *Sex and Money: Feminism and Political Economy in the Media.* University of Minnesota Press, Minneapolis.

Miller, K. (2002) *Communication Theories: Perspectives, Processes and Contexts.* McGraw-Hill, Boston.

Mills, K. (1988) *A Place in the News.* Dodd, Mead, New York.

Peters, B. (2001) *Equality and Quality: Setting Standards for Women in Journalism.* International Federation of Journalists, Brussels.

Robertson, N. (1992) *The Girls in the Balcony: Women, Men and the New York Times.* Random House, New York.

Sanders, M. and Rock, M. (1988) *Waiting for Prime Time: The Women of Television News.* Harper and Row, New York.

Steiner, L. (2000) The New York Times Women's Caucus, 1972–present. In: Burt, E. V. (ed.), *Women's Press Organizations, 1888–1999.* Greenwood Press, Westport, CT, pp. 164–70.

Tuchman, G. (1978a) The symbolic annihilation of women by the media. In: Tuchman, G., Daniels, A. K., and Benét, J. (eds), *Hearth and Home: Images of Women in the Mass Media.* Oxford University Press, New York, pp. 3–38.

Tuchman, G. (1978b) *Making News.* Free Press, New York.

Venema, S. (2003) Gay wedding announcements a growing trend. *Women's Enews,* January 5: www.womensenews.org (last accessed January 10, 2003).

Virtue, G. (1998) Media: changing the media's maxim. In: Anand, A. and Salvi, G. (eds), *Beijing! UN Fourth World Conference on Women.* Women's Feature Service, New Delhi, pp. 72–4.

Voices for Media Democracy (2003) Women's Institute for Freedom of the Press, Washington, DC: www.wifp.org/VoicesforDemocracy.

Weaver, D. (1997) Women as journalists. In: Norris, P. (ed.), *Media, Women and Politics.* Oxford University Press, New York, pp. 19–40.

WIFP (Women's Institute for Freedom of the Press) (2002) *Media Democracy: Past, Present, and Future.* Women's Institute for Freedom of the Press, Washington, DC.

7

Working, Watching, and Waiting: Women and Issues of Access, Employment, and Decision-Making in the Media in India

Ammu Joseph

Introduction

- On 14 October 2002, the top story on the front page of a multi-edition Indian newspaper, datelined Baghdad, was by the political editor of the English daily, reporting from inside Iraq. She happens to be a woman.
- In late 2001, women were conspicuous by their presence in the Indian media, covering the events of "9/11" and thereafter, and analyzing their implications – as correspondents and commentators, editors and anchors, interviewers and hosts of current affairs programs, especially on some high-profile television news channels and in the indigenous English-language press.
- In the early part of 2002, women played an active role in covering the "communal" conflagration in the Indian state of Gujarat. As the media provided on-the-spot reports from the internal battle-front, female bylines were very much in evidence in several newspapers and news magazines, and female broadcasters regularly appeared on a number of television news and current affairs programs, focusing public attention on the sectarian violence and its aftermath. Women were also prominent as media commentators analyzing developments in Gujarat as they unfolded. Like a number of their male colleagues, some women

reporters were threatened and at least one was physically attacked in the course of doing their jobs under difficult circumstances.

These recent examples of women journalists covering conflict tell one side of the story of women in the Indian media. There are obviously many other aspects to the question of women's participation in and access to the media, and the impact of the media on and its use as an instrument for the advancement and empowerment of women in the context of South Asia. This chapter attempts to describe the complex reality of the media and women in India, to highlight the challenges and opportunities presented by the prevailing situation, and to discuss some of the measures and strategies currently being essayed to enhance the potential of media to tackle gender-based disparities within the media and in society, as well as to empower women both as professionals and as citizens.

The Indian experience may be relevant beyond the country, and even the region, in view of the growing trend toward the globalization of media and communication, and the fact that recent international collaborations and exchanges on gender and media matters have revealed more commonalities than differences in the state of affairs in different parts of the world in this respect.

The apocryphal story about six blind persons and their descriptions of an elephant, based on the part of the animal they were able to touch and feel, comes to mind in the course of any endeavor to represent any aspect of India. The subcontinental nation is, arguably, the mother of all elephants and the Indian media certainly constitute one of her sizable pachydermatous progeny. Both defy definitive description. Under the circumstances, this chapter will merely provide glimpses of the whole, highlighting some issues concerning access, employment, and decision-making through examples from different sections of the media in India.

The range of issues that confront women in media professions in India and require attention from media professionals as well as organizations will be presented primarily through a summary of the situation, experiences and perspectives of women journalists working in the print media (see also Joseph 2000). For reasons of brevity, women's experiences in television are not discussed here at any length, although the limitations of the add-women-and-stir formula that is often expected to correct gender imbalances in media personnel and content can be clearly seen in the mixed signals emerging from that medium.[1]

The need for official policies to enable more women, especially from disadvantaged communities, to exercise their right to access and participate in media and communication will be highlighted through the experiences of women involved in community media initiatives.

The possibility of effecting positive change through media education and networking will be presented through two examples among the many initiatives underway in India.

And, finally, some ideas on policies and strategies that could help remove the remaining stumbling blocks in the path to women's effective access to and participation in the media will be listed for discussion and possible action.

Women in journalism: print media

The Indian print media currently include over 46,000 newspapers and periodicals; among them are more than 5,000 dailies, nearly 17,000 weeklies and 13,000 monthlies, and about 6,000 fortnightlies and 3,000 quarterlies. These are published in as many as 101 languages and dialects. The largest number of publications is in Hindi (nearly 19,000), followed by English (nearly 7,000), and Urdu (nearly 3,000). Forty-one Indian newspapers still being published in various languages are a century or more old (Malayala Manorama 2002).

Daily newspapers in India are believed to enjoy a total circulation of 130 million copies, of which the lion's share is accounted for by 200 big dailies. According to recent reports, the 350 largest newspapers are estimated to employ a total of about 5,000 reporters, 2,000 full-time correspondents, 5,000 stringers (informal employees who serve as correspondents, especially in far-flung areas of the country), and 5,000 editorial staff (AMIC 2002).

Appearance vs. reality

There are no current, credible, comprehensive data on all journalists in India, let alone on women in the Indian media. However, there is little doubt that the number of Indian women in the mainstream press had reached an unprecedented high by the dawn of the new millennium.

Female bylines have become commonplace since the early 1990s, not only in magazines and features sections but also on the news and editorial pages of dailies, including the front page. Apart from a large number of female staff reporters and subeditors (or copy editors), the Indian press currently boasts many women who are senior editors (including editors in charge of single editions of multi-edition dailies, political editors, – and financial editors), chief reporters, chiefs of bureaus, special and foreign correspondents, business and sports journalists, and columnists, not to mention magazine editors and feature writers. It also harbors some female photojournalists and even one or two female cartoonists.

Women journalists in India now write on a wide range of current events and issues, spanning a broad spectrum of subjects, including high-profile topics such as politics, business and economics, international relations, and what is euphemistically known as defense. A number of women have managed to storm the citadel of hard news coverage. Many are recognized for their reportage from various areas of conflict in and around the country, having broken exclusive stories and secured rare interviews with leaders of militant organizations operating in these hot spots. Several have been associated with some of the most sensational investigative scoops of recent years, including financial scams. Quite a few have also made names for themselves in the prestigious field of political reporting or analysis or both.

However, the exciting opportunities now available to a growing number of women journalists are not enjoyed by all or even most women in the profession. There are significant differences in the situation of women journalists across the country and the press. For instance, the growing number of women in the metropolitan media workforce has created the impression that the barriers that once restricted women's entry into the press have been overcome. But resistance to the recruitment of women still persists in many places and in certain sections of the press.

Similarly, the increasing visibility of women on television and in the indigenous English-language print media – generally known as the mainstream, national press because of its unique reach and influence – suggests that there are no more impediments in women's path to the top of the editorial pyramid. But many female journalists still experience slow and limited progress, if not total stagnation, in their careers. And the existence of a glass ceiling, which currently keeps women from occupying the very top spots in the editorial hierarchy (of newspapers in particular), is widely acknowledged, even by women who have reached relatively high positions within their news organizations.

The spectacular success of a number of women in a wide range of high-profile areas of journalism, hitherto assumed to be male terrain, implies that there is nothing to stop competent and determined women from fulfilling their professional dreams. However, the tendency to relegate women to particular functions and beats within the press has not completely disappeared. And many women allege that they are not given a chance to demonstrate their capabilities, especially in what is commonly, if erroneously, seen as hardcore, mainstream journalism.

Issues particular to the Indian media context

In terms of access and employment, gender-based problems are particularly acute in sections of the Indian-language press, which reaches a much larger proportion of the country's reading public than the more conspicuous English-language press. Commenting on the place of women in genuine journalist roles in Indian-language newspapers, Robin Jeffrey (2000: 177) concluded: "their numbers . . . were scant, the jobs few and the prejudices against them formidable."

Acknowledging that women's presence in what is generally known as the "language press" had registered some growth in recent years, he proposed that opportunities for women journalists could open up further, thanks to the increasing recognition that newspapers had to cultivate women readers. However, since the news media's new interest in female audiences derives largely from women's role as consumers and their potential as targets of advertisements for a wide range of products, the job opportunities it generates tend to be limited in both scope and potential.

Another factor that bears consideration in the context of access and employment is the reality of minorities within minorities. If race piggybacks on gender, and vice versa, in some parts of the world, in India class, caste, creed, and ethnicity often play a critical role in determining who, even among women, gains entry into the media and has the opportunity to rise in the profession.

There are at present no data on the socio-economic and cultural composition of the Indian press corps, let alone that of its female component. However, circumstantial evidence suggests that the representation of scheduled castes and tribes[2] in the media workforce is not only minimal but completely disproportionate to their presence in the population. As Jeffrey (2000: 164) put it, "on the overwhelming majority of Indian newspapers in the 1990s there simply were no Dalits." With gender compounding the disadvantages of caste, women from Dalit – not to mention Adivasi – communities clearly have even less access to media employment.

Similarly, the representation in the media of some of India's numerous religious minorities – notably Muslims – appears to be marginal. Here, again, women from these communities are undoubtedly doubly disadvantaged.

Common obstacles

Many of the issues confronting Indian women in journalism are similar to those faced by women in the media in other parts of the world, while other issues are more closely linked to specific social and cultural norms prevalent in Indian society.

Thus, for example, while women's perennial struggle to reconcile the conflicting demands of work and family is clearly a universal – almost existential – reality, women in India face particular problems due to family structures and expectations, as well as social attitudes. The long, late, and irregular hours and the erratic, unpredictable work schedules that characterize the profession, and the mobility it often requires, exacerbate the situation, especially for women from conservative families or communities and/or those who cannot afford to hire full-time domestic help.

The continuing controversy over women and night work exemplifies the dilemma of women who opt for a non-traditional career in what remains a tradition-bound society for all but a relatively small percentage of the urban population. If, on the one hand, women have to deal with objections or disapproval from families and communities, on the other they have to contend with employers who would be only too happy not to hire women or to relegate them to dead-end jobs.

For instance, a number of media establishments try to evade statutory responsibilities toward female employees (such as night transport or dormitory facilities) by either "excusing" women from the night shift or using the "problem" of night duty to justify not hiring women. Although many women journalists have successfully fought for the right to work on all shifts and believe that such parity is critical to professional advancement, others are ambivalent about the issue, mainly because of real anxieties about safety, domestic responsibilities, and family or social censure. A number of women seem to feel that they are damned if they do work at night and damned if they do not.

Breakthroughs and barriers

There is little doubt that women journalists have contributed significantly to broadening the scope of press coverage to include more and better reporting on and analysis of social issues in general and what are known as women's issues in particular. It is widely acknowledged within the media that they have played an important role in highlighting a wide range of issues related to human development and rights, social and economic justice, culture, and other vital aspects of life and society that were earlier neglected by a press traditionally preoccupied with politics (in the narrow sense) and government. Women have been noted for their coverage of social trends. They are also credited with having introduced more human interest into the media, even while covering hard news.

At the same time, it is difficult to state categorically that the presence and rise of women in the Indian media have had a perceptible, positive impact on mainstream journalism and media coverage as a whole. Women's capacity to influence the agenda, practice, and output of the media is currently limited by several factors:

- The number of women in key decision-making positions is still relatively small. Many successful women in media professions tend to adopt or, at least, adapt to the prevailing values and norms of the profession, like the majority of their counterparts elsewhere – in the media as well as in other professions. At present such conformity does appear to be an effective strategy for career advancement, since those who retain an alternative worldview seem to come up against the glass ceiling sooner rather than later.
- A third inhibiting factor is the apparent shift in the Indian media's priorities and preoccupations since the early 1990s, thanks to a number of developments – especially within the economy – that have affected many aspects of society, including the media. The increasingly market-driven nature of the media today has had a major impact on their perceptions of themselves and their role in society, which, in turn, is reflected in their content. Influential sections of the media – including some quality broadsheets – now seem obsessed with the lives of the bold and the beautiful, the rich and the famous, the pampered and the powerful, and consequently less receptive to the interests and concerns of those who do not belong to this charmed circle. In this altered

media environment there is obviously less time and space for in-depth coverage of serious issues, including many relating to gender.

- The rise of celebrity and lifestyle journalism through the 1990s and into the new millennium and its spread from glossy magazines into some mainstream newspapers appear to have special implications for women in the profession. While this change has certainly increased job opportunities and professional visibility, it seems in some ways to have led to a backslide. Young women entering the field since the early 1990s have found that they are more prone to be assigned to the contemporary equivalent of the "ladies' beat" of yore than their male colleagues. Rubbing shoulders with the glitterati can be a heady experience, especially for novices, until they discover that it may not pave the way to meaningful journalism – or, indeed, to the higher reaches of the profession.
- Finally, the Indian press, like the media everywhere, has a predilection for events, especially dramatic ones that involve or threaten violence or conflict. As a result, the gender-related issues that routinely receive the most media attention are those that fit into dominant perceptions of what constitutes news (see Joseph and Sharma 1994). Among these are violent atrocities, such as rape and dowry-related murder, and political hot potatoes, like the threat by a militant organization in Kashmir to disfigure or kill girls and women who ignore its edict on the wearing of the *burqa*. Women in decision-making positions within the media have not been able or willing to make an appreciable difference to definitions of news and hierarchies of news values.
- The media's continuing tendency to focus on events rather than processes often results in the neglect of many important issues concerning women – for example, the combination of chronic malnutrition and overwork that threatens the health of millions of women, and the initiation into public life of thousands of rural women elected to institutions of local governance from the mid-1990s onwards. Nevertheless, when such issues do get covered, it is thanks to women in the media, more often than not.

Women and journalism: television

The audio-visual media in India remained state enterprises until the early 1990s, with the monopolistic public broadcasters – Akashvani (All India

Radio) and Doordarshan (the national television network) – traditionally and tightly controlled by the Ministry of Information and Broadcasting. The advent of satellite television totally altered the Indian media scene, as foreign and indigenous private television channels began to beam programs into homes across the country. By late 2002, over 100 television channels in different languages were estimated to be available within the country, with some also reaching audiences in other South Asian countries and even farther afield.

According to recent reports, Doordarshan has 19,000 employees, of which about 4,000 are in production and news, while AIR employs 24,000 people, including 4,500 in news production. Private networks reportedly employ an average of about 1,700 people, although only about 500 are directly involved in production and news: outsourcing is a common practice (AMIC 2002).

There has been little documentation of women's involvement and experiences in radio and television and there are few data on their employment in these media. However, as in most parts of the world, women in India seem to have found it easier to break into broadcasting than into the press, especially newspapers. Thanks to official personnel policies, women found employment in the state broadcasting organizations from a relatively early stage. The satellite channels have further boosted women's visibility on the small screen, with women becoming increasingly conspicuous even in news programs, as both anchors and correspondents based in different parts of the country.

Of a batch of 21 young reporters recruited by Doordarshan (DD) in 2002, as part of its effort to revamp its news services, 16 were women.[3] However, senior positions were still overwhelmingly held by men. For example, within DD's news department in New Delhi, men occupied the top post as well as the five posts of director (news). Of the 10 news editors, only three were women; similarly, there were just three women among the 12 assistant news editors. The executive and chief producers (news and current affairs) were both male. And there were no women among the 12 program executives. Women were underrepresented in technical jobs, too, with none among the eight video editors and only three among the 33 camera persons (note: the official designation is still camera*man*).[4]

The private channels are less forthcoming with statistics on personnel. However, women are highly visible on most of them and at least some also have women in decision-making positions. For example, the managing director of the most high-profile bilingual, private, Indian 24-hour news channel is a woman, women often present its sports and business news (besides general news), and a woman journalist hosts two of its weekend current affairs programs.

Some of the more prominent female television journalists and personalities have already become public icons and there is no dearth of role models for girls aspiring to pursue careers in the media. Further, despite the difficulty of correlating content with staff in the absence of proper substantiation, it certainly appears that at least some types of gender-related issues make it into TV news and current affairs programs more often now than in the past, even if the treatment is sometimes somewhat superficial.

Women are active in the entertainment side of television, too, as writers and directors, hosts of talk, game, and music shows, and of course as actors. The relatively recent rise of women as creators of popular television serials (especially programs belonging to the soap opera and sitcom genres) raises critical questions about the impact of women's participation in and access to the media on the use of media as an instrument for the advancement and empowerment of women. The questions assume particular relevance and significance in view of the fact that women seem to constitute the primary target audience of TV serials.

Women, media, and community activism

In most discussions of the media in India, the focus is on middle- and upper-class, urban sections of the population. There is little information about media reach and consumption in the rural areas and among the socially and economically disadvantaged, urban or rural. This can be attributed at least partly to the fact that the two annual all-India audience surveys that generate media-related data cater primarily to the needs of commercial users of the media. The fragmented information that does exist provides only glimpses of the significant class- and location-specific differences in media access and participation.

Deficit

The broad-brush pictures painted by the supposedly nationwide surveys not only obscure the realities on the ground but reveal almost nothing about the media and women as a whole, let alone those from disadvantaged sections of the population. In one of the few Indian studies to focus some attention on the access of poor, rural women to the media (classified as a public resource), conducted in the mid-1990s (Batliwala et al. 1998), barely 15 per cent of the 1,171 women respondents from representative parts of Karnataka state reported regularly reading newspapers or magazines. About 55 per cent reported listening to the radio and 27 per cent said they watched TV programs at least occasionally. Interestingly, nearly half of those who reported watching TV (14 per cent) said their families did not own a TV set; the phenomenon of access without ownership suggests that they watch programs in a place other than their own home. Of those with access to TV, nearly 60 per cent said they were able to watch programs only occasionally (every couple of months), while 21 per cent reported watching once every third day or so.

The study also found that women saw television primarily as a medium of entertainment even though it had been originally and officially hailed in India as a means of mass education and awareness-building. According to the researchers, while almost all the women with access to TV watched films, and two-thirds watched serials, just over half viewed news and educational programs. When the program-wide distribution of viewers was placed against the entire female survey population, the proportion of those viewing news shows and information/education programs dipped even lower, to about 15 per cent. This is obviously more a comment on the quality, relevance, and viewer-friendliness of such programs (and, of course, on actual accessibility) than on women's attitudes to information and education, especially in view of the enthusiastic participation of village women in adult literacy programs designed with their interests and needs in mind.

In such a scenario, special efforts are clearly required to increase women's access to and participation in relevant and meaningful media and communication. A number of non-governmental organizations (NGOs) and some quasi-governmental entities have in recent times initiated community media and communication projects in order to serve the interests and needs of those who are not reached or are poorly served by the mainstream media. Such initiatives received a boost from a landmark judgment of the Supreme Court of India in February 1995, which declared that the airwaves were public property, ought to be free from state monopoly and control, and were to be used to promote the public interest in a pluralistic society. Although the judgment has been interpreted primarily as an argument in favor of private sector involvement in the broadcast media, NGOs have been trying to demonstrate that it is and should be seen as an affirmation of the right of the wider public to access, create, and run such media.

The following examples provide a flavor of the many, varied efforts currently underway to enable members of the disadvantaged majority, especially women, to access, participate in, and make decisions regarding media and communications:

- "Last year Chinna Narsamma, a 25-year-old farm worker, stood in ankle-deep water and reported on camera about the destruction of *bajra* and *jowar* (millet) crops." The story was aired on the Telugu-language channel of Doordarshan as well as on a private satellite channel in the local language. Narsamma is one of seven Dalit women of Pastapur (Medak district, Andhra Pradesh state) involved in a community radio project which grew out of the efforts of the Hyderabad-based Deccan Development Society (DDS) to train women in the use of video. The project now has a full-fledged FM radio station at Machnoor village, equipped with a 100-watt transmitter that has a reach of approximately 30 km. Program content is determined by Narsamma and her team, with inputs from the target audience, all of them members of rural communities within the project area. More than 100 hours of interviews, field reports, group discussions, songs, and dramas relating to community-specific needs and issues had been recorded by the women by 2000, and the tapes circulated for use in the villages covered by the project (Sen 2000).
- "Groups of men and women of this sunflower-draped village flash their newly acquired contraptions – Murphy radios – and get engrossed in listening to the programs . . . packed with village-centered news, views, plays and folk songs, all in their local idiom . . . broadcast on Mana Radio (Our Radio)," a new community radio station set up in Orvakal village in Kurnool district, Andhra Pradesh, by a women's self-help group, under the auspices of the Velugu project of the Society for Elimination of Rural Poverty (SERP) (Venkateshwarlu 2002). Run by members of the Orvakal Mandal Samakhya, who have made all the decisions about program content and schedules as well as broadcast timings, Mana Radio was field tested on October 2, 2002. According to Zubeida Bi, president of the women's bank that has also been launched by the project, "Earlier I thought that in radio the machine did all the

work. Now I realise that we are the machines that make the programs!" (cited in a Velugu/SERP press release).

- The Kutch Mahila Vikas Sangathan (KMVS), a group working toward the empowerment and education of rural women in Bhuj district, Gujarat state, runs a community radio project producing half-hour weekly programs that are broadcast by All India Radio, Bhuj. The programs, recorded in the local Kutchhi dialect, deal with a variety of issues of concern to women in the area, especially in the context of the roles and responsibilities of *panchayats* (institutions of local self-governance). The programs became the talk of the district within a few months of their launch (Mukhopadhyay 2000).
- Video SEWA, established in 1984 by the Self-Employed Women's Association (SEWA), a trade union of self-employed women engaged in a variety of activities, uses the visual medium to motivate, mobilize, organize, and train its members and to strengthen their organizations. For women workers who are members of the union, as well as the cooperatives that have emerged from it, Video SEWA tapes are a source of information as well as inspiration. For example, when *chikan* embroidery workers of Lucknow saw how their counterparts in Ahmedabad had taken to the streets to press for minimum wages, they planned a rally of their own. SEWA also uses the videos for advocacy. For instance, when leaders of its water campaign met with the state minister for water supply and showed him footage of their work on water harvesting, he apparently proposed that more such conservation activities be taken up under the leadership of women.
- The Video SEWA team includes eight full-time video camera persons and producers and another 20 part-time members who produce videos on a wide range of issues. They have produced more than 200 tapes, of which many copies have been sold. They also undertake work for other organizations. Among the team members are informal sector workers such as head loaders, vegetable vendors, and home-based workers who have undergone technical training in the use of video and now also function as trainers. Video SEWA members formally registered their cooperative, the Shri Gujarat Mahila Video Sewa Mahiti Communication Sahakari Mandali Limited, in 2002.[5]
- SEWA also uses satellite communications (satcom) to meet the demand for training among its members scattered across Gujarat in areas such as organization-building, *panchayati raj* (decentralized governance), and issues related to forestry and water. They have found that satcom

talk-back programs help maximize the reach of the training team, enabling it to serve the needs of a large number of groups in rural communities within a limited period and thereby increase the organization's outreach capacity for awareness-raising, experience-sharing, and learning (Nanavaty 2000).

- In addition, SEWA has taken the initiative to optimally utilize "new economy" tools for increasing the efficiency and output of the organization as well as the activities of its members. The SEWA ICT Cell, a recently initiated small unit, has rapidly expanded its reach to impact on a wide range of the organization's activities. SEWA hopes to substantially improve the efficiency, efficacy, and output of its family of 101 women's cooperatives and associations through the proper deployment of information and communications technologies placed in the hands of the poor through its cadre of grassroots leaders (cited in a briefing note from SEWA ICT Cell, received from the SEWA Academy).
- "A village woman walks into a center and asks for some health-related information. She is given all the details about her particular ailment and the name of a doctor who can attend to her." Village Knowledge Centers such as this one were launched in 1998 in Vellianur and four other neighboring villages in Pondicherry state by the Chennai-based M. S. Swaminathan Foundation as part of a project aiming to bring information technology to grassroots villages. The centers are run by trained volunteers, including women, drawn from the rural communities they serve (Siddharthan 2000).
- *Ujala Chhadi* (literally, "wand of light") is a monthly newspaper published from Jaipur, Rajasthan, whose purpose is to serve the needs of those who get left out of the mass-media market. The newspaper, priced at Rs2 (which is, incidentally, the price of many mainstream, commercial Indian newspapers), has 3,000 subscribers in the rural areas it serves; in addition it is read out to many others who cannot read or write. It emerged out of the government-initiated Adult Literacy Program and Women's Development Program in the state but has been published since 1993 by Vividha, a women's rights organization with a special interest in media. The decision to launch a "people's paper" was taken because "even regional language papers often do not serve all the needs of rural readers. Their definition of news leaves out much of what people in villages want and need to know about their own surroundings. Their style of presentation is also often not suitable for the person who can barely read." According to the editors, "We

> do not claim neutrality, we are on the side of the deprived segments of society – the lower castes, women, minorities – and committed to supporting all struggles for social justice" (quoted in Raghavan 2002). Many neo-literate readers of *Ujala Chhadi* have also become news gatherers, thus advancing the editors' commitment to participatory journalism (Mishra 2002).

While these and other such initiatives are obviously exciting and promising, the flip side is that, in the absence of enabling policies, they are doomed to remain small experiments with limited reach and utility, especially in the context of the country's vast area and population. This is especially true of attempts to make audio-visual media more accessible and participatory. There is little doubt that the time, effort, and funds spent on infrastructure and training, as well as on creating the programs – not to mention the enthusiasm they have generated – could be put to far greater use with official support.

For instance, the government's recent initiative to open up the community radio sector is unlikely to benefit the radio projects mentioned above. Its proposal, awaiting clearance by the cabinet of ministers at the time of writing (December 2002), stipulates not only that educational institutions alone would be eligible to apply for licenses but that the power of the transmitters cannot exceed 50 watts. These conditions appear to immediately rule out the possibility of the Pastapur project being granted a license because DDS is not a university, college, or school and its transmitter is too powerful. As a result, the radio programs eagerly produced by women will have to continue to be used for "narrowcasting," a process where audio cassettes are played to concerned relevant groups (Ninan 2002).

The Velugu and KMVS projects also seem doomed under this dispensation because neither is, technically, an educational institution. The newly launched Mana Radio currently circumvents the licensing problem because of its range (400 m) but its broadcasts are consequently limited to the confines of one village. The KMVS currently pays commercial rates to the licensed public radio station in order to broadcast public interest programs within its catchment area.

Clearly this is not the way to make optimal use of financial or media/communication resources. Further, the absence of official support in terms of policy and practice effectively prevents real access to and participation in media and communication by the very women who need information and education, as well as entertainment, the most. Ironically, FM radio licenses have been issued over the past few years to private, commercial media establishments serving the entertainment needs of the urban elite in metropolitan cities (they are at present, late 2002, not permitted to broadcast programs based on news and current affairs). Now educational institutions may join the ranks of those allowed to run radio stations, including FM channels. But women who are currently producing radio programs for their communities are no closer to being empowered to broadcast them even to their existing audiences.

Another aspect of the government's new proposal is also likely to limit the scope of local, participatory broadcasting: even licensed community radio stations will not be allowed to broadcast news or current affairs programs. If the definition of news and current affairs covers reports on matters of critical importance to local communities, such as Chinna Narsamma's story about the loss of crops in her little corner of the country, the purpose and utility of community radio would obviously be diminished.

Gender and agency in the media industry

The many, complex issues relating to women's participation in and access to the media, and its impact on and use as an instrument for the advancement and empowerment of women – especially in the Indian and South Asian contexts – clearly require a variety of responses at many different levels. A number of efforts are already underway to improve the situation. Two relatively recent initiatives – involving media education and networking – that seem to have the potential to effect change from within are described below. These processes are highlighted, despite the fact that they are still evolving, partly because they are relatively new to India and therefore exciting, but mainly because they may eventually be in a position to address a variety of issues of concern regarding the media and women.

Interventions among young people are generally believed to be more effective and sustainable than efforts to change attitudes and behavior in people at later stages of life. Media training institutes seem to be appropriate sites for strategies to bring about desirable changes in the media workforce – and thereby in the media workplace, media content, and, eventually perhaps, even media policy. Institutions offering journalism education in India are currently attracting as many bright young people as they can accommodate. Some even have a few international students, often from other developing countries. Most now have an equal number of male and female students; some have more women than men applying and qualifying for admission; in addition, a number of women's colleges offer communications courses at the undergraduate level. The majority of the professional institutions focus on helping students develop the skills necessary for media jobs.

However, in a conscious effort to sensitize young people undergoing training for careers in the media to important subjects that require but do not always receive media attention, a college of journalism in Chennai, Tamil Nadu, introduced some courses that seek to increase students' awareness and understanding of a range of issues, including those affecting various disadvantaged sections of society, such as women. One of these courses focused on gender. It was based on the premise that holistic, quality coverage of gender-related issues is an integral part of the media's role in a democratic society and that awareness of gender as a major force in society is a professional asset for all aspiring journalists, irrespective of the branch of journalism they choose to perch on. The course attempted to establish that there is a gender dimension to virtually every event, process, institution, and/or individual experience covered by the media. The course also highlighted the fact that some of the most interesting and innovative work emerging from different fields of knowledge, creativity, and action is informed by gender awareness.

The course sought to demonstrate that issues of gender – popularly but somewhat inaccurately known as women's issues – should be of concern to both women and men because they affect everyone. It questioned the tendency in the media to ghettoize gender and related issues, and highlighted the growing recognition that all issues are women's issues, that women's issues are human issues, and that women's rights are human rights. It aimed to challenge the traditional, artificial duality of "hard" and "soft" news/stories in the media, which privileges the former and relegates gender, among other equally vital issues, to the margins of the latter. It attempted to promote the integration of gender consciousness into media coverage across the board through an exploration of gender issues in the context of some key areas of standard journalistic coverage, such as violence, politics, economics, and culture. It also sought to demonstrate that human development in general and women's development in particular need to be on the agenda of the media. It tackled common myths and misconceptions about gender, patriarchy, feminism, and women's movements. In addition, the course included critical analyses of the media and gender.

The response from the young people was encouraging, with not just those who opted for the elective course but a number of other students, too, keen to work on gender-related stories and projects. An introductory lecture on gender to a new crop of students in 2002 was titled: "Does gender matter?" Those who replied with an emphatic "yes" seemed to outnumber the nay-sayers as well as the fence-sitters – and, significantly and encouragingly, several young men were vocal in their affirmation of gender as an important issue for future journalists to be aware of and sensitive to.

The introduction of such courses into the curriculum of media training institutes may be one way to ensure that gender-related and other important issues, including those of particular relevance to socially and economically disadvantaged sections of the population, are integrated into mainstream media coverage – to the extent possible in the increasingly market-driven media environment. By providing the time and space for young, aspiring journalists to explore such issues, and also examine their own attitudes and behavior, such courses may help new entrants into the media to make decisions that could help foster positive changes in the media workplace as well as in media content. They can also create opportunities for informal mentoring by gender-conscious faculty, which may be helpful to young women in media professions, especially during the early stages of their careers.

Networking and mentoring have been identified the world over as key strategies to empower women in the media and help them to overcome the obstacles in their career paths. The Network of Women in Media, India (NWMI), launched in January 2002 at the end of a national workshop preceded by a prolonged process of consultation and consensus-building, represents one attempt to employ those strategies in the Indian context. The network-building process began with a series of three regional workshops held over a period of 10 months in 2000–1, which enabled women journalists from different parts of India, working in a number of languages and various sections and levels of the press, to gather together to discuss issues of common concern and to explore the possibility of building professional networks at the local, state, regional, and national levels.

There was broad agreement among workshop participants on the need for multi-layered, informal networks of women journalists that could serve multiple purposes, both professional and societal. Apart from the obvious purpose of providing a forum for addressing issues related to the workplace, it was felt that such networks could facilitate career advancement through training and professional enrichment programs, as well as mentoring. In addition, it was agreed that platforms of this kind could help highlight ethical issues related to the media, as well as the vital role of the media in society, especially in a democratic and diverse country like India.

In the wake of the regional workshops, women journalists began getting together at the local and, in some cases, state levels to address common issues and interests and to take forward the process of network-building. In the few places where such groups were already in existence, the process provided the possibility of establishing links with women in media professions in other parts of the country. Groups in different centers (currently about a dozen) determine their own agendas based on local context, priorities, and needs.

The program for the national workshop was drawn up in consultation with women journalists across the country. The founding principles, aims, and objectives of the national network were determined through a process of intense discussion and debate among participants at the national workshop. The effort throughout has been to ensure that the network evolved through a collective, bottom-up process, responding to felt needs as they arose and/or were articulated by members. Meanwhile, local groups have been engaged in a number of activities aimed at broadening the horizons of media professionals and reflecting their varied concerns, especially with regard to gender, the media, and society. Many of these activities, initiated and organized by women in media professions, have attracted participation from journalists and other professionals of both sexes.

Technology is being utilized to facilitate communication among members of the local and national networks. Some local groups have established e-groups, or listserves, to share information and resources, exchange ideas and opinions, and plan and organize events. An NWMI website (www.nwmindia.org), developed by an editorial team scattered across the country, is due to be launched in February 2003 and is expected to provide a boost to the network-building process at the national level.

Through its evolution over the past couple of years the NWMI has helped bridge many existing gaps and divisions within the profession – between journalists working in different parts of the country in different languages and media, from different generations, and at different levels of the profession. As the network grows and matures it is expected to improve its capacity to address a wide range of issues relating to the media and gender, including but not only those concerning access, employment, and decision-making.

Conclusion

Much is happening but much remains to be done with regard to women's participation in and access to the media, and its impact on and use as an instrument for the advancement and empowerment of women in India. Of vital importance for further progress in this respect are more widespread awareness and acceptance about the relevance of the issue. At present there is little recognition – in official quarters or within media and related establishments – of the need for a gender perspective in media matters.

For example, the Working Paper on a National Media Policy, submitted to the government in 1996 by a subcommittee of the consultative committee set up by the Ministry of Information and Broadcasting, made no specific recommendations relating to women as consumers of and participants in the media or in terms of media representations of women. Similarly, in a section on "manpower needs" in a privately circulated discussion paper on media policy, there was no mention of gender as a factor to be taken into account while planning training for media professionals. A media-related study commissioned by a UN agency discussed strategies to reach younger viewers but made no mention of female audiences. In a national survey of media audiences the breakdown of occupations by gender categorized more than 77 per cent of women as "non-working or retired," whereas only 15 per cent of men were placed in that category.[6] Decision-makers who influence media policy, plan training and other interventions, determine the parameters of data collection, and so on, clearly need to be more aware of gender as a significant factor that impacts many aspects of society and the media.

Second, there is an obvious and urgent need for official policies to strengthen the role and use of media as instruments for the advancement and empowerment of women. The public broadcasters, which have come up with knee-jerk reactions to competition from private channels since the early 1990s, require a renewed mandate for public interest broadcasting in general and the promotion of women's interests through the media in particular. In addition, in the era of decentralized governance, the Supreme Court's directive on the airwaves as a public resource should be urgently implemented through the grant of licenses to community media initiatives that serve the information, communication, and entertainment needs of disadvantaged sections of the population, and enable members of local communities – especially women – to access and participate in the media.

Third, the sensitization of media professionals in both the public and the private sector, including those involved in entertainment programs, to gender and other such issues may help tackle the confusing and conflicting signals currently emerging from the media. Both institutes of media education and professional networks of women in media can help move this process forward.

Finally, the situation of women in journalism requires attention and action from a number of players. Some of the points below, which relate to the press, may also be applicable in the broadcast and internet-based media.

The Indian print media are almost entirely owned and managed by private companies, the bulk of them family-owned business enterprises. The potential for governmental intervention in the personnel policies of private media houses is minimal and, in fact, fast reducing as media managements increasingly side-step the recommendations of the officially appointed wage boards, which periodically prescribe salary structures for media employees in different categories of media establishments. In any case, most journalists – of both sexes – would balk at the prospect of official interference in media matters lest it compromise editorial independence. Self-examination and introspection leading to transformation from within would, therefore, be a more widely acceptable route to change.

Among the issues that may bear consideration by those who run media organizations are:

- the desirability of stated policies and transparent procedures with regard to recruitment, remuneration, promotion, work assignment, and other matters that affect professional access, employment, and advancement, in keeping with essential principles of gender justice and equity;
- the need to institute measures and mechanisms to counter or minimize the effect of negative gender-based attitudes and behaviors within media organizations, including implementation of the directives of the Supreme Court of India with regard to sexual harassment in the workplace;

- the possibility of systemic and structural adjustments in work schedules, not as a special concession to women, but in recognition of the need for all human beings to achieve a healthy balance between professional and personal life, which would, in turn, enhance both productivity and creativity;
- the practicability of institutional support to women – beyond the mandatory maternity leave – during particular periods in their lives when it would make a crucial difference to their ability to cope with the often conflicting demands of work and family. This would help to ensure that women's current and potential contributions to the field are not frittered away through the neglect of their felt needs and real problems, especially since many of these are rooted not in individual, personal foibles but in societal biases and inequalities, and in view of the fact that flexibility is now entirely feasible thanks to technological innovations.

Associations and/or unions representing journalists of both sexes can also play a role in ensuring gender justice and equity within media organizations by advocating or supporting initiatives and changes in policies and procedures, as well as measures and mechanisms to ensure the elimination of gender-based disparities and disadvantages in access, employment, and advancement (in addition to highlighting and countering problems of access and employment due to other factors such as caste, class, religion, and ethnicity).

Organizations, associations, and/or networks of women in the media can call attention to the need for change through research and documentation, dissemination of information, discussion and debate, advocacy and lobbying. They can also initiate mutually supportive strategies – such as the sharing of resources, training, and mentoring – to enhance women's confidence, capabilities, and potential for advancement within the media. In addition, they can address the problems of access to media employment faced by women from disadvantaged communities through special programs aimed at enabling and empowering them.

Institutions involved in media education can contribute to the process of transformation by sensitizing students to the importance of gender awareness, equality, and equity in all aspects of life, including professional life. These institutions can further contribute to democratizing the media by introducing policies that will encourage women, as well as men, from disadvantaged communities to access journalism education.

Meanwhile, it is a matter of some comfort that awareness and concern about gender-related issues are very much alive and kicking among a cross-section of women in media today, including young professionals. According to one young journalist, this is not just because they are women but because they consider such issues inherently important, involving a section of the citizenry that does not easily find a voice in the media. "Our generation has little idealism left," said another, "But the little that remains seems to be with the women" (cited in Joseph 2000: 60–2).

Key terms

Akashvani
community media and community projects
Doordarshan
glass ceiling
indigenous English-language print media
"ladies' beat" of yore
minorities within minorities
narrowcasting
people's paper

Questions for discussion

1. In what way is the story of six blind persons who each arrive at a different definition of an elephant after touching different parts of the animal used by Joseph as a metaphor for the media system in India?
2. Explain some of the disparities that separate women journalists from each other in India, according to Joseph.
3. What are some of the personal attributes that the author states determine how well an Indian woman journalist will do in her profession in India?
4. What are some of the barriers and breakthroughs that Indian women journalists have experienced in India, according to the author's research?
5. What efforts are underway to make broadcast media accessible to rural and lower-class women in India?

6 How has the journalism program at the Asian College of Journalism begun to sensitize students to gender-related issues in reporting? How are students responding, according to Joseph?

Notes

1 This is an edited version of a paper originally written for the United Nations Expert Group Meeting on the "Participation and access of women to the media, and the impact of media on, and its use as an instrument for the advancement and empowerment of women," organized by the UN Division for the Advancement of Women in collaboration with other UN entities, and held in Beirut, Lebanon, in November 2002. In the full text, I elaborate further on this point: www.un.org/womenwatch/daw/egm/media2002/reports/EP4Joseph.PDF. See as well other documents related to the meeting at www.un.org/womenwatch/daw/egm/media2002.

2 Castes and tribes officially recognized as having historically suffered social, economic, and political disadvantages; also known as Dalits and Adivasis respectively.

3 Personal inquiry of *Doordarshan News.*

4 Personal inquiry of *Doordarshan News.*

5 Information from SEWA's website: www.sewa.org and www.videosewa.org.

6 Personal correspondence with William Crawley, co-author with David Page of *Satellites Over South Asia: Broadcasting Culture and the Public Interest* (Sage, 2001).

References

AMIC (Asian Media Information and Communication Centre) (2002) *Communication Education and Media Needs in India,* reviewed on www.inomy.com by Rao, M., October 2002.

Batliwala, S., Anitha, B. K., Gurumurthy, A., and Wali, C. S. (1998) *Study on the Status of Rural Women in Karnataka.* National Institute of Advanced Studies, Women's Policy Research and Advocacy Unit, Bangalore.

Jeffrey, R. (2000) India's *Newspaper Revolution: Capitalism, Politics and the Indian Language Press.* Hurst, London.

Joseph, A. (2000) *Women in Journalism: Making News.* Media Foundation/Konark, New Delhi.

Joseph, A. and Sharma, K. (1994) *Whose News? The Media and Women's Issues.* Sage, Delhi, Thousand Oaks, CA, and London.

Malayala Manorama (2002) *Manorama Yearbook 2002.* Malayala Manorama, Kottayam.

Mishra, N. (2002) Message for the masses. *Times of India*, October 24.

Mukhopadhyay, B. (2000) Why AIR has completely ignored community radio. *Humanscape,* June, www.humanscapeindia.net/humanscape/hs0600/hs60013t.htm (last accessed November 11, 2002).

Nanavaty, R. (2000) Satcom for barefoot women managers. In: Bhatnagar, S. and Schware, R. (eds), *Information and Communication Technology in Development: Cases from India.* Sage, New Delhi, Thousand Oaks, CA, and London, pp. 163–67.

Ninan, S. (2002) Media pulse. *Hindu*, October 27.

Raghavan, M. (2002) *Ujala Chhadi*: a newspaper for village folk. *Hoot*, August 28. www.thehoot.org.

Sen, A. (2000) Voices waiting to be heard. *New Indian Express (Sunday Express)*, November 5; also reproduced on www.voicesforall.org.

Siddharthan, B. (2000) Global villages. *Humanscape*, June, www.humanscapeindia.net/humanscape/hs0600/hs6007t.htm (last accessed November 11, 2002).

Venkateshwarlu, K. (2002) Mana Radio. *Hindu*, October 6.

8
"Dangerously Feminine?" Theory and Praxis of Women's Alternative Radio

Caroline Mitchell

With powerful voices, women can organize, train, take collective action and ultimately build communities and a society based on self-determination.

Stuart and Bery 1996: 211

Introduction

"Dangerously feminine" (Skard 1989: 141) was a phrase used to describe Radiorakel, the first known women's radio station in Europe, which has been broadcasting in Oslo, Norway, since 1982. Women all over the world have used radio to campaign, entertain, inform, shock, and celebrate women's lives. Increasingly people spend time listening to radio more than any other mass medium (Downing 2001). This chapter explores the development of women's alternative media practice over the past few decades with particular emphasis on radio as a medium. Radio has been discussed and defined as a female medium in terms both of the intimate relationship women have with it as listeners, and of the program content that has been devised by or for them. Karpf noted that "radio has a special relationship with women's lives in that it is an explicit accompaniment to then – a commentary or a counterpoint" (1980: 43).

In this chapter, I explore how "woman friendly" the radio medium is in terms of an alternative media practice. I argue that radio is a particularly accessible medium for women in terms of how they can learn production skills and techniques, how they can work together to shape program schedules and tell their stories, and how it helps to meet their needs for information, education, and pleasure through a wide range of programming forms. I also look at the particular problems that women encounter fitting in their personal lives and commitments around the exigencies of being involved in a radio station, and suggest ways that radio station operations and structures can be made more women friendly. I argue that gendered radio training and community development are crucial to the survival and diversity of women's radio practice.

I document some of the key historical moments in the development of women's radio across the world. I do this in the context of defining radical, alternative women's media and looking at how the community radio sector is particularly important and fruitful as a site for women's radio practice. Case studies of Fem FM, the first radio station run by women in the United Kingdom, and Feminist International Radio Endeavor (FIRE), a feminist internet station from Latin America, are used to examine the wider concerns and issues involved in such a targeted media practice. I also focus on the particular structures of production, program content, style, and forms of (audience) address contained within women's radio output, in order to define the ways in which women's radio practice is different to mainstream processes.

In the final part of this chapter, using the many bold and exciting examples of women's radio across the world, I synthesize what constitutes feminist radio practices and discuss the conditions that best suit women's radio stations. Finally, I look to the future to see how women are adapting to technological and cultural developments, particularly women's use of sound and radio on the web.

Radio: a female medium?

> *Radio is one of the sites where gender is produced, reproduced, and transformed.*
>
> *Lacey 1996: 244*

Radio has been described as a medium that is particularly accessible and pertinent to women. It comes straight into the home and has long been considered a companion to women while they do their domestic work and numerous other things: travelling to work, washing up, doing the ironing, and so on. In its infancy, equipment manufacturers quickly realized that radio could be transformed from being a "boy's toy" into a medium with programs organized around the housewife's day and domestic routines (see Johnson 1990; Moores 1988).

From mainstream broadcasting histories it would seem that until the last two decades of the twentieth century, radio was a very male domain in which to work. Thankfully, feminist academics, and broadcasters themselves, have rectified this perception through revisions of history and biographical writings that have restored the work of previously underrated or "invisible" women pioneers of radio, from in front of and behind the microphone (for examples, see Shapley 1996; Hilmes 1997; Barlow 1999). Documenting women's radio experience is important in terms of keeping women's media activities visible and enabling a more balanced understanding of women's contribution to radio.

Excluded voices

Women who work in radio have long known that radio can be a more sympathetic and "fairer" medium for women because it concentrates on the female voice and not the female appearance. However in mainstream radio, until at least the 1970s, it was assumed that women's voices were unsuited to radio and that audiences, male and female, didn't want to listen to women. Both assumptions have been used as an excuse for not employing women in presentation roles (Gill 1993). McKay found that it was when women tried to speak out to *change* their situation that their problems really started:

> When women used the technology in support of the goals and activities of established institutions, they were applauded at best or ignored at worst. When they attempted to use it in ways that would lead to change in the traditional order and in women's customary roles, their right to use it was challenged. (McKay 1988: 187–8)

Contemporary research considers how women modify the pitch of their voice and sometimes their regional accent in order to sound more "acceptable" and to fit in with the prevailing ideology of particular broadcasting organizations (Michaels and Mitchell 2000: 244). Gill (1993) used critical discourse analysis (CDA) to examine program controllers' talk.[1] Gill's close analysis of how radio program controllers "justify" the lack of female DJs at radio stations demonstrates how male managers often blame audience attitudes for their own failure to employ women. Gill argues that the space for female listeners is still seen as male-defined; for example, in the relationship between the "husband substitute" DJ and the housewife audience. The sexualization of the male DJ's relationship with the female listener – constructing himself to replace the absent man in the woman's life – extends to fantasizing about a relationship with the female listener. Gill demonstrates how this shift is understood by a commercial DJ she interviewed:

> I think mid-morning radio has always been considered housewife radio. It isn't to the same extent now. Actually in some parts of the morning you have more men listening than women. But I think you still go for a female audience. I mean you flirt with them – that's exactly what you do for three hours. But what you've not got to do, is do it to the extent that it annoys the men listening. (cited in Gill 1993: 333)

In the US, as more women were heard on air, there was decreasing criticism and comment about women's voices being a barrier to industry entry: "There are no problems any more with women's voices being too high. There are standards for both men and women" (Cramer 1993: 165). Later in this chapter, we shall see how the relationship between listener and presenter and women's identities, as represented on air, change considerably as more women broadcast through women's community stations.

Feminist content on mainstream and alternative media

The relationship between the media and the feminist movement has been complex and often problematic. In terms of constructing a "public identity" for the women's movement, Steiner (1992: 121) notes that "At worst, mass media ignore, trivialize, or belittle the philosophies of the women's movement; at best they dilute or co-opt the major concepts." As van Zoonen comments, "feminism has not gained access to the media on its own terms" (1992: 453). She argues that mainstream media's construction of the women's movement in the Netherlands in the late 1960s and early 1970s shows that whilst certain discourses of feminism, for instance equal opportunities, were acceptable, political feminism was not. For van Zoonen, mainstream media perceived a gap between the interests of "ordinary women" and activists. She notes that even in this framework, there was some room for divergent views (1992: 474), and acknowledges that discourses of feminism in the 1990s are more diverse. This might be usefully applied to discussing radio representations of feminism, particularly where women are active producers of radio.

Historically, there have been criticisms (for example, Local Radio Workshop 1983) that mainstream radio has concentrated on a limited view of women's lives, concentrating solely on their domestic role. A notable exception is *Woman's Hour*, on the BBC in the UK, which has covered a wide range of topics since it started in 1946 and over the years has aired pioneering features about previously taboo subjects. Former *Woman's Hour* editor Sally Feldman said she took the "Twin Peaks" approach to programming – dealing with issues for women and issues from a woman's perspective (Feldman 2000). The program, which is broadcast every weekday with a repeat at weekends, is produced by and contributed to by female broadcasters, although men make some features.[2] It has a reputation for serious investigative reporting, for campaigning, and for sustained coverage of international women's human rights, childcare, and health issues. However, it has been criticized in equal amounts by its audience for being "too feminist" and "too traditional" and for items mainly being of interest to older women. Nonetheless, Karpf argues that *Woman's Hour*'s dual approach to content, covering domestic as well as public issues, is part of its success:

> Although its tone is still often Home Counties bungalow, *Woman's Hour* is the closest thing we have on national radio to a feminist program. It negotiates the conflicts in broadcasting to and for women, at times unsure how far to examine and interrogate the "outside world," without losing its focus on and validation of the domestic world. (Karpf 1987: 175)

A listener describes the program's importance to her in bringing the public activities of the women's movement into her private sphere: "In the 1960s I was too caught up with the family to get involved in the women's movement. I never went to demos or meetings but I found out what other women were thinking from the program" (cited in Murray 1996: 130). It

Box 8.1 Example of interviews and features from a *Woman's Hour* program[3]

Interview with actress Jessica Stevenson
Interview about female-dominated professions
Feature about the artistic career of Eva Hesse
Studio discussion about gender and close friendships
Interview and performance by Dorothy Masuku, a South African singer
Recipe for last-minute Christmas cake
Interview with minister about government initiative to help homeless women and children escape from domestic violence

should also be noted that since 1997, BBC World Service has broadcast a weekly women's program called *Everywoman.*

However, it is still the case that programs made from women's perspectives are in the minority within mainstream radio output. It is hardly surprising therefore that there is an emerging interest and activity in alternative media production, where women have more control over the content and process of program production and where women's voices, views, and creativity can be central to a radio station's agenda and output.

Women's cultural production and radical alternative media practice

Feminist media must also be passionate, fresh, new, interesting, or even dramatic (or it will be ignored even by feminists).

Women's Radio Fund, "Why feminist radio?"

As I have discussed elsewhere (Mitchell 2002), when we define women's cultural production it is important to discuss the distinction between women's production and feminist production. Bredin (1991) outlines a number of different levels and definitions of feminist cultural production. Feminist production should be *by* women but the fact that women are involved does not mean that it will be feminist. Feminist production should be about the politicization of culture in resistance to patriarchal oppression. Recognition of cultural factors surrounding different groups of women (such as race, class, and sexual orientation) is integral to a feminist ideal of eliminating oppression.

McLaughlin argues that feminists have not paid enough attention to the media in their discussions of the public sphere and the work of Jürgen Habermas, and that "the key axis of exclusion from the liberal public sphere was gender" (McLaughlin 1993: 604). She suggests that media should be foregrounded in a feminist theory of the public sphere and that feminist media studies should account for the public sphere. Women's interests can be transformed through forms of resistance, including setting up oppositional discourses. She argues the need for "new media developments and alternative forms of media and participation in order to develop new forms of public life" (ibid.: 616). Women's community radio stations could provide the setting for new discourses of women's communications to develop.

Bredin argues that feminist production should demystify the role of producer so that the boundaries between producers and consumers of culture are broken down: "A work is never inherently feminist but depends on a feminist consciousness shared by both producer and consumer" (Bredin 1991: 36). Coward discusses how feminism has redefined women's interests in terms of women being involved in production; for example, setting up women's production companies, or working as producers in control of program content (Coward 1984).

So, what might be the characteristics of a "gendered structure of media production" (van Zoonen 1994: 49) at a local level, where most women's programming operates? The specialist presses and TV production companies set up by feminists in the 1970s and 1980s (such as *Ms* magazine in the US, or Virago Publishing and the Broadside TV production company in the UK) were aimed at national audiences who identified themselves as feminist. Steiner notes the problem with the way that some women's alternative media projects frame women's issues: "women's media often alienate potential sympathizers with their highly particularized version of their cause and their audience; this provides an easy opening for ridicule and accusations of self ghettoizing" (Steiner 1992: 126–7).

The setting up of short-term women's radio stations like Fem FM, Elle FM, and Brazen Radio in the UK in the 1990s can be seen as a new way of women negotiating how their lives are mediated through radio. Women's community radio stations are clearly targeted at female audiences at a local level – in the UK, short-term licenses are only available for local use. However, the context of the way women identified themselves had changed. In research carried out in women's radio training groups (Mitchell 2002), of particular note was how women identified with the "f" word – feminism – and how they operated a form of self-censorship in program content.

In more established radical stations (for instance, in campus-based university stations), younger women have engaged and grappled with how to adapt to changing discourses and perceptions of feminism. Jana Razga tells the story of how one women's radio program, *Adamant Eve*, on CJSR FM in Edmonton, Canada, changed over a period of two years from being a program with one or two producers to one produced collectively. They changed the program content, which had been "mainstream feminist" and "intellectual," and dropped the feminist label ("the word has become so ambiguous and alienating") in order to make challenging but accessible programs, with more training for women who wanted to get involved (Razga 1995: 6).

Linda Steiner defined characteristics of Women's Alternative Media (WAM) after surveying a range of women's media across the world, from magazines and publishing ventures to record companies, TV production companies, and radio stations. According to Steiner, the main aim of WAM is to "express and celebrate" (1992: 123) the views of a wide range of women whilst using media as a tool to help the women's movement achieve its aims. From Steiner's survey (1992: 124–31), I have identified the key characteristics of women's media up until the early 1990s, although of course not all of them are necessarily present in each venture:

- Women are involved in most aspects of production and value the production experience offered.
- Women get involved in WAM "for the love of it" and because they are committed to doing something that helps the feminist cause; however, they often experience burnout.
- WAM aim at small, specialist, and committed audiences and are not profit-oriented, although they seek to cover their costs.
- WAM are often run by one or two women or structured as a collective with decision-making by consensus: participation from the readership/ audience is encouraged.

Box 8.2 *Adamant Eve* and "The Conscious Cunt"

One of the most controversial aspects of the program was the collective's decision to name its regular alternative health feature "The Conscious Cunt." Initially the station management saw the use of the "C" word as obscene. The program team, however, said they used the word according to its original meaning:

> which referred both to female genitalia and women with connotations of respect, wisdom and knowledge. It was our goal to educate our listeners, women especially, in order to bring to light the empowering origins of a word that has been so subverted that today in its slang usage, it is considered one of the (or even the most harmful profanities) directed towards women. (Razga 1995: 7)

The program devoted a special show to the issue and sought feedback from its listeners about the use of the word. There was an overwhelming positive response for the word being used and CJSR agreed that it could be used providing it was used in the correct context. This was seem by the program-makers as "a victory for freedom of expression, a victory for proactive radio programming and a victory for community involvement in community radio" (ibid.).

Much important work relating to women and radio has happened under the umbrella of "grassroots" development work in communications. Riaño (1994: 6) presents a useful typology of women, participation, and communication, which has four main categories of communication: development, participatory, alternative, and feminist. Notably, it is the feminist category that represents the optimum access, control, and ownership for women.

One of the first examples of feminist radio is the community station WBAI in New York, which introduced feminist programming from 1969, including taped consciousness-raising sessions (Steiner 1992). Radio Donna was a women's station linked to Radio Città Futura, in Rome. In 1979, women broadcasting a program about abortion and contraception were attacked and a fascist group set the studio on fire. Afterwards 50,000 women demonstrated in support of Radio Donna (Karpf 1980).

Community radio: participatory structures for women's radio

So what is alternative women's radio practice, how widespread is it across the world, and under what conditions does it take place, thrive, survive, or fail? The majority of women's stations and programming operate at "micro-"media level in stations that have community licenses. Community radio is radio made by and for the community it serves, set up on a non-profit-distributing basis, usually staffed by volunteers and run with an underlying ethos of enabling participation in all the activities of the station through access and training (Lewis and Booth 1989). Although they attract many women as volunteers, community radio stations often reflect the gender stereotyping of mainstream radio stations in staff and volunteer roles, despite having aims and charters that support equal opportunities. A Europe-wide survey of community stations found that men outnumbered women volunteers in all work areas apart from administration and finance. Where there were full-time paid staff, only 22 per cent were women (Lewis 1994).

In North America, the Women's Radio Fund (WRF)[4] has produced a useful list of feminist radio projects, services, and programs (mainly in the US) that women have set up with varying levels of organization, complexity, and radicalism, from acts of guerrilla radio[5] to nationally and internationally syndicated news programs and examples of individual women trying to set up viable commercial women's stations.

Since the 1990s, many African countries have a developed a community radio sector in response to the opening up of political systems. Community radio is used here to strengthen democracy and increase representation of people and issues that were previously ignored by mainstream media. Associations like the African Woman's Development and Communication Network (FEMNET) and Africa's Women's International Network (AMARC) organize training for women and campaign around issues of equality and representation. According to FEMNET, there are now six women's community radio stations in Mali and stations in Cameroon, Malawi, Senegal, and South Africa (Wanyeki 2002).

In one part of the Asia Pacific region, in New Zealand and Australia, community radio has existed since the 1980s. There is now a large sector of community, ethnic, and special interest stations there, and most stations have women's programming and women involved in the running of the station. In 1989, the Public Broadcasting Association of Australia produced

Radio Jill, a self-help training pack to encourage more women to learn production skills.

Asia is one of the least developed continents of the world in terms of women and community radio, although in some countries, like India, community radio is in the early stages of development and women in particular are playing an important role in establishing rural radio stations.[6] The Women's Feature Service in India (Anand 1996) has been an important source of news about feminism and women's issues.

In Latin America and the Caribbean, many countries have an established community radio sector with hundreds of stations, often in remote rural areas. There have been a number of innovative projects coming from this area of the world, including FIRE (see case study 8.1 below).

There are relatively few women's stations that have a track record of sustaining a broadcasting service over a number of years. Some stations that are missing from "official" broadcasting histories have been documented by feminist historians. One such station is WHER-AM, a commercial "all-girl" radio station in Memphis, Tennessee, which broadcast from 1955 up until the early 1970s (Meade 2003). Established in 1982 and still broadcasting, Radiorakel in Norway is the longest-running women's station in Europe (see also D'Arcy 1996 on Radio Pirate Woman in Ireland). Many stations run by and mainly for women have been temporary or short-term projects "showcasing" women's radio. In the mainstream radio sector, most radio stations run 24/7, so part-time, opt-out (from full-time stations), or temporary stations are frowned upon. However, Lacey argues that alternative stations should not use the same market-oriented criteria to measure success, and that short-term or part-time stations need not be seen as inferior. Indeed, "The very transience of community stations is something to be celebrated since it [militates] against not only complacency and repetition, but more importantly against the potential for reification that is so dangerous in identity politics" (Lacey forthcoming).

Women's activity in mixed gender stations

Most community stations across the world will have some kind of programming made from a female perspective. However, the way women are represented in stations has changed since the early 1970s, so that where there were once single programs representing women's interests there may now be women working across different programs as individual music presenters and in programs of specialist interest (Jallov 1992, 1996).

One programmer at the Ryerson University student station CKLN in Toronto described the mix of programs made by women:

> I do a weekly three hour music show . . . what is called an open format show . . . I play everything from experimental jazz to hard core punk, country and Celtic music. [W]ithin my show I concentrate on music made by women, written by, performed by or done by all women bands, or bands where there are a few women. I also concentrate on lesbian and feminist issues in the context of doing a music show. You also find programs at CKLN tying current affairs and politics into the music they are playing . . . We also have a gay and lesbian show and a number of feminist programs. We have an international women's music show, a women's jazz and blues show and a number of women doing other forms of programming.[7]

Bredin argues that most urban community stations in Canada have feminist programming of some kind, and notes that cities with the most active women's movements and other feminist media forms (such as a women's press) have the most radio programming. She is, however, critical of the impact of this programming and of the participation of women in programming roles at the stations, particularly minority ethnic women and lesbians. She suggests that "something more than complacent lip service to community radio as a 'participatory medium' and 'open forum' is required" (Bredin 1991: 39). She concludes: "despite its current limitations, feminist community radio is actively engaged in the politicization of culture and the affirmation of marginal experience that characterizes women's resistance to oppression everywhere" (ibid.: 40).

Radio listening clubs and radio as a feminist development tool

Radio is a medium that can cross large distances and reach communities dispersed over wide areas. I have observed that even the poorest communities have at least one radio, and listening is often a communal activity.[8] In many African countries, in rural areas, women have formed "listening clubs" where they listen to a program together and then record their opinions and comments onto tape, and these are relayed back to the program-makers for inclusion in future programs. These are funded by development organizations and are often in conjunction with public broadcasters (see Moyo and Quarmyne's work on radio listening clubs in Zimbabwe, quoted in Allen et al. 1996). More recently some of these clubs have developed into programs on community stations focusing on women, and even into community stations run mainly by women. In Mali, the solar-powered station Radio Douentza has regular women's programming, with local female producers and contributors making programs about education, health, local politics, transport, and farming. The station played a major role in raising awareness of the importance of sending girls to school.[9]

Feminist radio training/gender-sensitive training

> *In many countries women almost always only appear in the media when they are raped, in relation to prostitution and crime or when they win a beauty contest, and of course in commercials as good housewives, mothers, sex objects and beauty product consumers. If we want to change this . . . we have to portray women as active members of society.*
>
> *Millioretti n.d.: 1*

As women's stations and programs have become more established, attracting funding and status, women's radio training courses, "gender-sensitive training," and university courses in feminist journalism practice have contributed to defining a praxis of women's radio. In Tyne and Wear in the UK, the Bridge Women's Radio project set up a course in conjunction with a local university that included classes in confidence-building, technical and computing skills, program-making, writing for radio, women's studies, and radio station management. The course supported students with childcare provision and expenses, and employed women from previous courses as community tutors (Mitchell 2002). Research into women's radio training carried out at the time (Baxter 2000; Günnel et al. 1999) showed that resources needed to be available to women outside the station (enabled by portable machines and laptop editing) and that stations could make productive learning partnerships with under-represented groups in the community.

The Media Project, in Mozambique, has developed a multi-faceted approach to women and radio, including devising a formal "gender-sensitive journalism training" course for men and women and a national network of women in community radio.[10]

At Radio Lora in Switzerland, which has women's, feminist, and lesbian programming, they have a guide to radical feminist broadcasting (Millioretti n.d.). This advises women to implement news values that have women's perspectives at their core: this means using women's community centers, resource centers, and libraries for research, using female interviewees where possible, encouraging shy or unconfident women to have a voice, using music written, composed, and sung by women where possible, and in general reporting women as active – fighting their oppression rather being sorry for them. The guide eschews impartiality and objectivity and states that feminist journalists should "play an affirmative role in favor of women" whilst remaining critical. (ibid.: 3). At the University of Puerto Rico, Norma Valle says that feminist journalism isn't a theoretical course: "it has to be activism . . . they become part of the women's movement." She sees feminist journalists as playing an important role documenting women's history: "Don't just interview the men . . . find the women. Women have been ignored in history – they have been present but their presence hasn't been recorded . . . Journalism is tomorrow's history and we are recording it now, so when we record that history we must not ignore women's participation."[11]

Case Study 1 Feminist International Radio Endeavour[12]

Today, a huge cloud of transparent, clean smoke is coming out of the FIRE-PLACE. It has been possible because of the warmth of the alternative women's media movement, including those who are here, and those who have stayed behind in their countries, who are also spreading the word that women are here to demand our rightful place in society and in this Forum.

Music by Sinead O'Connor "Fire on Babylon"

The Hopi Indians of the Sierras in South America have an ancient story that talks about how, if one were able to fly beyond the earth, as you look back down, you would see, instead of people's bodies, the fire in them. Millions of fires: big ones, small ones, dwindling fires, and strong fires . . . little sparks in some, and shining flame on

> others. The fire that you would see in this FIRE-PLACE today is hot and strong.
>
> Music
>
> Welcome to Feminist International Radio Endeavor – FIRE – broadcasting live, at last, from the FIRE-PLACE at the Women's Alternative Media Action and Service Centre in Huairou, China. Venue of the Non governmental Organisations Forum that has brought together the sparks of women from all regions of the globe. Those who are here have also brought the light of the hot hearted protest for those who could not make it. (Script of the first live broadcast from the FIRE-PLACE at the UN World Conference on Women, Beijing, China, 1995, in Anfossi and Suarez/FIRE 1995: 8)

Feminist International Radio Endeavor (FIRE) is a unique feminist internet radio and alternative news program founded in 1991, based in Costa Rica and operating worldwide. It uses radio and new technologies to their fullest extent to communicate between women locally and globally, creating and affecting news flow, reporting international women's human rights, and thereby tangibly influencing the world information and news order in a gendered way. During its relatively short life it has set up daily short-wave radio broadcasts on Radio For Peace International, received in over 100 countries, and since 1998 it has had a strong presence on the internet, making regular web broadcasts (including marathon web casts lasting several days) in English and Spanish.

Central to FIRE'S ethos is making access to the means of communication as easy as possible. The women who make FIRE travel all over the world to be present wherever women are meeting together and feminist news is being made. These women possess a wide range of technical, journalistic, and communication skills and a huge amount of creativity, persistence, and energy. Wherever FIRE is present, they set up a FIRE-PLACE – a small, basic, but fully functioning radio studio connected to a phone line or transmitter. Two or three women from FIRE, including its indefatigable co-founder María Suárez Toro, set up everything themselves, and from this base they conduct interviews with women who come to the FIRE-PLACE to clarify, relay opinions, and offer perspectives about issues that do not necessarily get a hearing from the mainstream media. The FIRE-PLACE acts as a focus for feminist journalists and guest producers from all over the world to meet and organize interviews and broadcasts with conference delegates, setting up round-table discussions so that issues are covered from many angles and in depth rather than in the sound bites of the mainstream media. Rhonda Copelon, US feminist lawyer and women's human rights activist, described the role of FIRE as follows: "FIRE was a place where we could speak with journalists who were not putting us against the wall. We needed this kind of space as a way of holding our own voice" (Suárez Toro 2000: 55).

> One of FIRE's aims is to be a bridge between women and the mainstream media thus facilitating media access for underrepresented information, opinions and positions. Like many feminist alternative media organizations, FIRE sees training of women and girls in media techniques as a high priority and does this as part of its broadcasts. FIRE has used various tactics for enabling underrepresented voices to be heard. This has included diverting aggressive "pro-life" representatives by setting up a FIRE interview with them, thus allowing the other representatives of women's reproductive rights organizations to put over views uninterrupted in interviews. (Suárez Toro 1996: 231)

Maria Suárez Toro sums up her definition of feminist radio: "Doing feminist radio is giving back to woman the importance of her voice . . . and her importance in life . . . It is having one ear open to others and one ear listening to what is inside."[13]

Case Study 2 Fem FM[14]

> A unique experience – a knowledge that things can be done, can be different, doors can be opened. There are alternatives and women have a collective power that is inspiring . . . When people come together united by a compelling idea and a working spirit of co-operation and mutual trust, they can do anything. (Mitchell and Caverly 1993: 10)

Fem FM was the first women's station to broadcast in the UK. It lasted eight days in March 1992, but its development work with over 200 women went on for a year and its impact lasted far longer, providing a role model for subsequent stations across the UK.

Fem FM was based in Bristol, a multicultural city in the south-west of England with a vibrant arts and cultural scene as well as an active community and voluntary sector. Women who had a background in community, youth, and women's radio set up the station. They organized a steering group of about a dozen women, "head-hunted" for their skills, experience, and expertise in radio, music, technical matters, fundraising, training, community development, working with volunteers, publicity, and marketing. This group set about recruiting and training volunteers to carry out both the background work to setting up a station from scratch (including choosing a name, devising a jingle package, fundraising, and finding broadcasting and training premises) and devising and producing programming for the eight days on air. The station was run completely on voluntary labor and the women raised over £20,000 from sources including the Gulbenkian Foundation. The station as a whole was sponsored by an airline, which was keen to promote the fact that it had an all-female flight crew!

The aims of Fem FM were:

- to create a radio station with a distinct and different sound from a woman's point of view, representing the rich diversity of women's culture;
- to include coverage of events and celebrations for International Women's Day and Festival Fortnight in Bristol;
- to encourage women from different generations and backgrounds to debate issues of importance to them;
- to provide a service produced and presented by a mix of experienced and first-time broadcasters and to offer guest slots to prominent female broadcasters to promote the station;
- to provide a variety of training opportunities to first-time broadcasters to develop their radio and communication skills and to have access to airtime. (Mitchell and Caverly 1993: 1)

The broadcasts contained a mix of live and pre-recorded programs with a 60:40 music:speech content mix. Producers wanted the station to sound professional – it was important to them that as a representation of women's achievement in radio Fem FM did not sound amateurish or boring, a criticism often leveled at community stations. This had to be balanced with giving first-time broadcasters an opportunity to get real, live experience and to make a few mistakes in a supportive atmosphere. Women at Fem FM were keen to scotch the myth that they didn't want to apply for presentation work in radio (see Baehr and Ryan 1984; Gill 1993; Michaels and Mitchell 2000).

The program schedule included a variety of speech and special interest programs, including a program in three Asian languages, a daily youth program presented by young women, and a daily *Men's Hour*, and broadcasts were very well received. On Fem FM there were no specialist programs for lesbians, although gay women were presenters and producers of programs across the schedule.[15] The feedback from listeners was extremely positive, with women appreciating the way that the station addressed its listeners, female and male:

> Thanks for getting it together redressing the balance on the airwaves . . . the presenters are human and relaxing not trying to be cool and slick. If this is a women's touch, I like it . . . To all the wonderful dedicated women at Fem FM, thanks for the brilliant, exciting, interesting, fresh, riveting, powerful, stimulating, happy, strong, electric eight days of woman's radio. Bristol should be proud . . . Sounds fab, I haven't heard such good music for a long time . . . It's destroyed my tolerance for Radio 4: men talking to men . . . Brilliant, it just makes me realise what's missing off the rest of the radio . . . It's so wonderful and so good that I just have to tell you I am looking forward to it ending so I can get out of the house! (listeners cited in Mitchell and Caverly 1993: 8)

Box 8.3 Fem FM schedules: selected examples

Monday–Friday

7–9 FEM AM – morning magazine. Features: "Yoga on the radio," "My mum," "Women mean business" (sponsored by Aer Lingus). Great morning music from female and male artists.

9–11 SAYIN' SOMETHING – great music from female artists. Interviews with performers like Jean Binta Breeze and Sister Aisha.

11–1 UPFRONT – highlights women in the community – meeting the women who make our community tick.

1–2 WRITE NOW – showcases the best of women's writing and poetry from international, national, and local writers. Visit to a local writers' group each day. Serial: "Our Joyce."

2–3 INTERMIX – news, views, and music from women around the world.

3–4.30 GIRLS EXPRESS – by girls, for girls – but boys can listen too! DJs, competitions, interviews with women in the media, Green girls . . .

6–7 ARTERY – lifeline to the arts. Highbrow to lowbrow and the unexpected in between. Features cabaret, film, music, and sports. Interviews from the Bristol Women's festival and the Bristol music scene.

8–9 MEN'S HOUR

9–10 FEM CHOICE SPECIALIST MUSIC

Monday – Jenny B. Goode, Mean Women Blues
Tuesday – Pizarro presents Garage City
Wednesday – Jackie J. Wilson: Lovers Rock and Reggae
Thursday – Muthaland: Right on Rap collective
Friday – Tatiana: World Grooves

10–11 WORD OF MOUTH – brazen discussion programme where women talk about issues close to their hearts. Topics include "Whatever happened to feminism?" and "Who'd be a mother?" Presenters include Patti Caldwell (BBC Radio 2) and Jenni Mills (BBC Radio 4).

11-1 LATE NIGHT SOUNDS

Monday – Mrs Jones: The Cookin' Soul Kitchen
Tuesday – Nicky E: Roots Daughters and Crucial Cuts
Wednesday night at the Shebeen – Bluebeat 'n' Ska, Rhythm 'n' Blues, Rocksteady 'n' Soul
Thursday – Rankin' Miss P: Top Reggae
Friday – Angie D (Kiss FM): Soul, Jazz, Funk, and Blues

Women's radio as feminist media practice: new definitions and conclusions

Before bringing together broader definitions of women's and feminist radio practice and the conditions under which such radio might thrive, it may be helpful to describe what might be considered the *antithesis* of women's radio practice. Naughton[16] recounts how one of the stations in the new tier of community stations in South Africa was originally set up and designed by women. It produced informative programs based on a lot of research as well as interactive phone-ins. The space and production resources were shared between the women, the programming of the station was organized to allow for childcare responsibilities, and a system was set up for the local taxi firm to give women lifts to and from the station. Later, young men in the area started using the station more. They had different working styles, commanded more time using production resources, and wanted to program round the clock. Naughton says this "culture of the DJ" works against women's interests.

In previous work (Mitchell 2000, 2002), I've given some defining conditions for feminist radio practice drawn from researching women's radio activity in the UK and Ireland. Here, I would like to expand this to include a wider range of examples, particularly those from a more radical and alternative feminist radio practice.

The nature of feminist radio and gendered production

Feminist radio practice is underpinned by the principle that women have a right to broadcast on their own terms: use their voices, articulate their concerns, and tell their stories in order to represent their lives, their struggles, and their achievements. Women's radio has a multiplicity of voices, mediating local and global feminism(s), from radical feminist news agencies, stations, and programs to other examples of women's alternative radio, which involve participatory practices and alternative representations to the mainstream, but are not necessarily labeled as feminist. Radio bridging the space between public and private is an important aspect of feminist radio.

Radio conventionally uses informal language mediated through a range of program styles and genres. The discourse of women's radio emphasizes the use of everyday speech and the content is based on women's lives: women telling their stories in their own words, their own voices, unmediated by professional broadcasters. Integral to the practice of gendered production is that it enables women to have the skills, resources, and structures to access radio. Inherent to feminist radio practice is the concept of using radio as a tool for women's self-development, as gaining broadcasting confidence often aids self-esteem. Gendered production for men can revolve around their taking up an unequal amount of space, airtime and production resources. For women, production tends to be more about sharing space (for instance, co-presenting) training and skills, collective working and problem solving – oh yes, and having fun!

The nature of women's radio stations

Unsurprisingly, there is no single easily defined format for a women's radio station: in fact, efforts to make a women's commercial format have usually failed in the past.[17] Most women's stations are set up as community radio stations. Some women's radio stations are exclusively run by women: however, most are keen that their audience should include men and indeed they see radio as a bridge for men to understand and be informed about women. Increasingly women in community stations share airtime and resources with men, who are allowed to produce a limited proportion of the programs.[18] Most women's and feminist programming exists in a mixed-gender station. Increasingly women are taking up airtime in mixed stations not only in a "women's program" but also in specialist programs relating to women in some way and through music programming. However, it is clear that unless women have their representation, airtime, and resource needs formalized through a station's constitution, then this presence can be easily lost.

Unlike many WAM projects of the 1970s and 1980s, contemporary women's radio stations are not run as collectives, although there may be some collective working and/or decision-making by consensus in production and station management. Women's stations are often part-time or temporary, reflecting the commitment and energy that women with professional and domestic lives are realistically able to give to them. I have never known a community radio station that is not struggling for financial support. In the US, the setting up of a Women's Radio Fund (see n. 4), which partially supports FIRE and WINGS (see Werden 1996), is a good model that could be replicated at national, regional, or local level.

Women's training is seen to be essential in fostering women's involvement at every level in women's stations and programming. Empowering underrepresented sections of the women's community (for instance, working-class women, young single mothers, or migrant women) through partnerships and outreach, and making program material as part of this process, are crucial to enabling women's participation.

New directions for women's radio practice?

Women are moving into the internet and there is no doubt that the connections between local and global feminisms are being enhanced by the communications facilitated by this tool. Downing states that internet radio "offers extraordinary possibilities for national and global diffusion of radical interactive audio" (2001: 181). Chakravarty notes that in India, where the government has installed computer kiosks in the streets in major cities, radio and the internet still offer the greatest hope to women (cited in Byerly 2002). The web raises interesting challenges for women, and already the work of FIRE, of individual new media artists, and of alternative media practitioners shows that women are harnessing the potential of the web for networking, interactivity, and organizing. There is huge potential for fusions and crossovers with music, performance, art, and other forms of popular culture that can be facilitated through feminist media practice. Women's stations and news services are moving on to the web and stations are using it to browse for information that might be of use to their listeners. Women's Net in South Africa is one example of using this technique.[19] In the future it may be that the daughters of today's alternative radio women will run their own individual fanzine radio stations from their bedrooms.

Certainly, the internet is a wonderful networking and communications tool and a virtual extension of women's radio space, but as Norma Valle says, the other spaces where women meet, talk, and commune are as important:

> Radios have traditionally belonged to men, and we've listened to them all our lives. In setting up women's stations, we've empowered ourselves. But

> now marginalized and alternative radio must set up microphones wherever there are women: in the main square, in parliament, in the bedroom, the jails, in the kitchen – all places where women are present.[20]

Key terms

community radio
fanzine
gendered radio training
pirate radio
praxis of women's radio
radical alternative media
radical feminist broadcasting
Women's Alternative Media (WAM)
women's production vs. feminist production
women's radio practice

Questions for discussion

1. Why does Mitchell believe that radio is a medium uniquely suited to women's needs and use?
2. How does the author distinguish between "women's production" and "feminist production," with respect to radio programming? Why is such a distinction useful in understanding the evolution of women's relationship to radio?
3. What has been the role of women's collectives in producing feminist-oriented programming, according to Mitchell?
4. How has lesbian experience (and identity) been important in feminist radio programming, in the author's view?
5. What are the "principles of feminist radio practice," according to Mitchell?
6. In what ways does Mitchell see the internet and women's radio practice as a logical interface?

Notes

1 In CDA, language is studied in social context (Talbot 1998).
2 For details of the program and daily broadcast schedules see www.bbc.co.uk/radio4/womanshour.
3 From week beginning December 9, 2002. www.bbc.co.uk/radio4/womanshour/09_12_02/listen_index.shtml.
4 Women's Radio Fund, "Why feminist radio?", www.womensradiofund.org/intro.htm.
5 Guerilla radio is not defined by WRF, but I would distinguish this from unlicensed pirate radio in that it comprises individual acts of sabotaging mainstream and even alternative radio to radical feminist ends or setting up unlicensed broadcasts in war zones.
6 For information about women launching Mana Radio, India's first community station, see http://victoria.indymedia.org/news/2002/10/8747_comment.php. See also chapter 7 in this volume.
7 From an interview with CKLM programmer carried out by Caroline Mitchell, Dublin, 1991.
8 Since the invention of the wind-up radio and solar batteries, the radio has been cheaper to run.
9 Information about Radio Douentza taken from BBC World Service program on women's radio as part of the "Radiocracy" series in 2000.
10 See www.mediamoz.tripod.com/CR.
11 From an interview with Norma Valle carried out by Caroline Mitchell, Senegal, 1994.
12 FIRE can be found at www.fire.or.cr.
13 From an interview with Maria Suárez Toro carried out by Peggy Law of the International Media Project, Milan, 1998.
14 The author was one of the two coordinators of Fem FM.
15 See Nye et al. (1994) for further discussion about the history and practice of lesbian radio.
16 A community radio consultant, talking to the BBC as part of the "Radiocracy" series (see n. 9).
17 Viva! radio was the first commercial station in the UK to be aimed mainly at women. Broadcasting in London, it was on air for just over a year. See Mitchell (2000) for an account of why Viva! radio failed.
18 This happened at Radiorakel.
19 More can be found on http://radio.womensnet.org.za/about.htm.
20 From an interview with Norma Valle carried out by Caroline Mitchell, Senegal, 1994.

References

Allen, D., Rush, R., and Kaufman S. J. (eds) (1996) *Women Transforming Communications: Global Intersections*. Sage, London.

Anand, A. (1996) Starting up, staying there and moving on: the Women's Feature Service. In: Center for Mass Communication Research (CMCR) (eds), *Media in Global Context: Reader Two*. Center for Mass Communication Research, Leicester.

Anfossi, K. and Suarez, M./FIRE (1995) *Report: Voices of Women at the Fireplace: Non-Governmental Organizations' Forum on Woman and the U.N. Conference on Women, Huirou and Beijing, China 1995*. RAIF/FIRE, Ciudad Colon.

Baehr, H. and Ryan, M. (1984) *Shut Up and Listen! Women and Local Radio*. Comedia, London.

Barlow, W. (1999) *Voice Over: The Making of Black Radio*. Temple University Press, Philadelphia.

Baxter, A. (2000) *Powerful Voices: Training Women in Community Radio Production – Practical Ideas for Involving Women in Radio*. University of Sunderland, Socrates Program for Adult Education, Brussels.

Bredin, M. (1991) Feminist cultural politics: woman in community radio in Canada. *Resources for Feminist Research* 20, 1–2, 36–41.

Byerly, C. M. (2002) Facing Goliath: feminism and communication policy. *Con/text* (the Feminist Scholarship Division (ICA) newsletter). www.icahdq.org/divisions/feminist/context/2002Spring/04goliath.htm (last accessed January 19, 2003).

Coward, R. (1984) *Female Desire: Women's Sexuality Today*. Paladin, St Albans.

Cramer, J. A. (1993) A woman's place is on the air. In: Creedon, P. (ed.), *Women in Mass Communications* (2nd edn). Sage, London, pp. 154–66.

D'Arcy, M. (1996) *Galway's Pirate Women: A Global Trawl*. Women's Press, Galway.

Downing, J. D. H. (ed.) (2001) *Radical Media: Rebellious Communication from Social Movements*. Sage, London.

Feldman, S. (2000) Twin Peaks: the staying power of BBC Radio 4's *Woman's Hour*. In: Mitchell, C. (ed.), *Women and Radio: Airing Differences*. Routledge, London, pp. 63–74.

Gill, R. (1993) Justifying injustice: broadcasters' accounts of inequality in a radio station. In: Burman, E. and Parker, I. (eds), *Discourse Analytic Research: Readings and Repertoires of Texts in Action*. Routledge, London, pp. 75–93.

Günnel, T., Jankowski, N., Jones, S., Lewis, P., Klug, A., Mitchell, C., and Poysko, A. (1999) *Creating Community Voices: Community Radio and New Technologies for Socially Disadvantaged Groups*. (Year 1 report for Socrates Program for Adult Education, Sheffield.) AMARC-Europe, Strasbourg.

Hilmes, M. (1997) *Radio Voices: American Broadcasting 1922–1952*. University of Minnesota Press, London.

Jallov, B. (1992) Women on the air: community radio as a tool for feminist messages. In: Jankowski, N., Prehn, O., and Stappers, J. (eds), *The People's Voice: Local Radio and TV in Europe*. John Libbey, London, pp. 215–24.

Jallov, B. (1996) *Women's Voices Crossing Frontiers: European Directory of Women's Community Radio Stations and Women's Radio Production Collectives*. AMARC-Europe Women's Network, Sheffield.

Johnson, L. (1990) *The Unseen Voice: A Cultural Study of Early Australian Radio*. Routledge, London.

Karpf, A. (1980) Women and radio. In: Baehr, H. (ed.), *Women and Media*. Pergamon Press, London, pp. 41–54.

Karpf, A. (1987) Radio Times: private women and public men. In: Davies, K., Dickey, J., and Stratford, T. (eds), *Out of Focus: Writings on Women and the Media*, Women's Press, London.

Lacey, K. (1996) *Feminine Frequencies: Gender, German Radio and the Public Sphere, 1923–1945*. University of Michigan Press, Ann Arbor.

Lacey, K. (forthcoming) Continuities and change in women's radio. In: Crisell, A. (ed.), *More than a Music Box: Radio Cultures and Communities in a Multi-media World*. Berghahn, Oxford.

Lewis, P. M. (1994) *Community Radio: Employment Trends and Training Needs*. (Report of Transnational Survey.) AMARC-Europe, Sheffield.

Lewis, P. M. and Booth, J. (1989) *The Invisible Medium: Public, Commercial and Community Radio*. Macmillan, London.

Local Radio Workshop (1983) *Nothing Local About It: London's Local Radio*. Comedia, London.

McKay, A. (1988) Speaking up: voice amplification and women's struggle for public expression. In: Kramarae, C. (ed.), *Technology and Women's Voices*. Routledge and Kegan Paul, London, pp. 187–206.

McLaughlin, L. (1993) Feminism, the public sphere, media and democracy. *Media Culture and Society* 15, 599–620.

Meade, M. (2003) Skirting the airwaves: the "all-girl" radio of WHER-AM. Paper presented at the Radio Conference: A Transnational Forum, July 28–31, University of Wisconsin at Madison.

Michaels, K. and Mitchell, C. (2000) The last bastion: how women become music presenters in UK radio. In: Mitchell, C. (ed.), *Women and Radio: Airing Differences* Routledge, London, pp. 238–49.

Millioretti, B. (n.d.) *Feminist Perspectives in Radio Broadcasting*. Radio Lora, Zurich.

Mitchell, C. (2000) Sisters are doing it . . . From Fem FM to Viva! A history of contemporary women's radio stations in the UK. In: Mitchell, C. (ed.), *Women and Radio: Airing Differences*. Routledge, London, pp. 94–110.

Mitchell, C. (2002) On air, off air: defining woman's radio space in European woman's community radio. In: Jankowski, N. and Prehn, O. (eds), *Community Electronic Media in the Information Age: Perspectives, Findings and Policy*. Hampton Press, Cresskill, NJ, pp. 85–105.

Mitchell, C. and Caverly, T. (1993) *Fem FM 101: First in Women's Radio*. University of Sunderland, Sunderland.

Moores, S. (1988) The box on the dresser: memories of early radio and everyday life. *Media, Culture and Society* 10(1), 23–49.

Murray, J. (1996) *The Woman's Hour*. BBC Books, London.

Nye, S., Godwin, N., and Hollows, B. (1994) Twisting the dials: lesbians on British radio. In: Gibbs, L. (ed.), *Daring to Dissent: Lesbian Culture from Margin to Mainstream*. Cassell, London, pp. 147–67.

Razga, J. S. (1995) Adamant Eve: the story of a women's radio collective. *Radio Resistor's Bulletin*, Spring, 6–7.

Riaño, P. (ed.) (1994) *Woman in Grassroots Communication: Furthering Social Change*. Sage, London.

Skard, T. (1989) Norway: two edged s(word)s for women journalists. In: Rush, R. and Allen, D. (eds), *Communication at the Crossroads: The Gender Gap Connection*. Ablex, Norwood, NJ, pp. 132–41.

Shapley, O. (1996) *Broadcasting A Life*. Scarlet Press, London.

Steiner, L. (1992) The history and structure of woman's alternative media. In: Rakow, L. F. (ed.), *Women Making Meaning: New Feminist Directions in Communication*. Routledge, London, pp. 121–43.

Stuart, S. and Bery, R. (1996) Powerful grass-roots women communicators: participatory video in Bangledesh. In: Servaes, J., Jacobson, T. L., and White, S. A. (eds), *Participatory Communication for Social Change*. Sage, London, pp. 197–212.

Suárez Toro, M. (1996) Feminist International Radio Endeavor. In Allen, D., Rush, R., and Kaufman, S. (eds), *Women Transforming Communications: Global Intersections*. Sage, London, pp. 226–32.

Suárez Toro, M. (2000) *Women's Voices on FIRE: Feminist International Radio Endeavor*. Anomaly Press, Austin, TX.

Talbot, M. (1998) *Language and Gender: An Introduction*. Polity, Cambridge.

van Zoonen, L. (1992) The women's movement and the media: constructing a public identity. *European Journal of Communication* 7, 453–76.

van Zoonen, L. (1994) *Feminist Media Studies*. Sage, London.

Wanyeki, L. M. (2002) Community radio provides women a way to have their voices heard. *Nieman Reports* Winter, 75–7.

Werden, F. (1996) The founding of WINGS: a story of feminist radio survival. In: Allen, D., Rush, R., and Kaufman, S. (eds), *Women Transforming Communications: Global Intersections*. Sage, London, pp. 218–25.

Women's radio stations and contacts worldwide

World Association of Community Radios (AMARC)
AMARC-Europe Women's network
c/o AMARC Europe
15 Paternoster Row
Sheffield S1 2BX
Tel: +44 (0)114 221 0592
www.amarc.org/europe/women

AMARC International
3575 boulevard St Laurent
Bureau 611
Montreal, Quebec
Canada
www.amarc.org
International office for AMARC

Association for Progressive Communication (APC) Women's Program
colnud.apc.org/apcwomen

Feminist International Radio Endeavor (FIRE)
www.fire.or.cr

FEMNET femnet@Africa Online

Women's International Newsgathering Service (WINGS)
www.wings.org

9
Cyberspace: The New Feminist Frontier?

Gillian Youngs

> *If only Mrs Seton and her mother and her mother before her had learnt the great art of making money and had left their money, like their fathers and their grandfathers before them, to found fellowships and lectureships and prizes and scholarships appropriated to the use of their own sex . . . We might have been exploring or writing; mooning about the venerable places of the earth; sitting contemplative on the steps of the Parthenon, or going at ten to an office and coming home comfortably at half-past four to write a little poetry.*
>
> *Woolf 1993: 19*

> *Male supremacist ideology encourages women to believe we are valueless and obtain value only by relating to or bonding with men. We are taught that our relationships with one another diminish rather than enrich our experience. We are taught that women are "natural" enemies, that solidarity will never exist between us because we cannot, should not, and do not bond with one another. We have learned these lessons well. We must unlearn them if we are to build a sustained feminist movement. We must learn to live and work in solidarity.*
>
> *hooks 2000: 43*

Introduction

Can we reflect on cyberfutures grounded in the complexities of the feminist struggles of recent and more distant history, and if so, why is it helpful to do so at this point in time? These are the questions at the heart of the discussion in this chapter, which seeks to explore the interactive dynamics of cyberissues and major traditions in feminist thought and politics. The main themes are continuity and discontinuity, the past in the present and future, and the importance of recognizing that the internet era offers new contexts for old problems, just as much as it introduces fresh opportunities related to old contexts. There is a focus on two forms of politics: that of space and that of social interaction. These signal the *real* significance and impact of the so-called *virtual* realm of the internet.

Attention to the past is not just due to some deference to feminism's founding ideals, but is essential to consider the new life that is breathed into long-standing questions of inequality by the internet and its diverse meanings as a boundary-crossing communications sphere. In order to think clearly about how the internet has (actually and potentially) changed the world for women (directly and indirectly), it is worth reflecting on the role of spatial freedoms, or lack of them, in shaping gendered inequalities and identities, and to pause to think about the history related to women's networks, or lack of them, and their material and symbolic significance.

The two opening quotes by Virginia Woolf (1882–1941) and bell hooks (born 1952) come from two seminal texts of twentieth-century feminism, *A Room of One's Own* (Woolf 1993) and *Feminist Theory: From Margin to Center* (hooks 2000) respectively. They signal two broad themes in feminist critique. The first is the importance of women's relationships with women over time and the historical significance of the resources (or, more importantly, lack of them) that influence the circumstances, and opportunities, women can create for each other, and the kinds of legacies they are and are not able to leave behind for the benefit of women who follow them. And the second is the ways in which women's lives and the meanings generated within them for their own identities and identifications are *mediated* by the institutional power of patriarchy and individual men.

These perspectives indicate how women's solidarity, in historical as well as more immediate terms, has been, and continues to be, constrained, by the limitations on their access to interrelated resources (money, education, freedom to travel and discover) and by the patriarchal value system of relations, which prioritizes woman–man relations over woman–woman relations. hooks has been among leading black feminists who have stressed the racial, class, and other barriers built into that hierarchically white-over-black value system.

Thus solidarity must address the problem of "bourgeois white" feminism to recognize "the true nature of women's varied and complex social reality" (hooks 2000: 43–4). It must overcome the factually misplaced and "romantic" notions of "*common* oppression despite the value of highlighting experiences all women share" (ibid.: 44; my emphasis). "Women are divided by sexist attitudes, racism, class privilege, and a host of other prejudices. Sustained woman bonding can occur only when these divisions are confronted and the necessary steps are taken to eliminate them" (ibid.: 44).

In the internet era women continue to suffer from resource and relational constraints linked to the material conditions of patriarchy. The divisions among women, in socio-economic and other terms, could be argued to be even more challenging on the basis of some global economic developments. The growing inequality gaps within and across countries impact unevenly on women. Poverty is gendered, whether we are talking about the poorest parts of the world where the struggle for survival is a daily reality, or the vulnerabilities and restricted opportunities and resources of groups such as teenage mums, legal and illegal migrant workers, sex workers.

The long-standing feminist battle for gender equality in education is far from being fully won (see UNDP 2002), and the issue has particular pertinence as the internet begins to embed "information society" developments in economic, political, civil society, and cultural areas. The early feminist calls of Mary Wollstonecraft (1759–97) (1985) for the rights of women in the area of education bear re-reading in the context of these times of "lifelong learning," increased importance of science and technology, and constant pressures for innovation and reskilling in flexible market conditions (see, for example, Youngs et al. 2001). The new opportunities facilitated by the internet in this context can only be understood in any depth with due regard to the historically created gendered conditions of inequality and the policy imperatives they generate.

Cyberfeminism(s): the new politics of virtual space

We can celebrate what the internet brings for women and feminist politics and practice, while holding on to a critical awareness of the range of inequalities affecting women's capacities and possibilities in this realm.

It's partly a case of recognizing that discontinuities (the new) sit alongside continuities (the old), producing hybrid conditions of potential as well as actual empowerment and liberation constrained by real material and social (gendered) conditions. And, as indicated already, the resulting inequalities will not be the same for all groups of, or individual, women. On the contrary, there will be immense diversity, making the inequalities among women of as much concern as those between men and women, and as broad patterns of inequality as a whole.

Virtual space has been understood partly in "frontier" terms. It represents not just an additional social arena, or set of interrelating spaces, but a sphere, which in its nature sharply contrasts with other traditional social spheres. These traditional settings are physical, often clearly bounded locations or places – the home, the nation, the city, the council or parliament chamber, etc. The internet represents a new frontier in transcending, in significant senses, many of the physical constraints of, and boundaries between, such traditional settings. The internet is characterized by its cross-boundary nature, and in this way and others goes *beyond* the (physical and geographical) world we have previously inhabited.

Feminist theorists have been among the pioneers mapping, philosophically and practically, this new social terrain, interpreting its shapes and contours, shadows and openings, threats and prospects. They have explored the new freedoms, in terms of social and relational spaces and identities, that cyberspaces enable, and investigated woman–machine linkages, in terms of information and communication technologies (ICTs) and their significance for transgressions of patriarchal traditions of thought and practice and for new knowledge-building processes. The following discussion provides illustrations of these contributions from feminist theory and practice. Feminists have authored (to borrow a computer software term) the brave new cyberworld in theory and practice, and this work has added to and, in some ways, changed feminist traditions, as much as it has contributed to shaping what the internet actually means in the context of ideas, practices, and possibilities.

Two key themes in feminist analysis of the internet focus on disruptions to patriarchal boundaries, which have been definitive in constructing and maintaining unequal social relations of power between men and women. The first of these boundaries divides private spaces (those of home, family, private relations, the spheres of social reproduction) from public spaces (those of government and commercial institutions, the spheres of political and economic decision-making and influence).

Historically, women's lives and identities have been configured primarily in relation to the private, and men's lives and identities to the public. Despite the growing presence of women in public life in many parts of the world, the historic influence of the private/public boundary on gendered identities continues to have an impact on women's lives and potential. The fact that the work of social reproduction related to the private is distinguished from other kinds of work related to the public by its unpaid rather than paid status is influential in this regard (for a discussion of relevant issues in these areas related to ICTs see, for example, Youngs 2001b).

The second major boundary that has impacted on gender relations has been that dividing the national from the international sphere. Women have, in the main, suffered from a double domestication with respect to this boundary. For if they have been, and remain to a significant degree around the world, unequally present in or absent from the political and economic spheres of decision-making and influence in national settings, they have been even more unequally present in or absent from those realms in international settings. International relations has been, and in many senses remains, a bastion of masculinist principles and influence (see also Enloe 1989; Pettman 1996).

In the case of public/private and national/international boundaries, virtual space has particular significance for women and feminist work. The transgressive potential of the internet with regard to these boundaries, and their significance in maintaining different forms of patriarchal power and social structure, has implications for women's capacities both to relate to one another, and to make political, economic, and cultural contributions to their own and other societies, and to local, national, and international issues and processes, as individuals or collectively. The related areas of women's rights and campaigns against violence against women are key in this context. Women and women's non-governmental organizations (NGOs) have made extensive use of the internet to lobby for recognition of women's rights as human rights and to work against violence against women. The virtual sphere has enabled collective activity across national borders and the raising of the issue of violence against women – traditionally framed as a "private" issue in patriarchal terms – as a "public" issue on international agendas. These transgressions include, importantly, linking the similar *and* different kinds of violence against women occurring in different local contexts (see, for example, Harcourt 2000). This collective work is connecting the local and the global in embodied terms, which assert the gendered nature of social relations of power, demonstrate its impact on lives and communities, and work to change the multiple forms of destruction it causes.[1] This kind of virtual feminist work challenges the private/public and national/international boundaries that are foundational to the patriarchal mediation of women's lives, limiting their public influence in national settings and restricting it even further in the international realm of power politics and transnational corporate might.

Such feminist endeavors demonstrate that the existence of the internet, in crossing boundaries between public and private and national and international arenas, is actually and potentially revolutionary for women and feminist activism. But, and this is a very large but, it does not instantly, or in all cases of course even necessarily in the long term, wipe out the impact of the historically embedded nature of these patriarchally defined divides on the lives and potential of women and societies more broadly. Furthermore, the history of male domination in science and technology impacts on the relationship of women to the internet and the complex ICTs (hardware and software) that form it. Feminists have focused on the inequalities that have resulted from this history, but they have also considered the radical potential of the future.

The cyborg is a key motif in this context, representing the woman–machine interface as a hybrid harnessing the power of both and potentially transforming the script of male-centered science and technology into new possibilities (Haraway 1991, 1997; Plant 1997). The cyborg highlights the importance of issues of identity and agency in the new world of what Donna Haraway (1997) has termed "technoscience." Different kinds of creative and innovative forces are brought together in this world: "technoscience should not be narrated or engaged only from the points of view of those called scientists and engineers. Technoscience is heterogeneous cultural practice that enlists its members in all of the ordinary and astonishing ways that anthropologists are now accustomed to describing in other domains of collective life" (Haraway 1997: 50). In this vein, Sadie Plant (1997), for example, has spoken of digital women and the new technoculture. The traditions of science and technology may have been associated primarily with male rationality, but the fusion of communications and information technologies, which the ICT era represents, breaks new, disruptive ground. ICTs bring together the human and machine aspects of how and what we communicate. They bring the affective (emotional) and rational processes in terms of ideas and material forms into interactive connection in the most complex ways. In the ways that bodies and minds interact with them, ICTs represent extensions of our sensory world. What does it mean to send our love or a hug via electronic networks, to express political engagement or commitment, friendship, anger via them? In part, it is to use such networks as extensions of our being. The "zeros and ones" of the digital realm and the technologies that transmit them become the medium for what we feel and do.

Marshall McLuhan (1911–80) was one of the most radical thinkers of the twentieth century in assessing communications technologies (print, radio, television) as an integrated part of organic social and cultural change. Many of his perspectives seem prescient in the interactive and global times of the far more powerful ICT period:

> The computer is by all odds the most extraordinary of all the technological clothing ever devised by man . . . Since the new information environments are direct extensions of our own nervous system, they have a much more profound relation to our human condition than the old "natural" environment. They are a form of clothing that can be programmed at will to produce any effect desired. Quite naturally, they take over the evolutionary work that Darwin had seen in the spontaneities of biology. (McLuhan et al. 1997: 35–7)

In terms of our social interaction, the virtual world of the internet meshes with the apparently more concrete physical world we are used to occupying, so we have "immersive digital realities continuous with reality itself" (Plant 1997: 13). As Sadie Plant (1997: 143) argues, "the keystrokes of users on the Net connect them to a vast distributed plane composed not merely of computers, users, and telephone lines, but all the zeros and ones of machine code, the switches of electronic circuitry, fluctuating waves of neurochemical activity, hormonal energy, thoughts, desires."

The multidimensionality of the wired world combines communicative and machine processes in ways that are bound to produce unintended consequences, just as other communications technologies have before them. One example is the telephone:

> What was supposed to be a simple device for the improvement of commercial interaction has become an intimate chat line for both women and the men who once despised such talk. And as means of communication continue to converge, the Net takes these tendencies to new extremes. Its monitors and ports do not simply connect people who are left unchanged by their

> microprocesses. The roundabout, circuitous connections with which women have always been associated and the informal networking at which they have excelled now become protocols for everyone. (Plant 1997: 144)

The occupation of multiple spatialities and networks in the same timeframe is also a characteristic – home and cyberspace, workplace and cyberspace, etc. Loving, living, working, shopping, being politically active, all take place (potentially and actually) across cyberspace and other material spaces. Mobile devices (computers, phones) also ensure that we can be on the move when we are actually occupying these multi-function multiple spaces. We operate through interacting sets of technologies – internet, mobile telephone, car, airport, aircraft, train, etc. "Here and there" become as much about virtual space as about physical place, and connecting between "here and there" as much about access (in every sense of that word) to combinations of technologies as about travel or geography. Time increasingly takes over from space as a guiding logic of lived realities (for a feminist perspective on time, see Youngs 2001b).

Contemporary feminist struggles include diverse engagements with technical-political interfaces, efforts to understand and address different dynamics shaping the internet age, and gendered dimensions of it. In a world increasingly mediated by technologies, the problem of the (Western) masculinist (rational man) bias of science and technology in theory and practice features high on the list of priorities (for assessment of relevant areas see especially Harding 1998). There are complex ways in which women have been largely excluded and objectified by the structures and traditions of science and technology, confined and defined more often as low-level users rather than active participants, inventors, innovators, and policy-makers in them (see, for example, Cockburn 1985; Cockburn and Ormrod 1993). Women have been primarily identified as users of low technologies, such as household domestic equipment (washing machines, dishwashers, etc.) and technologies associated with support roles (secretary, clerk, etc.), like typewriters and word processors. The desktop computer revolution has put the much greater power of ICTs in the hands of increasing numbers of women (Harcourt 1999; Green and Adam 2001).

"Access" has become a key political term in relation to the internet, although the extent of its vast range of meanings in this context has been far from fully interrogated to date. The term captures directly linkages between technological and social processes. It also draws attention to the dangers of a reductive and simplified, technocratic, instrumental approach to such issues, and the contrasting problematics and challenges of historically and power-sensitive contextualized approaches. On the one hand, access is *simply* regarded as concerning bits and pieces of technological hardware, software, and communications links, their availability and the ability to use them effectively or not. On the other hand, concern is more productively turned not only to such issues, important as they are, but also to the social (for example, gendered and socio-economic) factors that influence different kinds of active or passive identification with such technological processes, and varying levels of opportunity and competence to take part in, or have interest in, actually *shaping* them as well as *using* them:

> Feminist studies of technology have emphasized that, in addition to gender structures, gender symbolism is important in making technologies a male domain. Technologies have a masculine image, not only because they are dominated by men, but also because they incorporate symbols, metaphors and values which have masculine connotations. (Rommes et al. 2001: 245; see also Wajcman 1991)

Empowerment: networking and beyond

There are very different kinds of empowerment associated with the internet. The realm of networking is fascinating and key if we are looking at continuities in feminist politics in these cybertimes. Networking has always been as fundamental to feminist politics as it has been to other kinds of politics, and as much a matter of collaborative work to validate and establish new (more liberated and equal) identities as one of collective endeavors to intervene critically in policy processes, engage in different forms of activism, and organize to support women's activities and interests. The challenges of networking for women have included increasing the free flow of their association across public/private divides, addressing their multiple burdens of work and care inside and outside of the home, their often unequal presence and influence in institutional and commercial settings, and their unequal access to resources. Development is one of the major areas of women's networking. For example, Development Alternatives with Women for a New Era (DAWN):

> is a network of women scholars and activists from the economic South who engage in feminist research and analysis of the global environment and are committed to working for economic justice, gender justice and democracy. DAWN works globally and regionally in Africa, Asia, the Caribbean, Latin America and the Pacific on the themes of Political Economy of Globalization; Political Restructuring and Social Transformation; and Sexual and Reproductive Health and Rights, in partnership with other global NGOs and networks. (DAWN, www.dawn.org.fj)

DAWN, founded in 1984, in common with many women's organizations, has a web presence that is multifunctional, including, for example, information on its research and global advocacy. Its multilingual content, French, Spanish, and Portuguese as well as English, indicates the breadth of its outreach.

ISIS International Manila (www.isiswomen.org) explains on its website that it is:

> a feminist NGO dedicated to women's information and communication needs. Documenting ideas and visions. Creating channels to communicate. Collecting and moving information. Networking and building links. We focus on those advancing women's rights, leadership and empowerment in Asia and the Pacific. With connections in over 150 countries, we also keep up with changing trends and analyses concerning women worldwide.[2]

ISIS International, formed in 1974, focuses on a variety of media including ICTs. The section of its website devoted to them includes research, reports, and links to other online resources on women and ICTs.

Such websites and the advocacy and informational roles they outline demonstrate how women are using the internet collectively, and in diverse ways, to work strategically for change. Women's NGOs have created elaborate new spaces for women's politics, activism, knowledge, and information-sharing on the web. These are spaces of presence and community-building through links to other organizations. The internet has facilitated such multi-purpose networking for women. This is important because networking cannot be taken for granted in quite the same way as it can for men, who traditionally have had far more free access to public places of association, whether in formal or informal settings (such as politics, sport, pubs). And even though women in many societies have increasing presence in such places, this does not necessarily wipe away issues of inequality affecting them. The patriarchal gaze that continues to assert the associated dualisms of man/woman, public/private, active/passive, etc. is not so easily escaped, extending pervasively its disciplinary effect on identities and behaviors (see work on discipline by Foucault 1979).

Escape from such circumstances, and collective contestation of them, has been a long-standing characteristic of feminist practices. Women-to-women interaction is one of the priorities. This is a recognition of many things. Perhaps most important among these is the constriction of women's expression under patriarchal, or what would be regarded as "normal," social conditions. This exposes the pressures on individuals to conform to such conditions, in the recognition that real penalties can result from acts or expressions of non-conformity. But it also stresses the significance of the silencing of such expressions. This silencing has concrete effects, too, not least for female identity and consciousness. Isolated within patriarchal conditions of conformity, a woman's individual thoughts against such conditions, while silenced and not shared with others, have limited potential either for herself or for others. Acts of self-expression and communication are understood as intrinsic elements of liberation in feminist practice, hence the importance of creating "safe" environments such as women's groups of different kinds. These provide usually temporary opportunities for abstraction from normalized patriarchal conditions, from the disciplining which leads to conformity in such circumstances. There is, of course, no suggestion that such abstraction is ideal or complete in any sense, but it offers at least a challenge to dominant conditions, which can lead to different, empowering kinds of knowledge-sharing (Youngs 1999: 61–2; see also Foucault 1984).

The internet represents an extension of women's communicative space and offers challenges to the private/public and national/international (social and physical) boundaries, which have traditionally constrained them. This is not to claim that the internet is a safe space for women *per se*. It has its risks and dangers like any other social space. It has its more public areas such as open websites and chatrooms, for example, where one may encounter racist and sexist material and attitudes, and various forms of harassment. It has more private areas such as email and private discussion lists, which can offer safer contexts for exchange and exploration, although they of course can also be intruded on by unwanted and sometimes offensive mail items. And no one would claim the internet writ large as a liberational haven for women. The amount of pornography and sexploitation on the internet would be sufficient to counter such an idea (see Hughes 1999).

The internet reflects, and in some ways extends, traditional patterns of power and oppression, as well as opening up opportunities for new forms of politics, collaboration, and contestation. Access to this new communicative space, opportunities to explore its potential and find productive places within it, have been identified as part of contemporary feminist politics. Activists have stressed that such politics must include specific issues affecting women who are marginalized, such as migrants and sex workers. Part of the challenge here is to provide the kind of access appropriate to their particular needs; for example, mobility. Thus a "network" in this context could be vans equipped with a range of informational and other services in addition to internet access:

> Such an approach – technology not isolated in offices, not connected to formal education, not touted as a new religion, not pushed as a "right," but instead associated with coffee, sandwiches and chat – would not appeal to everyone. Some women might not be able to take seriously a computer in a van, or have time for it. Others might learn to type and send their own e-mail or look for their own information on the Web. The vans themselves would *be* a communications technology connecting travelling women who rarely avail themselves of services located in inhospitable buildings and neighborhoods. (Agustín 1999: 155)

The importance of cyberspace for women was a driving force of Dale Spender's (1995) groundbreaking work *Nattering on the Net: Women, Power and Cyberspace*. The direct enthusiasm of the book, and its no-nonsense approach to breaking through the mystique of computers, aimed "to put human beings at the center of computer culture" (ibid.: xiv). Her long view, focusing on the print revolution and the expansion of readership, and the expanded authorship possibilities of the internet era, addresses power and communication and the changes in what it means to be marginalized. For example, illiteracy has been a powerful marker of marginalization in print-based societies and it is doubly so in textually dense multimedia information societies.

Spender's book, coming fairly early on in the development of the internet environment, was in part a call to action for women, and as such, encouraged women to empower themselves in this new virtual sphere. The approach identified getting online as a political act in itself, not least to contribute to ensuring that the growth in women's knowledge production of recent times was passed on and expanded further. "The more women have put in over the past decades as information-makers, the more knowledgeable and wise the society is able to become. And this is why we simply cannot afford to permit white male dominance of the new communication technologies" (ibid.: xxv).

Technological inequalities have come to the fore generally in relation to information society developments, whether we are thinking about gaps between the richest and poorest parts of the world or individual societies, or those between men and women. The "international" context of these considerations has particular significance for new trajectories in feminist thought and activism. Thanks to the internet, cyberfeminist work crosses national boundaries in ways that are revolutionary. If we look, for instance, at ISIS International's website section on Asia-Pacific Women on the Net,[3] instant access is provided to a range of regional organizations, networks, and mailing and discussion lists on women's issues. Importantly, this makes visible a wide range of work that women are involved in, but equally importantly, it offers the opportunity for those connecting to gather easily material related to women from a geographically extensive range of sources, and to network further for advocacy and other purposes. The collective endeavors of women can operate across local and global settings, working to connect issues and policy processes, lobby, and build new communities of interest. The internet has already had a significant impact on the reach of women-to-women communications. This is demonstrated by the number of virtual networks linked to the women's NGO websites discussed above and the diverse kinds of communication and work they are involved in, and these are just a few examples of the new forms of virtual presence and politics that women and women's NGOs are engaged in globally.

Part of the empowerment facilitated by the connectivity of the internet for women is the opportunity to build cross-cultural knowledge and politics about women's lives, problems, desires, and ambitions for their local and wider communities. Encountering "difference" is intrinsic to such work, rich in the opportunities and challenges of creating new and distinct threads of feminist theory and practice. Learning and listening are key, as are building connections between different settings, face-to-face meetings, cyberdiscussions, and activism. There are new feminist skills involved in cyberpolitics. Wendy Harcourt (1999: 14) has offered an evocative description: "My image is . . . of circles, or of throwing a stone in a lake and watching the circle widen and increase. Or the wind blowing with many voices intertwined trying hard to hear and bring them together. Or of finding a political space which is both local and global/feminine and safe."

Such a perspective signals clearly the degree to which cyberfeminism(s) are breaking new ground that relates to new forms of shared encounter, being, and endeavor in the new conditions of cyberspace:

> Women working in the home are linking with others for support in terms of managing children and other domestic pressures. Women in high tech factories in Asia are organizing across North–South lines with the international support of NGOs on health work conditions including women's special needs for example on night shift. And using the UN process women have brought local concerns to the forefront of the international agenda, analyzing women's needs in each region and connecting to political leaders willing to support a women's agenda internationally. (Harcourt 2000: 21)

This is happening individually for women, and, importantly, in collective settings in grassroots and community groups, national and international networks, NGOs, etc. NGOs focused on women's issues have been at the forefront of building and utilizing cybernetworks and linking them up to other, more traditional forms of communication, such as fax, telephone, and newsletter, to ensure that the informational and activist reach of the internet extends well beyond those who have direct access to it (see, for example, Gittler 1999).

Technological empowerment has been a high priority for much feminist activist and policy-oriented work at global and local levels, helping to reorient feminist and women's politics more strongly within the context of "technoscience" (Haraway 1997). The work of organizations such as the Association for Progressive Communications: Internet and ICTs for Social Justice and Development (www.apc.org) have been influential. APC's Women's Networking Support Programme (WSNP) celebrated its 10th anniversary in 2003. When it launched in 1993, it played a major part in facilitating ICT and networking processes for NGOs in relation to the Fourth World Conference on Women in Beijing in 1995:

> APC served as the primary provider of telecommunications for NGOs and UN delegates during the preparatory process and on-site for the Fourth World Conference on Women in 1995. To ensure that information and communications systems were available before, during and after the conference, APC worked closely with the organizing UN divisions, the NGO planning committee, and many women, NGOs and information providers. APC's support and services ensured that partnerships and progress made at the conference continued on-line long after the event was over. These

> efforts established computer networking as a powerful mechanism enabling women and women's NGOs to participate in an effective and timely fashion in the initiatives launched at the Beijing Conference. (Farwell et al. 1999: 104)

Such programs focus on deep empowerment for women in relation to ICTs promoting gender transformative strategies and policies.[4] This deep empowerment addresses the gendered inequalities defining the history of technology writ large, not just in relation to ICTs, and the importance of the involvement of women not only in the generation as well as the use of technology, but also in decision-making and control processes related to technology, to work toward the transformation of the current gender inequalities:

> WNSP's starting point in building a gender and ICT framework is to examine the relationship of gender and technology as a whole. One of the issues that the global women's movement has addressed is that of women's marginalization and invisibility in all aspects of technology. A framework that is useful in analyzing gender and ICT is the newly emerging cultural analyses of technology. This framework understands both technology and gender not as fixed and given, but as cultural processes which (like other cultural processes) are subject to negotiation, contestation, and, ultimately transformation. This "technology as culture" perspective goes further than the current viewpoint of women's exclusion from full participation in technological work. In the cultural analyses of technology, technologies are "cultural products," "objects" or "processes" which take on meaning when experienced in everyday life. Whereas technology has been defined as a predominantly male perspective, change comes through a total re-evaluation and appropriate remuneration of women's skilled and technical tasks. Given this framework, transforming the gendered relations of technology is not merely focused on gaining access to knowledge as it is, but with creating knowledge itself. This means being involved in the level of definition, making meanings and creating technological culture.[5]

WSNP's focus includes policy and advocacy work, research and information, developing training methodologies and materials, and supporting emerging national and regional internet-based networks. It has developed a gender evaluation methodology (GEM) to help establish whether ICTs are improving women's lives and gender relations, and bringing about positive change at individual, institutional, community, and broader social levels:[6]

GEM is intended to meet the needs of ICT practitioners seeking appropriate gender analysis tools and frameworks for their information and communication technology (ICT) interventions. The tool is for APC WNSP members as well as other practitioners who share a common commitment to gender equality and women's empowerment in ICTs, including:

- ICT initiatives for social change;
- project managers and project staff using ICT in projects without a specific gender or women's focus;
- evaluators working in the IT field;
- donors and development agency staff working in the IT field;
- gender focal points that support women's and IT issues;
- policy makers;
- ICT planners;
- consultants in the area of gender and ICTs.[7]

Uses and possible uses of GEM include assessing the impact of: internet cafés for girls and women; rural women's information centers; ICT training initiatives aimed at disadvantaged young women; and women's networking initiatives using ICTs.[8] Such developments indicate the embedded significance of technologies such as ICTs to women's lives and potential, and the relevance of addressing gender inequalities to broader societal possibilities. In many ways, these developments require the revisiting of history, and the rethinking of technology and its relation to politics in broad terms, and to feminist struggle in particular. The international orientation of organizations like APC also facilitates the integrated consideration of a whole range of inequalities in addition to gender; for example, between North and South, or between rural and urban environments.

Feminist activism and politics are increasingly taking place on the internet and are increasingly concerned with the inequalities linked to the technologies shaping it and the policy processes concerning it. The technical-political nexus helps us to understand at least a part of the dynamics driving the theory and practice of contemporary feminism. This discussion has illustrated that this nexus is helping to generate new questions about gender inequality and new mechanisms for thinking about the effects of it in direct relation to ICTs. If this is a new frontier for feminism, it is as much about looking back through new critical lenses as finding new ways to move forward.

The implications of such assessments are that gendered histories of technology count, and that increased rates of technological change, such as are now associated with the socially diverse roles of ICTs, make them count even more. Gender gaps and their associated identity formations, as far as they have existed, threaten to become even more deeply entrenched. This entrenchment operates across the public–private divide, reflecting the pervasive nature of women's subordination more generally in this respect. Questions of the waste of women's creativity (or the different degrees to which it has actually been harnessed) in relation to technological possibilities have different and socio-culturally specific historical antecedents across the world. And it may be that these questions are all the more pressing in a global sense, as the technologies that facilitate continually intensifying "connectivity," within as well as between societies, increasingly contribute to defining what "the social" is, as well as the individual's places and potential within it (Youngs 2001a; see also Youngs 2002).

Cyberspace: what kind of feminist frontier?

This discussion has suggested that if cyberspace is the new feminist frontier, it is a complicated, multi-faceted, and contradictory one. In common with most frontiers, it brings with it exploration, adventure, a sense of the unknown, and the excitement, dangers, risks, and fears that are associated with these. It brings challenges and hopes in equal measure, individually and collectively. There are chances to forge new paths, to revisit old ones, to find ourselves and each other in new circumstances. The many meanings and possibilities in play here are far too numerous and rich for this small chapter to do any more than just scratch the surface of them.

In doing so, two themes have been a prime focus. The first is the deep relevance of cyberspace to the fabric of feminism, to its past concerns and their continued relevance to wider considerations of inequality and empowerment. If anything, the issues surrounding internet use, access to it, and deep empowerment in relation to it make feminism and its struggles of the past more relevant than they ever have been. Priorities such as equal rights to education, and problems of the male-centered traditions in science and technology, which have limited women's overall presence and influence in these major fields, count more than ever in a world increasingly defined by "information" and diverse technological processes associated with its production, storage, exchange, and manipulation.

There is a simple truth that is worth stating, and that has wider significance. It is quite likely that we would be confronting a rather different information age in contemporary times if women had played, over recent history, as big a role as men in shaping what led toward it. Such are the missed opportunities of human history that feminists, in so many diverse ways, have endeavored to highlight in their philosophy, theory, and activism. Feminism may be first and foremost about women and the unequal relations among them and between men and women. But its transformative implications are for societies *as a whole*, and this is a point too often missed in caricatures of feminism.

Society as a whole benefits if all within it are allowed and enabled to make the fullest possible contribution, drawing on all their capacities and gifts. This relates to all areas of inequality, as feminists, among others, frequently argue. Inequality is often a multiple condition touching on a range of factors, such as the socio-economic, racial, or ethnic, categories of citizenship, and gender. Inequalities within societies are as important as those between them. This is the frame in which information society developments are being addressed.

At a time of unprecedented technological development and economic integration, the gaps between the richest and the poorest in the world are among those causing most concern: "amid the wealth of new economic opportunities, 2.8 billion people still live on less than $2 a day. The richest 1 per cent of the world's people receive as much income each year as the poorest 57 per cent. And in many parts of Sub-Saharan Africa the lives of the poorest people are getting worse" (UNDP 2002: 2).

The internet reflects the concentration of wealth and technology in the richest countries. In 2002, a total of 72 per cent of internet users lived in the high-income countries of the Organization for Co-operation and Development (OECD), which have 14 per cent of the world's population (UNDP 2002: 10). If such trends continue, the information revolution could threaten to embed historically established inequalities, rather than lessen them. These kinds of concerns are central to debates regarding the digital divide surrounding the World Summit on the Information Society (Geneva 2003/Tunis 2005), organized by the International Telecommunication Union (www.itu.int/wsis). As UNESCO (2002) has argued:

> This divide accentuates disparities in development, excluding entire groups and countries from the benefits of information and knowledge. This is giving rise to paradoxical situations where those who have the greatest

> need for them – disadvantaged groups, rural communities, illiterate populations, or even entire countries – do not have access to the tools which would enable them to become fully fledged members of the information society.

Gender is one of the intersecting aspects of the global digital divide, and critical work on gender and science and technology contributes to the broader understanding of that divide and ways in which it can be addressed. This brings us to the second main theme of this chapter: the boundary-crossing qualities of feminism in the cyber-era. Access to the internet has heralded a new stage of feminism with regard to the international reach of women and the NGOs that represent their interests. Virtual technologies are facilitating women's collective endeavors in diverse ways, including consciousness-raising, intervention in policy processes, and project-driven innovations, as illustrated above.

Importantly, this process has contributed to bringing feminist theory on "technoscience" (Haraway 1997) into ever closer connection with the priorities of feminist practices, advocacy, and activism. In the international theory-, practice-, and policy-related work I have been involved in on ICTs, I have noted what seems to me an interesting development in this regard. Women's encounters with one another – the similarities and differences in their lives, problems, and aims – have been interwoven with their contrasting experiences or lack of experience with ICTs, different views of the potential contribution of ICTs to community, family, and individual life, and critical perspectives on restricted (Western-centric) notions of "knowledge" associated with ICTs.

Those I have learned from have enhanced and made more complex my initial feminist sense that part of the problem with the "information society" is that what counts as knowledge is too readily assumed; and furthermore, that the international reach of the internet could be much more actively used to *share* and discover new and established knowledge, including knowledge about technology and its potential applications. I have learned that one of the most radical potentials of the internet is cross-cultural consideration of assumptions attached to it and other associated "high" (Western) technologies. Women thinkers and practitioners have demonstrated how *located* perspectives on ICTs indicate just how diverse their applications can be, from "indiginal mapping" in the Pacific, providing online cultural information to connect today's cyberkids to ancestral knowledge (Bray-Crawford 1999; see also Aloha Quest, www.alohaquest.com), to the building of cyberlinks between rural and urban women in Australia (Lennie et al. 1999).

As much as the internet is about the future, it is also about opportunities to revisit the past and reconnect it with the future – for example, in relation to lesser-known, forgotten, or suppressed forms of knowledge – and to do so in networks, involving growing numbers of people in that knowledge. This is true for feminist knowledge, which as part of the networked world is now more readily accessible to growing numbers of people. There are many pioneers on this feminist frontier of cyberspace and many temporary and more permanent communities exploring, creating, and building. Fatma Alloo (1999: 161), from Tanzania, puts the challenge well:

> For me the interesting question is how can we use the Internet and the spaces being created as different cybercultures to produce an enabling environment where information is used as a tool to better people's lives. What is crucial is that the participation of different people in communities should feed into a creative system of change which improves the livelihoods of all, and not only of the "haves." This is the challenge we face not only in Zanzibar but also in the global realm of cyberculture which we are trying to build.

Key terms

"bourgeois white" feminism
cyberfeminism
cyberfutures
cyborg
double domestication
gender evaluation methodology (GEM)
hybrid conditions of empowerment
"indiginal mapping"
information and communication technologies (ICTs)
information society
located perspectives
low technologies
patriarchal boundaries

patriarchal gaze
spatial freedoms
"technoscience"
virtual space

Questions for discussion

1 Youngs begins her discussion by observing the factors dividing women. Identify some of these and explore how they serve to inhibit women's solidarity, according to the author.
2 How does Youngs use the public–private dichotomy to develop an explanation of boundaries that define women's experience? How does she say the internet helps to transgress, or overcome, such boundaries?
3 Youngs adds a second dichotomy, national–international, to her discussion. How does she say this relates to women and cyberspace?
4 In what ways does the author believe that the internet empowers women?
5 In what ways does the author also find the internet reinforces what she calls "traditional patterns of power and oppression"?
6 How does Youngs explain the important role of non-governmental organizations (NGOs) in helping the internet to become a political organizing tool for women?

Notes

1 See for example, Human Rights Watch Women's Rights Division, www.hrw.org, Women's Rights section.
2 See www.isiswomen.org, "About Isis" section.
3 See www.isiswomen.org, "Women's Link" section.
4 See www.apcwomen.org/gem/gend_analysis.htm.
5 Ibid.
6 See www.apcwomen.org/gem/all.htm.
7 See www.apcwomen.org/gem/whois.htm.
8 See www.apcwomen.org/gem/whosafrica.htm#amarc.

References

Agustín, L. (1999) They speak, but who listens? In: Harcourt. W. (ed.), *Women@Internet*. Zed Books, London, pp. 149–55.

Alloo, F. (1999) Information technology and cyberculture: the case of Zanzibar. In: Harcourt, W. (ed.), *Women@Internet*. Zed Books, London, pp. 156–61.

Aloha Quest www.alohaquest.com (last accessed December 1, 2002).

APC (Association for Progressive Communications: Internet and ICTs for Social Justice and Development), www.apc.org (last accessed December 1, 2002).

Bray-Crawford, K. (1999) The ho'okele netwarriors in the liquid continent. In: Harcourt, W. (ed.), *Women@Internet*. Zed Books, London, pp. 162–72.

Cockburn, C. (1985) *Machinery of Dominance: Women, Men and Technical Know-How*. Pluto Press, London.

Cockburn, C. and Ormrod, S. (1993) *Gender and Technology in the Making*. Sage, London.

DAWN (Development Alternatives with Women for a New Era), www.dawn.org.fj (last accessed December 1, 2002).

Enloe, C. (1989) *Bananas, Beaches and Bases: Making Feminist Sense of International Politics*. Pandora, London.

Farwell, E., Wood, P., James, M., and Banks, K. (1999) Global networking for change: experiences from the APC women's programme. In: Harcourt, W. (ed.), *Women@Internet*. Zed Books, London, pp. 102–13.

Foucault, M. (1979) *Discipline and Punish: The Birth of the Prison* (trans. A. Sheridan). Penguin, London.

Foucault, M. (1984) The order of discourse (transl. I. McLeod). In: Shapiro, M. (ed.), *Language and Politics*. Blackwell, Oxford, pp. 108–38.

Gittler, A. M. (1999) Mapping women's global communications and networking. In: Harcourt, W. (ed.), *Women@Internet*. Zed Books, London, pp. 91–101.

Green, E. and Adam, A. (eds) (2001) *Virtual Gender: Technology, Consumption and Identity*. Routledge, London.

Haraway, D. J. (1991) *Simians, Cyborgs and Women: The Reinvention of Nature*. Routledge, New York.

Haraway, D. J. (1997) *Modest_Witness@Second_Millennium. FemaleMan©_Meets_OncoMouse®: Feminism and Technoscience*. Routledge, London.

Harcourt, W. (1999) Cyborg melody: an introduction to women on the net (WoN). In: Harcourt, W. (ed.), *Women@Internet*. Zed Books, London, pp. 1–20.

Harcourt, W. (2000) Women's empowerment through the internet. *Asian Women* 10, 19–31.

Harding, S. (1998) *Is Science Multicultural? Postcolonialisms, Feminisms and Epistemologies*. Indiana University Press, Bloomington, IN.

hooks, b. (2000) *Feminist Theory: From Margin to Center* (2nd edn). Pluto Press, London.

Hughes, D. (1999) The internet and the global prostitution industry. In: Hawthorne, S. and Klein, R. (eds), *Cyberfeminism: Connectivity, Critique and Creativity.* Spinifex, Melbourne, Vic., pp. 157–84.

Human Rights Watch Women's Rights Division, www.hrw.org/women (last accessed December 1, 2002).

ISIS International Manila, www.isiswomen.org_(last accessed December 1, 2002).

Lennie, J., Grace, M., Daws, L., and Simpson, L. (1999) Empowering on-line conversations: a pioneering Australian project to link rural and urban women. In: Harcourt, W. (ed.), *Women@Internet.* Zed Books, London, pp. 184–96.

McLuhan, M., Fiore, Q., and Agel, J. (1997) *War and Peace in the Global Village.* HardWired, San Francisco.

Pettman, J. J. (1996) *Worlding Women.* Routledge, London.

Plant, S. (1997) *Zeros and Ones: Digital Women and the New Technoculture.* Fourth Estate, London.

Rommes, E., van Oost, E., and Oudshoorn, N. (2001) Gender in the design of the digital city of Amsterdam. In: Green, E. and Adam, A. (eds), *Virtual Gender: Technology, Consumption and Identity.* Routledge, London, pp. 241–61.

Scott, A., Semmens, L., and Willoughby, L. (2001) Women and the internet: he natural history of a research project. In Green, E. and Adam, A. (eds), *Virtual Gender: Technology, Consumption and Identity.* Routledge, London, pp. 3–27.

Spender, D. (1995) *Nattering on the Net: Women, Power and Cyberspace.* Spinifex, North Melbourne, Vic.

UNDP (United Nations Development Programme) (2002) *Human Development Report: Deepening Democracy in a Fragmented World.* Oxford University Press, New York and Oxford.

UNESCO (2002) World Summit on the Information Society, http://portal.unesco.org/ci/ev.php?URL_ID=2228&URL_DO=DO_TOPIC&URL_SECTION=201&reload=1036403349 (last accessed December 1, 2002).

Wajcman, J. (1991) *Feminism Confronts Technology.* Polity, Cambridge.

Wollstonecraft, M. (1985) *Vindication of the Rights of Woman* (first published 1792). Penguin, London.

Woolf, V. (1993) *A Room of One's Own/Three Guineas* (first published 1929 and 1938). Penguin, London.

Youngs, G. (1999) Virtual voices: real lives. In Harcourt, W. (ed.), *Women@Internet.* Zed Books, London, pp. 55–68.

Youngs, G. (2000) Women breaking boundaries in cyberspace. *Asian Women* 10, 1–18.

Youngs, G. (2001a) Gender and information societies: creative challenges and testing opportunities. Paper from International Roundtable on Lifelong Learning, Beijing, July 1–3, 2001.

Youngs, G. (2001b) The political economy of time in the internet era: feminist perspectives and challenges. *Information, Communication and Society* 4(1), 14–33.

Youngs, G. (2002) Feminizing cyberspace: rethinking technoagency. In: Parpart, J. L., Rai, S. M., and Staudt, K. (eds), *Rethinking Empowerment: Gender and Development in a Global/Local World*. Routledge, London, pp. 79–94.

Youngs, G., Ohsako, T., and Medel-Añonuevo, C. (eds) (2001) *Creative and Inclusive Strategies for Lifelong Learning: Report of International Roundtable 27–29 November 2000*. UNESCO Institute for Education, Hamburg.

Index

Index

Index

Index